7.

...ony
...silence
30/-

THE POWER
TO SILENCE

THE POWER TO SILENCE

A History of Punishment in Britain

ANTHONY BABINGTON

Robert Maxwell : Publisher

London

Copyright © 1968 Anthony Babington

First published by Robert Maxwell: Publisher
4 Fitzroy Square, London W.1
A division of Pergamon Press Ltd.

Printed and bound in Great Britain
by A. Wheaton and Co., Exeter

08 007060 4

889032

365.942   10/7/69

Contents

PART ONE: THE HERITAGE

Chapter

PART TWO: FACING THE PROBLEM

"The power of punishment is to silence, not
to confute."

(Johnson's Sermons*)*

"The Criminal Law thus proceeds upon
the principle that it is morally right to
hate criminals and it confirms and justifies
this sentiment by inflicting upon criminals
punishments which express it."

*(Sir James Fitzjames Stephen, Judge of
the High Court of Justice, Queen's Bench
Division,* A History of the Criminal Law of
England, 1883*)*

"We were impressed by the argument that
the greatest deterrent to crime is not the
fear of punishment but the certainty of
detection."

*(Report by the Advisory Council on the
Treatment of Offenders, H.M. Stationery
Office, 1960)*

Foreword

I FIRST saw the inside of a prison in 1951 when I was in Manchester acting as Marshal to a High Court judge, Sir Geoffrey Streatfeild.

It was the judge himself who suggested that I should visit Strangeways. "If you are going to have anything to do with the criminal courts," he said, "you should see for yourself the conditions under which prisoners serve their sentences."

Accordingly, he arranged with the governor that I should spend a morning seeing as much as I could of the interior of the prison.

I imagine that my initial reactions were little different from those of any free person who steps inside the heavy gates of a full-security prison. The sensation of claustrophobic heaviness when one surveys the vast, dark walls; the vivid impression of the hopelessness and futility which seem to linger on the atmosphere with the sullen intensity of a hovering storm. And then the harsh inhospitability of drab cells with their small grill-windows. The complete lack of privacy and the feeling of eyes all around you, continually watching.

It was only when I met the prisoners that I seemed suddenly able to reorientate myself. Five or six years before I had finished my service in the army, and now walking round with the governor and hearing him talking to the convicts seemed to be rather like accompanying a commanding officer on a barrack inspection.

The principal lesson I learnt from my visit that day was that the population is not divided into two district species, the law-keepers and the law-breakers. There is no "we" and "they" in this matter, nor are there any perceptible lines of demarcation. A growing acceptance of this truth has led in recent years to an ever-increasing interest in the penal system.

The subject of penology is as complex as it is vast and the modes of punishment which are used by the courts of a nation are a measure of its standard of humanity and enlightenment. In a civilised democracy like our own there is no adult citizen who can evade his share of responsibility for the judicial penalties which are being carried out in his name. When a prisoner was led to the gallows the whole nation became his executioners; when an offender was flogged the whole nation became the wielders of the whip. And even each time a criminal is imprisoned all of us become his jailers. Penal sentences are authorised by Parliament and Parliament is elected by universal franchise.

In the past far too little thought has been given to the objects and the methods of punishment and far too little research has been made into the consequences of the various permissible sentences. People hold an amazing diversity of views on this subject. On one extreme are those who think that punishments are becoming absurdly lenient. They advocate a wider imposition of the capital penalty, a reintroduction of flogging, and far harsher prison conditions. A surfeit of deterrence, they say, is the only way to deal with the mounting crime wave. But if, in truth, the sole purpose of punishment is to deter, then there should theoretically be no limits to the severity of court sentences and no limits to the barbarity with which they are carried out. For instance, if the unvarying penalty for the convicted shoplifter was execution in a public place, there can be little doubt that the prevalence of this particular offence would be greatly diminished.

On the other extreme are the radicals and the humanitarians who experience a slight feeling of uneasiness at the thought that we are punishing our wrongdoers at all. Now that the most obnoxious penalties have been eradicated from our penal system these people are constantly urging a further alleviation of the hardships of prison routine. There are quite a few who feel that in this age of greater understanding and wider compassion the caged and segregated life of the prisoner is in itself becoming more and more of an anachronism.

However, if the object of punishment is really to punish, then the penalties inflicted by the courts must be intentionally distasteful to the criminal. It is argued that the punitive effect of a prison sentence will be directly proportionate to the hardships and inconveniences of prison existence. I remember a client of mine, a confirmed recidivist, telling me before his trial that he was not particularly concerned at the prospect of serving yet another term of imprisonment. "I wouldn't have told you that a few years ago," he added, "but prison's becoming cushier and cushier nowadays."

Where does the right solution lie? At what point do the requisites of social order coincide with the dictates of humanity? In the pages which follow I have not sought to answer those questions, but merely to provide some factual information which might be helpful in finding the necessary answers. For it seems to me that before one can reach any reasonable conclusions on this vast and complicated matter it is advisable to consider the history of punishment from the earliest times; to study the ways in which the various methods, conditions and theories were originated, varied and developed; to find out, in fact, how we have progressed to the stage at which we are standing today. Although similar factors were applicable the world over, for the sake of brevity and for convenience I have confined myself for the most part to the situation as it existed in Britain.

I should make it clear at the outset that I am not a penologist or a criminologist, and neither am I a social historian. In compiling this book I have not endeavoured to unearth any new or unusual material; indeed, I have only consulted the rather obvious authorities as I am writing for the layman rather than for the expert.

Having explored the British penal methods of the past it might have been appropriate to discuss the system we are using at the present time. But so many well-informed authors have delved extensively into this subject over the last decade that a further exposition, coming from my pen, would be merely superfluous. Instead, I have tried in the final section of the book to set out some of the tendencies and suggestions which have been shaping the development of the treatment of offenders during recent years. This is an age of reform, and tremendous changes in the penal system lie just ahead. One can only hope that the majority of them will be for the best.

Acknowledgements

I SHOULD like to acknowledge the help and encouragement I have received in preparing this book from Mr. A. V. Mindham, Chief Clerk at Bow Street Magistrates' Court, and from Miss Mary Hamilton, Mr. W. W. Badger, Mr. M. Fenner, and Mr. Barry Swinney, Probation Officers at that Court.

Also I am much indebted to Mr. Eric Stockdale, Barrister-at-Law, for his invaluable advice and for referring me to so many useful books of authority.

Finally, I should like to thank the governors and the members of the staffs of the various prisons and penal establishments I have visited for their infinite patience and their unvarying courtesy in showing me around and in answering all my questions.

PART ONE

THE HERITAGE

Chapter One

Origins of the Penal System

WE TAKE it for granted these days that every sovereign state possesses an inherent right to formulate its own criminal code and to seize and punish all those who offend against its laws. I certainly do not wish to criticise, to justify, or even to analyse this assumption. My only concern at this juncture is to see how it came into being.

In the primitive stage of civilisation crime, as we understand the word, did not exist. It was considered both just and proper in inter-tribal skirmishes for the victors to reap their vengeance on the vanquished by murdering their males, raping and enslaving their women, and by stealing their land.

Within the tribes the idea of communal responsibility for the preservation of order gradually gained acceptance and it became the custom that if one member was slain by another, the family of the victim had the right to kill off a relative of the murderer.

Later in time, when the corporate ownership of movable and immovable property by the whole tribe gave way to ownership by individuals within the tribe, the kinsmen of a murdered person frequently compounded their right of revenge by accepting a payment in kind, for instance by way of arms, of cattle, or of land, from the family of the killer instead of demanding their recompense in blood.

As soon as kings and governments had decided that they themselves were entitled to a share in the compensation, the notion of fines and state-controlled penalties automatically came into being. It was perhaps a fairly logical step for the State, having assumed its interest in the preservation of the lives of its subjects, to undertake a further responsibility for the protection of their property. In this way the distinction was conceived between private wrongs, or civil injuries, on the one hand, and public wrongs, or crimes against the whole community, on the other. The former became punishable at the suit of the individual, and the latter at the hands of the State.

During the regal period of the Roman Empire, before the full flowering of the Roman system of law, the line of demarcation between private and public wrongs was still vague and arbitrary. It seems probable that the State only undertook the prosecution of offenders who had committed crimes of treason or murder, and even in the case of murder the position was complicated by the fact that there was a religious necessity for the kinsmen of the murdered man to appease his household gods by taking vengeance against the family of the slayer.

Since the State in those times had little or no machinery for enforcing the prescribed penalties, it was usually left to the victim of a crime to exact his own retribution. For instance, it was permissible for a man who found his wife or his daughter in the act of adultery to kill her lover on the spot, and a thief who was apprehended by night could likewise suffer immediate death at the hands of his captor. There was also a class of offences which were considered to be so serious that they removed the wrongdoers completely from the protection of the law. Henceforth they became outlaws with no further rights to life or to property, and anyone who chose to slay them could do so with impunity. The crimes which had this effect included the removal of a boundary stone, the slaughter of a plough-ox, a father killing or exposing his infant in a manner contrary to the prescribed rules, and a child who maltreated his or her parents. If the criminal possessed any property it was confiscated by the State, but his actual killing was a matter for the public at large.

There were other crimes in that period which carried penalties less than death—for instance, slavery, banishment, flogging, and imprisonment—but here, too, it was left to the injured party to pursue the offender and to enforce his punishment personally.

Inside the family the paterfamilias combined the functions of lawmaker, judge and jury in all matters appertaining to domestic relationships. It was he alone who decided whether or not one of his womenfolk had committed adultery or if a child of his had been guilty of undutiful behaviour. His powers of punishment were unbounded and included the right to impose and to carry out a sentence of death.

In the course of time it became customary for the criminal, when captured by the person he had wronged, to seek to compound his offence and thereby to evade the penalty authorised by the law. The practice received official recognition to such an extent that when a dispute arose regarding the proper payment to be made by way of compensation the matter could be taken before the supreme appellate tribunal, the king himself. The king then heard the arguments and pronounced his judgement. There can be little doubt that this development contributed towards the centralised administration of the criminal law and to the enforcement of penalties by the State rather than by the private individual.

It was during the reign of Servius Tullius, the sixth king of Rome in the fifth century B.C., that the first real effort was made to separate public wrongs, which we now call crimes, from private wrongs, now known as torts. The effect of the Servian reforms was to leave public wrongs in the hands of the king and to refer all private wrongs to a special panel of judges, to be tried in accordance with established principles and a set procedure.

The distinction between public and private wrongs was preserved in the following century by the XII Tables, the first codification of the Roman Law. The XII Tables also adhered to the doctrine that offences against the public order were the concern of the whole community. In its desire for self-protection the community was entitled to punish the offender by the most rigorous means, and among the penalties which the Tables prescribed were hanging, beheading, flogging to death, burning at the stake, and hurling from the Tarpeian rock.

To some extent the XII Tables permitted a continuation of the ancient principle of retribution against the criminal by his victim, but the right to personal vengeance was considerably modified and restricted. For example, a thief who was apprehended by night could still be slain by his captor, but if he was caught in the daytime he might only be killed if he offered resistance by force of arms. On the whole, however, there was a far greater emphasis on a system of punishment under the control of the State.

In later years the demarcation between public and private wrongs has been adopted by every reputable system of law. So has the principle that the executive of a nation possesses an undeniable right to inflict punishment on the criminal. The fundamental objectives of this punishment—certainly in its earliest conception—were retribution and deterrence. It followed that the more barbarous the punishment, the more effective the deterrence and the more satisfying the retribution.

Chapter Two

Torture

WE ARE told that torture as a punishment has always been illegal in English common law. This may well be so, but the fact remains that the use of torture in many of its most brutal forms has featured in our penal system throughout the ages.

Prior to the Norman Conquest both mutilation and branding were recognised criminal penalties. Even during the sixteenth century an Act in the reign of Henry VIII decreed mutilation as the punishment for any person who used violence in a royal palace. Under the same monarch another Act was passed providing that murder by poisoning was to be punished by boiling to death, and it is said that three or four people suffered this fate before the Act was repealed shortly after Henry VIII had been succeeded to the throne by his son.

I shall refer in another chapter to the barbarous procedures which were used in the infliction of the capital sentence for treason, but I want for the moment to consider the use of torture as such.

The Magna Carta (1215) sought in indirect language to provide sanctity against torture and later the Bill of Rights (1689) provided in express terms that cruel and unusual punishments ought not to be inflicted by the courts.

The English judges have always pronounced against the use of torture, though admittedly, in past ages, the sincerity of some of their official dicta on the subject must remain a matter of some doubt. One finds the great Chief-Justice Sir Edward Coke, in the reign of Queen Elizabeth I, declaring in his Institutes that "There is no law to warrant tortures in this land nor can they be justified . . .", yet he is on record, when presiding at a criminal trial, as commending his Queen for her mercy in "not torturing or racking" a defendant. Even Sir Thomas Smith, the Regius Professor of Civil Law at Cambridge University during the same period, who was an opponent of all forms of brutality, was directed by warrant in 1571 to carry out tortures on a number of recalcitrant prisoners.

However, the fact remains that torture was usually imposed extra-judicially, and in 1628 the judges declared that it was unlawful for a man to be tortured on the rack because, they said, "no such punishment is known or allowed by our law".

Mutilation was a punishment which was frequently applied in the Anglo-Saxon period. It took various forms, and an attempt was generally made to relate it to the particular offence for which it was inflicted. Sometimes the hands were cut off, sometimes the feet, and sometimes both hands and feet. Facial mutilation was also practised; for example, the removal of the nose, the ears, or the upper lip, or, perhaps, for more serious crimes, the excision of the eyes.

As recently as 1731 a man named Joseph Crook was sentenced to have both ears cut off, both nostrils slit, and to be branded on the nose. We are told, in a contemporary report, that he endured his punishment "with undaunted courage".

It has been said that there have been only two known instances in which a warrant to torture has been authorised by an English judge, but it is difficult to verify whether or not this claim is, in fact, true. Certainly a royal warrant to torture was issued in 1310, and in the fourteenth century a commission reporting on the conditions in Newgate Gaol alluded to the employment of torture against the prisoners there.

In spite of the fervent protestations to the contrary by the judges and jurists of medieval times, torture appears to have been introduced in Britain during the fifteenth century as a recognised extra-judicial penalty. It was about this time also that the rack was first used in the Tower of London. From then on, especially under the Tudor monarchs, torture was practised wholesale. In the reign of Queen Mary, and even more so in the reign of Queen Elizabeth I, the rack in the Tower was in constant use.

The rack, as is generally known, was a mechanism for stretching and dislocating the limbs of the victim. Under the Tudors another form of torture was also used, known as the "scavenger's daughter". This squeezed up the victim into a ball, a direct contrast to the form of suffering imposed by the rack.

Amongst many others to undergo torture at this period was Edmund Campion, the Jesuit, who was imprisoned in the Tower in 1581 on charges of exciting the people to rebellion and holding treasonable correspondence with foreign powers. After being brutally treated he was executed at Tyburn at the end of that year. In 1606 Guy Fawkes, whose stupendous courage has been given far too little credit by posterity, was subjected to prolonged torture in an effort to make him disclose the identities of his confederates in the Gunpowder Plot. On this occasion King James I issued his personal instructions: "If he will not otherwise confess," wrote the monarch, "the gentlest tortures are to be used first on him and so on, step by step, to the most severe and so God speed the good work." The involvement of the deity in this context must be a matter for some surprise, but it does, at least, reflect the general attitude of the time that a criminal had forfeited all right to be treated with any sort of consideration or humanity. Eventually, when the "good work" was completed and Guy Fawkes was taken to the scaffold, we are told that "his body being so weak with torture and sickness he was scarce able to get up the ladder".

Torture in British law was used for two real purposes. Firstly as a means of punishment, and secondly in order to induce confessions which would not, or could not, be given voluntarily. It was very widely practised by the Star Chamber, that infamous court which never made any claim to practise the common law. It should be remembered that the Star Chamber was not controlled by the official judiciary, but was constituted of members of the Council and the Privy Council reinforced at times with judges or bishops sitting as supernumeraries. This court was most active under the Tudors and Stuarts, and was finally abolished by the Long Parliament in 1640.

A peculiar form of torture known as *peine forte et dure* (the strong and hard pain) was practised on prisoners who refused to plead to an indictment. The purpose of such a refusal was usually an attempt by the accused to evade the forfeiture of his property and possessions which followed automatically on a conviction for felony. The origin of this procedure is obscure, but it may have derived from a thirteenth-century statute which stated that "such persons as will not put themselves upon inquests of felonies at the suit of the King shall be put into hard and strong prisons". Hard imprisonment was succeeded by a far more cruel process at the beginning of the fifteenth century when the judges advised that if prisoners stood mute:

> the marshal should put them in low and dark Chambers, naked except about their waist; that he should place upon them as much weight of iron as they could bear, and more, so that they should be unable to

rise; that they should have nothing to eat but the worst bread that could be found, and nothing to drink but water taken from the nearest place to the gaol, except running water; that on the day in which they had bread they should not have water, and *e contra*; and they should lie there till they were dead.

The early volumes of *State Trials* contain numerous references to prisoners being "pressed to death", right up to the early years of the eighteenth century, though out of humanity the weight used was normally sufficiently heavy to ensure a quick death, and sometimes a sharp stone or a piece of wood was placed under the victim's back to hurry his end. Frequently a prisoner undergoing this form of torture would repent of his former obduracy and beg to be given another opportunity to plead. Whether or not he was released and brought back into court depended entirely on the whim of the trial judge.

Sometimes a preliminary, milder torture was applied at the start so that the recalcitrant prisoner would have a chance of changing his mind. This consisted of tying the thumbs as tightly as possible with whipcord. Both men and women were subjected to this procedure, and we read that in 1721 a girl called Mary Andrews continued in her refusal to plead until three cords had been broken on her thumbs.

The last occasion on which the press was employed was in the year 1726, although it was not officially abolished until the reign of George III.

Under the Criminal Law Act of 1827, if a prisoner remains silent when asked to plead to an indictment, a jury is called on to decide whether he stands "mute of malice" or "mute by visitation of God". If the jury's verdict is "mute of malice", a plea of "not guilty" is entered and the trial proceeds accordingly. On the other hand, if the verdict is "mute by visitation of God", for instance if the prisoner happens to be deaf and dumb, then means are discovered, if humanly possible, to convey to him what is taking place.

Chapter Three

The Pillory

THE various forms of suffering which man can inflict upon man include not only the agony of physical torment but also the mental and emotional anguish of humiliation.

This fact was accepted as one of the fundamental tenets of punishment in this country from the earliest times.

A thirteenth-century ordinance dealing with the penalties for bakers in the City of London who adulterated their bread reads:

> If any default shall be found in the bread of a baker in the City, the first time, let him be drawn upon a hurdle to his own house through the great street where there be most people assembled, and through the great streets which are most dirty, with the faulty loaf hanging from his neck; and if a second time he shall be found committing the same offence, let him be drawn from the Guildhall through the great street of Cheepe, in the manner aforesaid, to the pillory, and let him be put upon the pillory, and remain there at least one hour in the day.

The pillory, or stretch-neck, was a form of punishment which was used in most European countries. It was probably introduced in Britain during the Anglo-Saxon era. The principal function of the pillory was to expose the offender to the maximum public ridicule and the physical discomfort entailed in the exhibition was largely incidental. There was no set pattern for the structure : indeed contemporary sketches depict a number of different designs. The majority of pillories held only one person, but there were others which accommodated two or even more prisoners.

The most usual type of pillory consisted of a platform raised several feet above the ground and surmounted by a wooden post with an attached frame. The victim was made to stand on the platform with his head and his hands secured through apertures in the frame. When a prisoner was sentenced to stand in the pillory it was usual to state on how many occasions and for what lengths of time the punishment was to take place.

By a statute in the reign of Edward I, a pillory was to be so constructed that an offender would suffer "no peril" to his body. However, it was customary at one time to add further to the humiliation by shaving off a man's hair and his beard before he was locked into position. A woman, too, was liable to have her head completely shaved before she suffered the punishment.

The pillory was never intended as a severe form of punishment in this country, and consequently it was used only for what were considered to be lesser offences. An Act which was passed as early as 1266 set out a comprehensive list of pillory offences. These included using deceitful weights and measures, perjury, and libellous and seditious writings. In later years it was used for punishing prostitutes, brawlers, and "common scolds".

The tumbrel, or ducking stool, was also used as an instrument of punishment for scolding women. According to the volume of Burns, Justice of the Peace, which was published in 1845, it was employed "for ducking them over head and ears in water, and especially muddy or stinking water".

During the seventeenth century there was a considerable divergence of opinion amongst the judicial purists as to the proper wording of a pillory sentence. Soon after his appointment to the office of Chief Justice in 1689 the celebrated lawyer Sir John Holt adjudicated on the issue. "To stand in the pillory or on the pillory is the same thing in judgement", he said. "The judgement is now to be set in and upon the pillory."

The judges not only had a discretion in deciding how often and for what duration a prisoner should stand in the pillory, but they could also specify, if they chose, the exact location in which the punishment was to take place. In sentencing Elizabeth Collier in 1680 the judge told her that she was to be :

> put on the pillory three several days in three several public places; in the first place . . . it is thought fit that she stand, as near her own house as conveniently can be, between the hours of twelve and one, for one hours space at the May-pole in the Strand, on the most notorious day. (I think there is a market near that place, let it be on that day.) And at another time, that she stand in Covent Garden on a public day, the like space of time. And at a third time that she stand at Charing Cross on the most public day, for the space of one hour.

During the seventeenth and eighteenth centuries the pillory was used increasingly for political offenders, and as a result there were often demonstrations by hostile crowds. The prisoner, powerless to defend himself, was treated to every indignity and sometimes even to violence. Ordinary criminals, too, were liable to suffer at the hands of an unruly mob.

In a footnote to the case of Elizabeth Collier (1680), in the seventh volume of *State Trials,* the editor says:

> It may, therefore, well deserve the consideration of a judge who inflicts the punishment of the pillory (as it becomes at present the great occasion of mobs and riots) whether it can be reconciled to the original intention of the law in this mode of punishment; as also if this riotous scene ends in the death of the criminal, whether he is not in some measure accessory both to the riot and the murder. . . . The chief intention of setting a criminal in the pillory is that he should become infamous, and known for such afterwards by the spectators. Can an offender, whose face is covered with rotten eggs and dirt be distinguished, so to prevent his gaining a new credit with those who have occasion afterwards to deal with him?

Mr. Emlyn, who contributed the preface to the second edition of the *State Trials,* published in 1730, also had his doubts about the practical application of this form of punishment.

> As to the pillory [he wrote] that is intended to expose the offender to shame and infamy, and to mark him out to the public as a person not fit to be trusted, but to be shunned and avoided by all creditable and honest men. Never did the law design that he should be exposed to the peltings of a mob, or the assaults and injuries of a furious rabble.

The judges themselves were not unaware of the disgraceful scenes which took place around the pillory. Sir Francis North, the Lord Chief Justice, when sentencing Nathaniel Reading in 1679 to be "set in the pillory for the space of one hour in Palace yard in Westminster", added:

> We have reason to suspect that the rage of the public will be so great against you that it might endanger your life. Therefore, we have taken care to give a charge to the sheriff and the justices that the peace might be kept and that no ill consequences may happen to you, but only the shame and infamy to which you are condemned; and which you do deserve as well as any man that was ever convicted.

Since there was in those times no regular police force to maintain law and order, it was left very much to the discretion of the local officials what precautions, if any, should be taken against the unruliness of the mob. When the Rev. Kinnersley and William Hales stood in the pillory as part of their punishment after a conviction for forgery, a number of constables armed with long staves were specially hired to hold back the crowd and to prevent them, as is said in the official report on the trial, "from their usual diversions in such cases". A typical "diversion" is described by George Wilkinson in *The Newgate Calendar*:

> The mob [he says] no sooner saw the prisoners exposed in the pillory than they pelted them with stones, brickbats, potatoes, dead dogs and cats and other things. The constables now interposed but being overpowered the offenders were left wholly to the mercy of the enraged mob. The blows received occasioned their heads to swell to an enormous size, and they were nearly strangled by people hanging on to the skirts of their clothes.

Sometimes the assailants were caught and punished for their violence. In 1732 two men were convicted of murder at the Old Bailey for killing a prisoner in the pillory "by pelting him with cauliflower stalks".

Indeed, the scenes at the pillory must at times have degenerated into something very much akin to a public stoning. Such an instance occurred in 1756 when four men—M'Daniel, Barry, Eagan, and Salmon—were sentenced for being accessories before the fact to highway robbery. M'Daniel and Barry stood together in the pillory at Hatton Garden "and were so severely handled by the populace," says the official report, "that it was with the utmost difficulty that one of the sheriffs and the keeper of Newgate, who stood on the balcony just by prevented their being utterly destroyed; and so great was the mob, that peace officers found it impossible to protect the prisoners from their fury". In spite of the behaviour of the crowd on that occasion the two other convicted men, Eagan and Salmon, were forced to stand in the pillory three days later and "were instantly assaulted with showers of oystershells, stones, etc., and had not stood above one half-hour before Eagan was struck dead, and Salmon was so dangerously wounded in the head that it was thought impossible he could recover".

Towards the end of the eighteenth century the crowd surrounding the pillory was often sympathetic to the prisoner, especially if his offence had been political in nature, and not infrequently the whole occasion turned into a popular demonstration in his favour. Thus, with bloodshed, on the one hand, and martyrdom, on the other, it became clear that this form of punishment had ceased to achieve any useful purpose.

After 1806 the pillory was only used for offences of perjury and subornation. In 1837 it was abolished completely and the courts were given authority in its stead to order imprisonment with or without hard labour, or a fine, at their discretion.

Although, as has been seen, prisoners were only placed in the pillory for a comparatively short duration of time in Britain, and the essence of the punishment was humiliation and indignity, in other countries the same system was used essentially for the infliction of privation and discomfort for sustained periods.

The stocks, which operated on a similar principle to the pillory except that the victim was seated and his ankles were locked in the frame in addition to his head and wrists, was habitually used as a punishment for Negro slaves in America. Professor Kenneth M. Stampp has quoted an entry from a plantation record book, kept towards the beginning of the nineteenth century, which states that an offending slave is to be kept "so secured in a lonely, quiet place, where no communication can be held with anyone, nothing but bread and water allowed, and confinement extending from Saturday, when they stop work until Sabbath evening".

In England the victim was usually left in the stocks for not more than about six hours. The stocks had, in fact, a dual purpose, for not only were they used as a form of punishment but they also provided a means of securing a wrongdoer when there was no other convenient place where he might be detained.

The House of Commons suggested in 1376 that every village should provide itself with a set of stocks, and in 1406 it became compulsory for every town and village to have one. Gradually the whip and the stocks became the principal forms of punishment which were meted out by justices of the peace.

Usually the offences punished by placing in the stocks were of a fairly trivial nature—drunkards, gamblers, vagrants, and such like. The punishment, too, was fairly slight on the face of it, but in many ways the deliberate exhibition of a helpless prisoner to public indignity and mass intolerance can be a more inhuman penalty than the calculated infliction of pain. Certainly, to a sensitive temperament the agony could be more bitter and the after-effects more lasting.

Amongst my memories of wartime scenes is one which has remained undimmed throughout the course of the intervening years. It is of the market square in a French town on the morning following its liberation by a column of Allied troops. A wooden platform had been erected at one end of the square and in front of an excited, jeering crowd a number of local girls who had fraternised unduly with the occupying German army were led up to suffer the penalty of their transgressions. First of all they were held down on the platform while their heads were completely shaved. Then they were led around the centre of the town with an escort from the French Forces of the Interior, through streets packed with shouting, taunting spectators. One girl passed very close to me on this procession of shame. She was only about 19 or 20 and was tall and slender. From the stubble of hair that remained on her head one could see that she had been blonde. Her face was scratched and still bleeding from the rough treatment she had received on the platform and there were stains of blood on her grubby white jumper and her faded blue skirt. She glanced at me momentarily as she went by and I have never before seen such appalling suffering and anguish in any human eyes.

I sometimes think, if that memory is still so vivid for me, what must it be like for the woman herself?

Chapter Four

The History of Corporal Punishment

THERE are still in existence a number of very ancient parish and municipal records which show entries of payments made to persons for the administration of whippings. Indeed, flogging appears to be one of the oldest forms of punishment ever used in this country.

Women as well as men were at one time liable to be whipped, and the punishment was usually carried out in public, the victim being tied to a cart's tail or else to a special fixture known as a whipping post.

Flogging was always considered the appropriate penalty for vagabonds, vagrants, and beggars. A statute passed in the reign of Henry VIII provided that a vagrant should be tied naked to the end of a cart and beaten with whips "till his body should be bloody". With a nice sense of propriety Queen Elizabeth I had the Act slightly amended so that the victim would no longer receive his punishment stark naked, but would only be stripped to the waist.

Just as hanging was at one time the automatic penalty for common law felonies, so a whipping automatically followed a conviction for a common law misdemeanour—and even for a statutory misdemeanour when no other penalty was specifically authorised.

Thus from Norman times until the early days of the nineteenth century, corporal punishment was habitually inflicted on prisoners of both sexes for a vastly differing range of offences.

It is difficult for a person living in this country today to visualise the bestiality of some of the punishments of former times. Perhaps the only way even to begin to appreciate the horror of what took place is to turn to the accounts of the eye-witnesses of the period. One observant onlooker watched a public whipping in 1829.

> A poor boy, aged about thirteen years [he wrote] was flogged at the cart's tail a distance of nearly 150 yards, for stealing a pair of shoes, and his screams after the second lash were heart-rending. He continued to shriek and cry, "Oh, Lord! Oh, Lord!" during the whole distance and on being placed in the cart at the conclusion the wretched child seemed too weak to support himself—his back was dreadfully lacerated. A considerable crowd was collected.

Another witness of the flogging of two men in the yard of the Old Bailey in 1830 recounts : "it appeared to astonish the medical gentlemen in attendance that the culprits bore ninety-one lashes with such apparent fortitude. Our astonishment and indignation were aroused when we saw at the back chamber of a house, a matron of seventy, and four damsels in their non-age, laughing at the writhings of their guilty fellow-creatures."

Even during the eighteenth century, judges and magistrates were almost as prone to order corporal punishment for women as they were for men. In 1764 a woman was whipped at the cart's tail in Enfield, and in 1769 in Nottingham a girl of 19 was ordered to be stripped to the waist and publicly whipped in the market place.

During the eighteenth century the legislature obviously continued to have a high regard for this particular form of punishment as it was authorised as a sentence for offences committed under two separate statutes, one of which was passed at the beginning and one at the end of the century. The Diplomatic Privileges Act, 1708, was an obscure enactment for the protection of foreign ambassadors and their staffs who were serving in this country. The Act provided that anyone convicted of an offence under its various sections "shall suffer such pains, penalties and corporal punishment" as may be imposed. The Knackers Act, 1786, was directed against persons (again, both males and females) who were convicted of slaughtering horses and cattle without a licence. The penalty clause laid down that an offender "may be sentenced to such public or private whipping as the court may direct".

In the nineteenth century there were a number of radical alterations in the law with regard to flogging, as well as a first attempt in this country to clarify public policy with regard to corporal punishment as a whole.

An Act passed in 1817 stated that "judgment shall not be given or awarded against any female convicted of an offence that such female offender do suffer the punishment of being publicly whipped". Another Act in 1820 completely abolished corporal punishment for women whether such punishment was carried out in public or in private. A few years later the Vagrancy Act, 1824, considerably curtailed the power of the magistrates' courts to impose sentences of whipping on men. Up to this, one justice sitting alone had had jurisdiction to order any vagrant to be publicly whipped. By the 1824 Act a vagrant only qualified for corporal punishment on a second or subsequent conviction for a vagrancy offence, and even then he had to be committed to quarter sessions for sentence. The term "vagrant" covered a wide assortment of offenders, including anyone sleeping out, begging, fortune-telling, gaming in a public place, peddling without a licence, wilfully neglecting to maintain his family, and exposing his person with intent to insult a female. The 1824 Act also provided that quarter sessions might imprison the vagrant for any period up to twelve months "and may further order, if they think fit, that such offender (not being a female) be punished by whipping at such time during his imprisonment, and at such place within their jurisdiction, as according to the nature of the offence they in their discretion shall deem to be expedient". These whippings were to be carried out in public as a heightened indignity to the victim. At this time corporal punishment was still the general penalty for all common-law misdemeanours. An Act of Parliament in 1827, which abolished benefit of clergy and the general punishment of death for all felonies, also provided that anyone who should henceforth be convicted of a felony under a statute which laid down no special penalty for the offence in question should be liable to transportation or imprisonment and, if a male, "to be once, twice or thrice publicly or privately whipped".

It is strange to notice how in the decade from 1820 to 1830 the legislature seem to have adopted such an indecisive—even a contradictory—attitude towards corporal punishment. On the one hand, women were excluded from the penalty and vagrants became less likely to receive it; on the other, the range of offences for which it could be ordered was considerably extended. All this happened within an era when the public and the official conscience was being mildly stirred by a movement for penal reform. There were then, as there always have been, a large number of people who regarded a flogging as the ideal form of punishment, swift and inexpensive to administer and providing a direct retributive satisfaction to the honest and law-abiding community.

From time to time for more than a century past voices have been raised in this country calling for the introduction of corporal punishment against any class of offenders which, at that particular moment, has aroused the public indignation. This exact process occurred in the year 1842. In May of that year, when the young Queen Victoria was out driving in her carriage with the Prince Consort, a psychopathic youth named John Francis pointed a pistol at her from the roadside. The pistol had been faultily loaded and could not, in fact, have been fired. Four weeks later the Queen was again in her carriage when an almost identical incident occurred and a second psychopath was arrested. It was realised by the royal advisers that the motive behind these incidents was largely one of exhibitionism, but the only offence with which the culprits could then be charged was the capital felony of high treason. In fact, Francis, who was undoubtedly more in need of treatment than punishment, was sentenced to death, the sentence later being commuted to transportation for life. In an atmosphere of mounting public anger the Treason Act, 1842, was rushed through Parliament. It created certain new offences, including the discharging or aiming any firearm at or near the person of the sovereign, for which the punishment was to be transportation for seven years or imprisonment. In addition, while he was serving his sentence the offender was to be "publicly or privately whipped, as often and in such manner and form as the court may order and direct, not exceeding thrice".

Such was the temper of the House of Commons when the Treason Act was being debated that one member was acclaimed for describing it as being "a measure calculated to mark with the contemptuous execration of the whole nation those brutal attempts on Her Majesty's life".

Corporal punishment has, in fact, never been ordered under this Act.

A few months after the passing of the Treason Act the Commissioners on the Criminal Law submitted a report to Parliament. In it they voiced the first official misgivings about the efficacy of flogging as a punishment for adult offenders, although they specifically excluded from their argument the type of offenders who pointed firearms at the sovereign, for whom they considered whipping to be a suitable, even a highly desirable, form of penalty. The report of the commissioners is of particular interest in view of the fact that it preceded by more than a hundred years the eventual abolition of corporal punishment as a judicial penalty in Britain. In the first place, said the commissioners, there seemed to be very little logic in the separation of offences into those which were and those which were not punishable by whipping.

> We see no reason [the report went on] for confining this species of punishment to the limits within which it is now applicable, if resort to it be advantageous either in respect of deterring or correcting offenders. If, however, the efficacy be not established by experience, we should certainly be inclined to reject it altogether, except in the instance in which it has lately been imposed by the legislature* as constituting a signal mark of ignominy. We think that, so far from extending this species of punishment it would be better to reject it, except in the instance to which we have alluded, and a few, if any others, which it may be proper to mark with signal reprobation. It is a punishment which is uncertain in point of severity, which inflicts an ignominious and indelible disgrace on the offender and tends, we believe, to render him callous and greatly to obstruct his return to any honest course of life.

These comments bore fruit surprisingly quickly. In 1861 a series of important Acts were passed consolidating the law in regard to offences against the person, larceny, forgery, malicious damage, and coining. Between them these Acts embraced a large proportion of the offences then being dealt with by the criminal courts. However, none of them provided the penalty of corporal punishment for persons over 16 years of age.

As it happened, floggings were at that time being ordered less and less for common law misdemeanours, and the effect of the 1861 legislation was virtually to restrict corporal punishment to offences committed under four statutes : the Diplomatic Privileges Act, 1708; the Knackers Act, 1786; the Vagrancy Act, 1824; and the Treason Act, 1842.

Two further reforms were introduced by the Whipping Act, 1862. The first provided that no person should be whipped more than once for the same offence, and the second that all future whippings should be carried out in private.

At this time no one was suggesting that the whip was not a suitable instrument for the punishment of male juvenile delinquents. In fact the tendency was to increase rather than to decrease its availability for this class of offender. An Act passed in 1847 gave justices the power to deal summarily with persons under the age of 14 who were charged with simple larceny. If they convicted a boy of the offence they could order him to be whipped instead of

* The Treason Act, 1842.

or as well as sending him to prison. Since there were then no special prisons for juveniles in those days this provision was probably a merciful one as it made it possible for the young offender to return to his home after the flogging was over. The crop of Acts passed in 1861 also made provision for boys, this time under the age of 16, to be punished for certain offences by being "once privately whipped in addition to a term of imprisonment". The reason for the compulsory term of imprisonment being added to the whipping is probably that these offences were considered to be far more serious than the petty larcenies dealt with by the 1847 Act.

It might have been, and it probably was, thought by a number of people that the 1861 legislation had marked a turning point in the use of corporal punishment as a sentence on adult offenders and that from then on the tendency would be towards a gradual restriction on its employment by the courts. However, in the summer of 1862 there was a sudden outbreak of robberies with violence in the London area, and again and again the victims of these attacks were garrotted, that is to say, half-strangled by the thieves to render them incapable of resisting. Throughout the autumn and winter of that year the crime wave continued amidst the mounting concern of the public.

Eventually, after a Member of Parliament had been set upon, garrotted, and robbed on his way home one evening, a clamour arose for special legislation to deal with this new terror of the streets. Several back-benchers immediately introduced a Bill to make garrotting an offence punishable by flogging. This Bill, which passed into law as the Garrotters' Act, 1863, never obtained the official backing of the Government. In fact it was described by the Home Secretary as a piece of "panic legislation after the panic had subsided". Garrotting and robbery with violence were already punishable with penal servitude for life, but under the new Act the offender could be sentenced, in addition, to be "once, twice or thrice privately whipped". This was, of course, a complete reversal of the policy laid down by the Whipping Act, 1862, to the effect that no person should be flogged more than once for the same offence.

The Garrotters' Act broke new ground inasmuch as it required that a court when ordering a whipping must specify not only the number of strokes to be dealt but must also name the instrument with which the punishment was to be administered. The choice lay between the cat and the birch, with the prescribed maximum of twenty-five strokes of the birch for offenders under 16, and fifty strokes with either the cat or the birch for those who were over 16.

As it happened, the epidemic of robbery with garrotting had died out before the Garrotters' Act became law, but owing to the wide definition given to the crime—"attempting to choke, suffocate or strangle any person with intent thereby to facilitate the commission of any indictable offence"—the Act was subsequently employed against offenders who had half-strangled their victims, not with an intention to rob, but in the course of an attack or a sexual assault.

During the last quarter of the nineteenth century the power of justices of the peace to order whippings for male juvenile offenders was considerably increased, probably because the legislature was at a loss to devise a more suitable form of punishment for the young. At the same time informed opinion was inclining more and more to the view that in general flogging was an unsuitable punishment for adults. But this tendency was not reflected in the Statute Book, for in 1898 a Bill was introduced into Parliament which created two new categories of vagrant, a man who lived on the immoral earnings of a prostitute, and a man who himself solicited for an immoral purpose. Since under the Vagrancy Act of 1824 vagrants could be punished by flogging, this measure indirectly widened the number of offences for which corporal punishment could be inflicted.

Although the Vagrancy Act, 1898, created two new categories of vagrant, it was principally directed against men who lived on the earnings of prostitutes. A special inquiry had been set up in 1881 and had unearthed the disquieting fact that British girls were being systematically introduced into foreign brothels by paid agents operating in England. As a result, the Criminal Law Amendment Act of 1885 had made it an offence, punishable with up to two years' imprisonment, to procure women or girls for immoral purposes. A League of Nations report published many years later said of this Act that it had been successful in its purpose and that the recruitment of women and girls in this country for the purposes of prostitution abroad had been virtually eliminated. But the general public in the closing stages of the nineteenth century was firmly convinced that the white slave traffic in England was continuing to grow. As a result a great deal of attention was focused on the habits of prostitutes, their pimps, and their sponsors. It seems fairly clear that one result of this interest was the inclusion in the Vagrancy Act, 1898, of the offence of living on immoral earnings of a prostitute. Alarm about the supposed large-scale white slave traffic mounted rapidly in the early days of the twentieth century until— in 1912—Parliament passed another Criminal Law Amendment Act and once again, for the third time in seventy years, allayed the apprehension of the public and fulfilled their own sense of duty by extending the penalty of whipping to an entirely new class of offender. Hitherto the men who procured women or girls for immoral purposes had been punished with a maximum of two years in prison. By the new Act they could also receive a flogging with the maximum number of strokes not being specified. For the sake of tidiness the two offences concerning male persons who importuned and those who lived on the immoral earnings of prostitutes were removed from the 1898 Act and embodied in the 1912 Act. There was, however, a difference in the penalties for the three offences. Procurers could be sentenced to a whipping for their first offence, but in the case of the importuners or immoral earners the sentence was only permissible on a second conviction.

The Criminal Law Amendment Act, 1912, has the distinction of being the last statute in this country which made a new offence punishable by whipping. It is true that the Larceny Act of 1916 contained some clauses permitting corporal punishment, but this was merely a consolidating measure as all the offences concerned were previously punishable by whipping under the Garrotters' Act.

By the Criminal Justice Administration Act, 1914, no person could be sentenced to corporal punishment unless he were convicted under some statute which expressly authorised such a penalty. The effect of this provision was, in brief, that the courts were deprived of their power of ordering corporal punishment for common law misdemeanours, a power which had not, in fact, been exercised for a great many years. The Act also laid down that no person should be whipped more than once for the same offence. A clause in the selfsame terms had been included in the Whipping Act, 1862, but, it will be remembered, this was deliberately contravened a short while later by the penalty clause of the Garrotters' Act, by which a defendant could be ordered a whipping once, twice, or three times.

Following the 1914 Act the law in regard to corporal punishment remained unaltered for thirty-four years until its final abolition in 1948.

Chapter Five

Methods and Abolition of Corporal Punishment

IN THE summer of 1938 Mr. Walter Elliott, then the Home Secretary, set up a Departmental Committee under the Hon. Edward Cadogan to study the whole question of corporal punishment as a penalty for criminal offences. This committee, some of whose members actually witnessed sentences of corporal punishment being carried out, investigated the system with meticulous care and described in their report the exact procedure of a judicial flogging.

Of the instruments used for inflicting the punishment, the Cadogan Committee described the birch as being "not a rod or a cane but a bundle of birch twigs—somewhat similar in appearance to the broom or besom used by a gardener for sweeping up leaves but less bulky and not having a wooden handle. The twigs are bound together at the thick end to form a handle, and the remainder is left free so that the loose ends of the twigs form a spray." There were three different types of birch, varying in size and weight, the particulars and dimensions of which were carefully regulated. For instance, the birch used on adults had an overall length of 48 inches and weighed 12 ounces; that used for boys over 10, an overall length of 40 inches and weighed 9 ounces; and finally that used for boys under 10, an overall length of 34 inches and a total weight of 6 ounces.

"The cat-o'-nine-tails", said the committee, "is composed of nine lengths of fine whipcord, whipped at the ends to prevent fraying, and attached to a short handle." Again, the weight and dimensions were laid down precisely. The tails had to be 33 inches long and the handle $19\frac{3}{4}$ inches long (if there was some subtle reason for not enlarging the length of the handle by another quarter of an inch, thus bringing it up to a round figure of 20 inches, it was not stated in the report). The total weight of the instrument was 9 ounces. The committee emphasised that there was no truth in the popular belief that some types of cat were made of leather and that they were either knotted or else were weighted in some other way.

The Cadogan Committee explained that an adult prisoner who was committed for trial on a charge which rendered him liable to corporal punishment was usually detained in custody until he was tried, to enable the prison medical officer to assess whether he was mentally and medically fit for a flogging. If the prisoner had been allowed bail the doctor's opinion would be based on a physical examination only. When the court decided to impose a sentence of corporal punishment the number of strokes would be stated. "In practice," says the report, "the courts appear to have worked to a maximum of 36, or even 24 strokes." In recent years* very few offenders have been sentenced to more than 24 strokes. The prisoner could not be taken away and flogged directly after his sentence had been passed because he was allowed a statutory period of ten days in which he could lodge a notice of appeal. However, if the ten days elapsed and he had not appealed he was again examined by a prison doctor and the flogging was carried out. If he appealed unsuccessfully, of course, he might not receive his flogging for a matter of weeks after the original sentence had been passed.

The Cadogan Committee found that there was no universal requirement that a youthful offender should be medically examined before he was birched. In most police forces it was customary for a police surgeon to see the boy before his punishment was carried out, but "in some districts", said the committee, "this medical examination takes place only if it is suggested by the court or by the parents, or if for some other reason there are grounds for believing that the boy might not be fit to undergo the punishment".

Although a notice of appeal against an order for birching might be lodged on behalf of a juvenile offender at any time within fourteen days of the making of the order by a court of summary jurisdiction, the sentence was not usually postponed for that period. "Unless the parent or other representative of the child signifies his intention to appeal against the order the birching is normally carried out at once—sometimes immediately after the rising of the court and almost always on the day on which the order is given." Although this practice was highly improper from the legal point of view, it was undoubtedly much kinder to the juvenile awaiting the punishment.

* The Cadogan Report was published in 1938.

The parent or guardian of a child had the statutory right to be present during the birching but, not surprisingly, parents very rarely availed themselves of this harrowing privilege.

There may be many people who still imagine that a judicial whipping vaguely resembled a conventional flogging at an English public or preparatory school. This is, however, very far from being the truth. The miscreant schoolboy through a sense of personal pride and in conformity with a long-established tradition submits himself to his beating in a mood of passive stoicism. On the other hand, the victim of a judicial whipping was bound by no prescribed code of conduct; indeed, in the case of an adult, he might well have been a vicious and recalcitrant thug who was just commencing a fairly lengthy prison sentence. Many recipients of the cat and the birch might have been expected to put up some sort of resistance either before or during the flogging. Therefore a system had to be devised to ensure that they were adequately secured.

The Cadogan Committee described what took place. Firstly, in the case of adults :

> A prisoner who is to undergo corporal punishment is strapped to an apparatus, known as a triangle, which is best described as a heavier and more solid form of the easel used to carry a blackboard in a schoolroom. His feet are strapped to the base of the front legs of the triangle. If the cat is to be administered, his hands are raised above his head and strapped to the upper part of the triangle. If he is to be birched, he is bent over a pad placed between the front legs of the triangle and his hands are secured by straps attached to the back legs of the triangle. In both cases he is screened, by canvas sheeting, so that he cannot see the officer who is administering the punishment. The birch is administered across the buttocks, on the bare flesh. The cat is administered across the back, also on the bare flesh, so that the ends of the tails fall on to the right shoulder-blade. When the cat is to be administered, a leather belt is placed round the prisoner's loins and a leather collar round his neck, so as to protect these parts from any injury which might arise from a misdirected stroke. Both the Governor and the Medical Officer of the Prison must be present throughout the execution of a sentence of corporal punishment. The punishment is administered by a prison officer selected for this purpose by the Governor of the Prison, and Governors always take care to select for this duty a steady and experienced officer, who can be relied upon to administer the punishment dispassionately. This officer receives a special allowance of 2s. 6d. for this duty. The strokes are delivered at deliberate intervals—the normal rate is not faster than ten or fifteen strokes a minute—the time being counted by the Chief Officer of the Prison. The Medical Officer stands in a position where he can see the prisoner's face, and he has a complete discretion to stop the punishment at any time, if he

considers that on medical grounds it is undesirable that it should be continued. If a punishment is so stopped, the remainder of it is remitted. At the conclusion of the punishment local dressings are applied, and the Medical Officer gives any other treatment which may be required. In practice, it is only on very rare occasions that the prisoner needs any attention from the Medical Officer; and there have been very few cases in which he has not been able to walk back to his cell without assistance.

Secondly, in the case of juveniles:

> The punishment is usually administered in a cell or private room either within the precincts of the court or at a neighbouring police station. The birch is applied across the buttocks, on the bare flesh. The method most commonly adopted is to bend the boy over a low bench or table. His hands, and sometimes his feet also, are held by police officers. This is done in order to ensure that he shall not move, for if he moved a stroke of the birch might fall on some more sensitive part of the body. This method, though probably the most common, is not universal. In some Police Forces one constable takes the boy on his back, drawing the boy's hands down over his shoulders; another constable holds the boy's feet, drawing his legs round the sides of the first constable; the first constable then leans forward, and the birch is applied by a third. We have also heard that in one Police Force the custom is for one constable to bend the boy over and hold his head between his knees, while a second officer administers the birch. And in one district the boy is strapped to an apparatus similar to the triangle used for corporal punishment in prisons.

The prison officer who administered the flogging to an adult, according to the Cadogan Report, "delivers each stroke with the full force at his command". The committee were assured by very experienced witnesses that a birching, as administered in prison, was almost, if not quite, as painful as a flogging with the cat.

> There is no truth [they said] in the suggestion that the blood flows freely during the infliction of the punishment. Both the cat and the birch are apt to break the skin, but they cause only minor superficial abrasions, which bleed only a small extent. Simple emergency dressings are sometimes applied, but the local physical effects of the punishment seldom require any special medical treatment.

A prison medical officer, having passed a man as fit for a flogging, only occasionally had to intervene and to stop the punishment before the full number of strokes had been applied, and he always did so when he thought that the victim was about to faint.

I have discussed this aspect of physical injury with Sir Bernard Shaw, a retired judge of the Colonial Service, who as a magistrate in Kenya Colony from 1926 to 1936 frequently had to impose sentences of corporal punishment and who had also been present when they were carried out. The instrument used, he told me, had been a cane and the upper limit had been 24 strokes. "This form of punishment", he said, "must have been agonisingly painful and the strokes left little weals. The scars would, in my opinion, have become inconspicuous in time and probably would have eventually disappeared altogether." Sir Bernard told me that in his youth he had lived near a large convict prison in British Guiana.

> In those days [he said] the cat was quite a common form of punishment and although I never witnessed a flogging I was not infrequently aware that one was taking place as I could hear the strokes and the cries of the victim. On one occasion when I was passing close to a working party of prisoners I saw the marks of a flogging with the cat on the body of one man and there could be no doubt at all that very extensive and very serious permanent damage had been done to the skin.

The Cadogan Committee were perfectly satisfied that the medical examination undergone by a prisoner was sufficient to ensure that nobody who would be liable to suffer lasting physical consequences was ever subjected to corporal punishment. They were gravely disturbed, however, about the mental effects of a flogging on a prisoner whose character and disposition made him an unsuitable subject for this form of punishment. Prison governors and medical officers had informed them that they did not have the sufficient opportunity of assessing a man's temperament before a sentence was passed and that "corporal punishment is sometimes ordered by a court in cases which from this point of view are not appropriate for this form of punishment".

Unfortunately, the Cadogan Report did not quote the views and reactions of any of the men whose duty it had been to actually administer the floggings. This omission was partially rectified in a *Report on Corporal Punishment* by the Home Office Advisory Council on the Treatment of Offenders in 1960. Here it was stated that : "Some former police officers who had been called upon during their service to administer the birch to juvenile offenders told us of the disgust which this aroused in them (one having gone so far as to refuse, at the risk of dismissal, to carry out this task a second time), while others said it left them quite unmoved and unaffected."

The report of the Cadogan Committee recommended that the use of corporal punishment as a judicial penalty both for adults and for juveniles alike should be entirely abandoned. The reasons for this conclusion, based on the most painstaking researches, are set out in full in the 150-odd pages of the report, but as they are not relevant to the context in which I write I do not intend to elaborate on them. Suffice it to say that the committee was eventually driven to the conclusion that corporal punishment could only possibly be justified on the basis of its value as a deterrent. In an effort to determine whether flogging had some special element of deterrence not provided by other available methods of punishment the committee, with the co-operation of the Home Office and New Scotland Yard, had analysed the records of 440 prisoners who had been convicted of robbery with violence during the period between 1921 and 1930, and had compared the later histories of those who had and those who had not received a flogging. The committee found that the subsequent criminal records of the men who had been flogged were even worse than those of the men who had simply been sentenced to periods of imprisonment or penal servitude.

The committee had also studied records and statistics relating to other offences for which corporal punishment had been employed as a penalty. At the end of their researches they commented:

> We have been unable to find any body of facts or figures showing that the introduction of a power of flogging has produced a decrease in the number of offences for which it may be imposed, or that offences for which flogging may be ordered have tended to increase when little use was made of the power to order flogging, or to decrease when the power was exercised more frequently.

Both the reasoned arguments and the conclusions of the Cadogan Committee were, perhaps, irresistible. Their recommendation that corporal punishment should be abolished was accepted by the Conservative Government who were then in office and it was intended to introduce a section to this effect in a new Criminal Justice Bill which was in process of preparation. But the Bill was shelved on the outbreak of war in 1939 and it was not until the Labour Government came to power in 1945 that Great Britain finally decided, as most other civilised nations had done a great many years before, to abolish flogging as a sentence of the courts. This was achieved by Section 2 of the Criminal Justice Act, 1948.

In point of fact, corporal punishment had been ordered comparatively rarely during the final epoch when it had been available as a penalty. In the early years of the twentieth century a large number of juveniles were sentenced to receive a birching. The annual figure for England and Wales from 1900 to 1920 varied between 1380 and 5210. From that time forward there had been a considerable tailing off in these numbers and between 1930 and 1936 the yearly total only once exceeded 200. Indeed, by the end of the 1930's the use of corporal punishment as a judicial penalty for juvenile offenders had almost died out completely as the courts had turned to more modern and more progressive forms of treatment.

Although from the year 1916 there had been seven different Acts of Parliament under which the superior courts could order a whipping, the penalty was virtually employed only for offences of robbery with violence, and even then in a small proportion of the cases. For the rest, the number of sentences of corporal punishment for each of the offences of indecent exposure, importuning, and living on the immoral earnings of prostitutes worked out at an average of less than one a year.

The percentage of men who were convicted of robbery with violence in England and Wales and were sentenced to corporal punishment was :

From 1921 to 1930   32·3%
  1931 to 1940   30·3%
  1941 to 1948   14·1%

The total numbers of sentences of corporal punishment during the last five years in which it could be awarded by the courts of this country were :

1944   68 sentences
1945   39 sentences
1946   48 sentences
1947   58 sentences
1948   26 sentences

In January 1960 the Home Secretary, Mr. R. A. Butler (now Lord Butler), asked the Advisory Council on the Treatment of

Offenders to consider whether there were grounds for the reintroduction of any form of corporal punishment as a judicial penalty. Mr. Butler informed the Council that there appeared to be considerable support, both in Parliament and in the country, for the reinstatement of this sentence and that as it was being suggested that new types of crime and new types of criminals had arisen since 1948, it was desirable that there should be a fresh review of the matter in the light of post-war trends in crime and of current opinions on the treatment of offenders.

The Advisory Council not only studied the Cadogan Report but they also considered statistical and medical evidence and results of the experience in other countries. They published their report in November 1960.

The Council faced the fact from the outset that the general feeling in this country seemed to favour a return to corporal punishment.

> A public opinion poll [they said] the results of which were published in March 1960, indicated that 74% of the population considered that corporal punishment should be the penalty for some offences and while the interpretation of the results of this poll requires some caution, they are, in fact, supported by the opinions expressed by our own correspondents and in letters received by the Home Office during our enquiry. . . . The Lord Chief Justice* was good enough to submit to us a memorandum which he had previously circulated among all the other judges of the Queen's Bench Division and other persons concerned with the administration of the criminal law. The great majority of those whom he consulted agreed with him that the reintroduction of judicial corporal punishment in certain circumstances might be desirable, but there was a minority who disagreed.

Nevertheless, the Council concluded : "Having studied the views expressed to us and all the available evidence, we consider that the findings of the Cadogan Committee are still valid, and have come unanimously to the conclusion that corporal punishment should not be reintroduced as a judicial penalty in respect of any categories of offences or of offenders." They added : "There is no evidence that corporal punishment is an especially effective deterrent either to those who have received it or to others."

---

* Lord Goddard.

Chapter Six

Corporal Punishment in Prisons

THE punishment of disciplinary offences in prisons and the sentencing of lawbreakers in the criminal courts are naturally governed by vastly differing considerations.

For one thing the prisoner, owing to his circumstances, is ineligible for any penalty involving either an immediate deprivation of liberty or the payment of a monetary fine. For another, the maintenance of obedience and good order amongst the prison population is so essential that the scale of punishment for breaches of prison rules has always been rather severe.

For a long time flogging has been regarded as the obvious punishment for major infringements of prison discipline. Indeed, in the early gaols the use of the whip was frequent, brutal, and indiscriminate.

The first really serious attempt to control the internal system of prison discipline was made by Sir Robert Peel, as Home Secretary, with his Gaol Act of 1823 which amended and consolidated all the previous legislation in regard to local prisons. By this Act the gaoler or keeper of a prison was empowered to deal with minor offences himself, but graver offences were to come before a board of specially appointed visiting justices. In the case of a prisoner who had been imprisoned for a felony, or who was undergoing a sentence of hard labour, the visiting justices could punish him with what the Act referred to as "personal correction". Before they awarded a flogging, however, the board had to satisfy themselves of the prisoner's guilt by a proper inquiry taken under oath. A few years later it was provided that the visiting justices could impose a maximum sentence of 36 strokes with the cat or the birch to prisoners over 18 and a maximum of 18 strokes with the cat or the birch to prisoners under that age.

The Transportation Act, 1824, which set out the conditions under which prisoners sentenced to transportation were to be treated while they were detained in this country, authorised the superintendent or overseer of convicts to inflict "such moderate punishment or correction as shall be allowed by one of His Majesty's Secretaries of State" on any convict who was guilty of misbehaviour or disorderly conduct. The "moderate" punishment allowed was the same as the visiting justice could award, 36 or 18 strokes according to whether the convict was above or below the age of 18.

In 1850 the power to order the flogging of a convict was transferred from the superintendent or overseer mentioned in the Transportation Act to the directors of convict prisons, and in 1877, when local prisons became the responsibility of the State, a similar jurisdiction, which had formerly been allowed by the visiting justices, was thenceforth exercisable by a new body known as Visiting Committees. The members of these committees were, in fact, the local justices of the peace who were empowered to supervise prison discipline, to inquire into the complaints of the prisoners, and to adjudicate on serious infringements of the prison rules.

A new prison rule was introduced by the Home Secretary in 1878 specifying the offences which could qualify a prisoner for corporal punishment. The rule stated:

> The following offences committed by male prisoners convicted of felony or sentenced to hard labour will render them liable to corporal punishment.
>
> 1. Mutiny or open incitement to mutiny in the prison; personal violence to any officer or servant of the prison; aggravated or repeated assault on a fellow prisoner; repetition of insulting or threatening language to any officer or prisoner.
> 2. Wilfully and maliciously breaking the windows or otherwise destroying the prison's property.
> 3. When under punishment wilfully making a disturbance tending to interrupt the order and discipline of the prison, and any other act of gross misconduct or insubordination requiring to be suppressed by extraordinary means.

Between 1870 and 1900 floggings were administered only to roughly 1 per cent of the inmates of convict and local prisons every year. Some indication of the comparative infrequency of this form of punishment can be seen from the statistics for three separate years selected at random, during this period:

Year	Daily average number of prisoners in convict and local prisons	Total number of floggings
1872–3	22,026	259
1883–4	22,865	225
1893–4	15,632	137

A Departmental Committee on Prisons in the year 1895 reported :

> During recent years there has been a distinct move forward in the direction of mitigating the severity of prison punishments. The use of the entirely dark cell has been discontinued . . . and the figures show that corporal punishment has decreased in a striking degree in local prisons. In convict prisons the total number of instances also shows a marked decrease but the percentage remains about stationary.

The departmental committee also endorsed a prison standing order which stated that "discipline is not better maintained by resorting commonly to severe punishment, which should be reserved for use when milder measures have been tried unsuccessfully and when it is necessary to apply them on particular occasions".

In 1896 Sir Matthew White Ridley, who was then Home Secretary, investigated the details of all sentences of corporal punishment in prisons inflicted during the preceding period of twelve months. He found that in local prisons 97 men had been flogged, 19 with the cat and 78 with the birch, and that out of this total only 24 had had the punishment inflicted for violence to a warder or to a fellow prisoner. An important fact which came to light from Sir Matthew's inquiry was the very wide discrepancy in the number of strokes which had been ordered for identical offences in different prisons.

In the following year, 1897, a new prison rule was introduced affecting all local prisons, which greatly reduced the range of offences for which corporal punishment might be inflicted. Henceforth, flogging was only to be awarded for the following offences :

(a)   Mutiny or incitement to mutiny.
(b)   Personal violence to any officer or servant of the prison.
(c)   An act of gross insubordination.

Similar rules were put into operation in convict prisons so that a uniform system became applicable to every gaol in the country.

The Prison Act, 1898, brought about a further restriction in the offences for which a prisoner could be flogged and reduced their number to two. These were mutiny or incitement to mutiny and gross personal violence to a prison officer. The Act also provided that the only prisoners who could be flogged were those who were serving sentences of penal servitude or hard labour and those who had been convicted of felony.

When Borstal institutions came into being in the early days of the present century the provisions of the Prison Act, 1898, with regard to the infliction of corporal punishment, were also extended to them. This created a somewhat anomalous situation. A Borstal sentence was wholly different from a sentence of either hard labour or of penal servitude, so it followed that under the 1898 Act the only inmates of Borstal institutions who could be punished by flogging were those who had been convicted of felony. As the distinction between felonies and misdemeanours was by no means indicative of the gravity of an offence it meant that it was largely fortuitous whether or not a Borstal boy was eligible for corporal punishment.

One might have expected that corporal punishment would have been administered fairly frequently in borstals but, in fact, during the first thirty years after these institutions were founded there was an average of less than one flogging a year in all the borstals in England. The use of corporal punishment was also decreasing for adult prison offences over the same period. In the early days of the present century about 40 prisoners were flogged every year; by the close of the 1930's this number had fallen to an annual average of less than 10. By the 1960's only about three recommendations for prison floggings were made each year out of which probably one or two were actually confirmed by the Home Secretary.

In the course of their report in 1938 the Cadogan Committee considered the use of corporal punishment for prison offences. They said :

> We have heard evidence from a large number of prison officials—Prison Commissioners, Governors, Medical Officers and senior prison officers—and from representatives of the Boards of Visitors and Visiting Committees. All these witnesses had close personal experience of prison administration, in many cases extending over a large number of years. Without exception they were all convinced that corporal punishment exercises a definite deterrent influence in checking offences of violence against officers, but they all stressed primarily the deterrent effect on others.

The Committee concluded :

> We are thus satisfied that the fear of corporal punishment does exercise a strong deterrent influence in restraining violent prisoners who would otherwise commit serious assaults on prison officers; that no other penalty would operate as an equal or sufficient deterrent; and

that, as it is imposed for prison offences, corporal punishment is not open to the main objections which can be urged against it as a penalty imposed by the courts for offences against the criminal law. . . . We have come to the conclusion that the time has not yet come when this power (i.e. of flogging in prisons) could safely be abandoned. We consider that it should be held in reserve as the ultimate sanction by which to enforce prison discipline; but we think that it should continue to be used very sparingly and we hope that in the course of time, as the character of the prison population improves and there is less need for purely repressive measures, it will be found possible to dispense altogether with the use of this form of punishment.

In the years which followed the close of the Second World War a considerable relaxation took place in the relationship between prison officers and prisoners, and with the abandonment of many of the harsher forms of discipline of the past and the amelioration of some of the more rigorous discomfitures of prison existence, an atmosphere was created in which the prisoner was considerably less likely to offer violence against those whose task and duty it was to supervise him.

Finally, on 1 October 1967, by Section 65 of the Criminal Justice Act, 1967, corporal punishment in prisons and prison institutions came to an end.

Chapter Seven

Capital Punishment

THERE can be few stronger or more persistent desires to the primitive instinct than the total destruction of one's enemies. This inclination exists both on the personal and on the collective level and it has lain at the roots of punishment since the very earliest times.

Not only must one's enemy be utterly destroyed, but his destruction must be brought upon him in as agonising a manner as can be devised. In this way his death will both heighten one's own sense of retribution and achieve the maximum deterrent effect on one's other potential adversaries.

The form of penal execution most favoured in England has usually been death by hanging. However, at various stages of history other methods of judicial killing have been practised. At one time it would appear that ordinary criminals were beheaded, for there is a reference to this form of execution in the Parliament Rolls for 1314, and again, about the same period, there are several allusions to beheading in the official Yearbooks.

I have already mentioned the Act, in the reign of Henry VIII, which prescribed boiling to death as the punishment for murder by poisoning. Another form of judicial killing, principally used with women prisoners, was death by burning. At one time women were liable to this penalty if they had been convicted of high treason or petty treason—a term which embraced a number of different offences including husband murder and all forms of witchcraft. The executioner was permitted to strangle the victim at the stake before the flames had actually taken hold of her clothing, but whether he did so or not appears to have been left very largely to his own discretion and there were cases when the executioner declined this act of "mercy" through fear of being caught in the flames himself. Sometimes arrangements were made for the woman to be hanged just prior to the stake being set alight. A description of such an execution in the year 1722 has been left to us by an onlooker:

> The prisoner [he says] was clothed in a cloth made like a shift, saturated with tar, and her limbs were smeared with the same inflammable substance, while a tarred bonnet was placed on her head. She

was brought out of the prison barefoot and being put on a hurdle, was drawn to the place of execution near the gallows. Upon arrival, some time was passed in prayer, after which the executioner placed her on a tar barrel at a height of three feet against the stake. A rope ran through a pulley in the stake and was placed around her neck, she herself fixing it with her hands. Three irons also held her body to the stake and the rope being pulled tight, the tar barrel was taken aside and the fire lighted . . . she was probably dead before the fire reached her as the executioner pulled upon the rope several times whilst the irons were being fixed.

Hanging was substituted for burning as the official form of death for women in 1790.

The execution of males who had been convicted of treason had its own special complement of brutalities and horrors with which I will deal later.

Under the Saxon and Danish kings of England, criminals were also killed by drowning and hurling from rocks, the latter method being a custom borrowed from the Romans.

William the Conqueror abolished capital punishment and substituted mutilation for all major offences; but gradually, in the years that followed, execution was introduced as the penalty for more and more crimes until in the year 1819 there were said to be some 180 offences punishable by death. These included many offences which we would at the present time deem to be trivial —as, for instance, associating with gipsies and stealing turnips from a field.

Even Sir Edward Coke, who was appointed Chief Justice of the King's Bench in 1613 and was by no means regarded as a benevolent or a humane judge, wrote in his third Institute : "What a lamentable case it is to see so many Christian men and women strangled on that cursed tree of the gallows, insomuch as if in a large field a man might see together all the Christians that, but in one year throughout England come to that untimely and ignominious death, if there were any spark of grace or charity in him, it would make his heart bleed for pity and compassion."

As recently as 1810 Sir Samuel Romilly was telling the House of Lords that there was "no country on the face of the earth in which there were so many different offences according to law to be punished with death as in England". And in 1830 Sir Robert Peel said in the House of Commons : "It is impossible to conceal from ourselves that capital punishments are more frequent and the criminal law more severe on the whole in this country than in any country in the world."

Transportation greatly reduced the number of executions and from the 1830's onwards the austerity of the law was somewhat mitigated. Statistics show that in 1831 sentence of death was passed on 1601 prisoners for all sorts of offences. This total, incidentally, includes only 14 persons convicted of murder. By 1838 the number of death sentences had fallen to 116, of which 25 were for murder. Not all these criminals were in fact executed, a proportion being reprieved in both of the years I have mentioned.

The punishment for murder was identical with the punishment for all minor capital felonies save that it seems to have been the custom to hang the murderer's corpse in chains directly after the execution. This procedure, known as gibbeting, was given statutory authority by an Act of 1752 which left it to the discretion of the judge whether or not this particular part of the sentence was to be enforced. The 1752 Act also required that the bodies of executed murderers should be delivered to surgeons for dissection. Gibbetings were carried out in Britain even in the nineteenth century, the bodies sometimes being left to hang for a year or more. According to official records the last known gibbeting occurred in Leicester in 1832. The penalty was abolished in 1834.

Hangings were a public spectacle attended by large crowds of morbid sightseers. In a following chapter I will deal in greater detail with the ritual which grew up around judicial executions.

The old volumes of *State Trials* provide us with a number of eye-witness accounts of the hanging of condemned men and women. The contemporary reporters took as much care in describing the final scenes as they did to detailing the earlier judicial proceedings in court. Great importance was always attached to the final speech from the scaffold, and a good deal of trouble was taken by the authorities to persuade prisoners to make a full confession before they died. Whether this was for the good of the condemned persons' souls or to salve the official consciences for the monstrosities which were about to be committed on the victims, one does not know.

In the ninth volume of *State Trials* there is a report of a trial which took place at the Old Bailey in 1682 when four men were charged with murder. Three of them, named Borosky, Vratz, and Stern, were convicted and the account concludes with the following description of their executions :

> On the 10th March following they were all three executed in Pall-mall, the same place they had committed the murder. . . . Captain Vratz would make no confession but persisted in denying what the others had owned; never did man die with more resolution and less sign of fear and disorder; his carriage both as he was led along and at the place of execution was astonishing; he was not only undaunted, but looked cheerful and smiled often: when the rope was put about his neck he did not change colour, nor tremble, his legs were firm under him; he looked often about on those who stood in balconies or at the windows and seemed to fix his eyes on some particular persons; three or four times he smiled; he would not cover his face as the rest did, but continued in an undaunted manner, looking up to the heaven with a cheerfulness in his countenance, and a little motion of his hands. Being asked if he had anything to say to the people, he said no. When they had stood about a quarter of an hour under the gibbet, after being tied up, they were asked when they would give the signal for being turned off; they answered they were ready; so a little while after the cart was driven away and thus ended their lives. Captain Vratz was permitted to be buried, but Stern and Borosky were hanged in chains.

The procedure for hanging a woman was identical with that for hanging a man. A young woman named Mary Blandy was executed in Oxford in 1752, having been convicted of the murder of her father. The final scene is again described in the *State Trials* for that year. The chronicler tells how a clean white handkerchief was placed over the victim's face. He goes on : "Her hands were tied together with a strong, black riband and her feet, at her own request, almost touched the ground. The number of people attending her execution was calculated at about 5,000, many of whom and particularly several gentlemen of the university, were observed to shed tears."

Mary Blandy, we are told, was left hanging for half an hour, but the narrative does not disclose how soon a merciful oblivion intervened to terminate her agony.

The worst barbarities of all were reserved for men who had been sentenced to death for high treason. The procedure of execution was comprised of six stages :

1. The prisoner was "drawn" to the gallows. In the early days he was literally dragged along the ground behind a cart, and to add to the ordeal sharp and jagged stones were sometimes put down along the route it would take. Later this part of the

punishment was alleviated and the prisoner was carried on a hurdle or a sledge.

2. The prisoner was hanged by the neck and was cut down whilst he was still alive.
3. His bowels were skewered from his body and his private parts were cut off.
4. Whilst the prisoner was still living his bowels were burnt in his presence.
5. His head was cut off.
6. His body was chopped into four quarters which remained, technically, at the monarch's disposal.

Time and again this nightmarish procedure was carried out in all its scarcely credible brutality, but gradually, as there are limits beyond which even a psychopathic sadist will not travel, the officials directly concerned with the hideous ceremonial found ways of mitigating its savagery. It is said that most executioners delayed the cutting down until they believed the prisoner to be dead, and often some of the other elements in the punishment were quietly omitted.

On the other hand, high treason was regarded as a personally mortal offence by the monarch and by the principal advisers to the throne, and since the main object of public executions was to inspire terror into the minds of the onlookers, it was considered that the maximum effect would be achieved by as great an exhibition of savagery as could be staged. For this reason there were usually a number of influential persons who were anxious that the cruelty of the proceedings should not be mitigated to any appreciable extent.

Sometimes, indeed, the executioners received special instructions to pile on the atrocities. Such an occasion was the execution of the first seven of the young conspirators after the discovery of the so-called Babington Plot in the autumn of 1586. Alan Gordon Smith, who made a close study of all the contemporary documents, has described the scene in his authentic and knowledgeable book *The Babington Plot*.

> On the morning of the 20th of September [writes Mr. Gordon Smith] they were drawn on hurdles from the Tower of London—Ballard leading; then two by two, Babington and Savage, Barnwell and

Tichborne, Tilney and Abingdon. The processions passed through the thronged streets of the city and so out along Holborn to a point where, just off the road, in the fields towards St. Giles, a scaffold had been constructed, surmounted by a high gallows. A dense crowd of onlookers were assembled all about it—some truculent, some curious, some inwardly sympathetic—and they strained to catch what they could of the conspirators' last words.

Most of the young men involved in this plot were only of undergraduate age. The leader, Anthony Babington, was, in fact, still a student at the Inns of Court. Early in his life he had inherited large estates at Dethick, near Matlock in Derbyshire, and in common with a number of the "landed gentry" of the time was studying law, not with the intention of becoming a practising barrister but to give him a sounder knowledge for the management of his family property. The basis of the conspiracy was religion. Babington had been secretly converted to the Church of Rome and had become involved in an underground system of communication between the imprisoned Mary, Queen of Scots, and her contacts in France. Later he had been persuaded to plan a coup by which Queen Elizabeth was to be deposed and the Catholic Queen of Scots was to be placed on the throne in her stead.

When they reached the place of execution the seven conspirators made their final speeches from the scaffold. Alan Gordon Smith's account continues :

The crowd inevitably had been impressed by the youth and demeanour of the seven; but when the punishment began, a sentiment of mere pity was kindled to one of horror and indignation. For it was apparent, immediately, that the hangman had received instructions. Ballard was the first taken. After one swing from the gibbet he was cut down alive and disembowelled. While the rest averted their faces, Babington, the next to suffer, stood calmly covered, looking on indifferently at everything that was done. He also, when his turn came, was taken from the gibbet alive. "Parce mihi", he was heard repeating as long as he was still breathing. Savage, a heavier man, broke the rope as soon as he was jerked from the cart and immediately on falling was seized by the executioner, castrated, ripped up and disembowelled alive. The other four were dealt with in a similar fashion. According to the official account of Camden, after hanging they were all cut down, "their privates cut off, bowelled alive and seeing, and quartered— not", he confesses thoughtfully, "without some note of cruelty".

Towards the end there had been no mistaking the dangerous change that had come over the crowd, and the Privy Councillors, who had been present, represented to the Queen that, with the seven others remaining, it might not be judicious to proceed to the same extremities.

The following day when the seven remaining conspirators were executed it was noticed that a similar degree of diabolical cruelty was not repeated.

As soon as all these fourteen young men had been dispatched it was considered prudent to issue an official statement in the name of the Queen absolving her from any responsibility for what had taken place during the first day's executions. In the light of accumulated information Mr. Gordon Smith dismisses this statement as a "cowardly official lie". It read: "The Queen, being informed of the severity used in the executions the day before, and detesting such cruelty, gave express orders that these should be used more favourably and accordingly they were permitted to hang till they were quite dead, before they were cut down and bowelled."

To complete the retribution the estates of all the conspirators were forfeited and the whole of their families, irrespective of their ignorance of the entire affair, were thrown into disgrace. However, this dishonour was by no means indefinite as soon afterwards, in 1611, the son of Anthony Babington's younger brother was appointed to be Protestant Bishop of Londonderry.

Sometimes the hangman used to use his own crude methods to extinguish the life of a half-dead prisoner before he proceeded to the official barbarities which were involved in the ritual execution for high treason. In the *State Trials* series for the year 1746 there is reported the public execution of one Francis Townley. The account reads:

> After he had hung six minutes he was cut down and having life in him as he lay upon the block to be quartered, the executioner gave him several blows on his breast, which not having the effect desired, he immediately cut his throat after which he took his head off; then ripped him open and took out his bowels and heart, and threw them into a fire, which consumed them; then he slashed his four quarters; and put them with the head in a coffin and they were carried to the new gaol at Southwark where they were deposited till Saturday, August 2nd, when his head was put on Temple Bar, and his body and limbs suffered to be buried.

The reporter of these proceedings adds, with a touch of compassion: "This unfortunate person was about 38 years of age, born near Wigan in Lancashire, of a very good family . . . the morning of his execution, and even at the fatal place, he showed no manner of signs of dread, but said he hoped he should be happy in the next world."

Sometimes the sovereign, as an act of leniency, would order that some of the more horrible incidents of a treason execution should not take place. Thus, the official account of the execution of Edward Despard and several others in 1803 recounts that they :

> were severally hanged, after being suspended for nearly half an hour they were cut down, and their heads severed from their bodies; the executioner exhibiting each head separately to public view said, "This is the head of a traitor". . . . The King graciously remitted the execution of the remainder of the sentence and their bodies were delivered to their respective friends.

In 1814 the parts of the formal execution for high treason which related to disembowelling and burning the intestines were abolished.

There is an official record of an execution for treason in 1817 in which the prisoners were hanged, after which their bodies were beheaded. The death warrants were signed on that occasion by the Prince Regent and it is said that the poet Shelley was amongst the onlookers. The three victims were Jeremiah Brandreth, William Turner, and Isaac Ludlam. The executioners wore masks to prevent identification and a force of infantry and cavalry with drawn swords surrounded the scaffold. One account states that when the decapitations took place a "terrifying shriek set up and the multitude ran violently in all directions". Another report says that, "At the hideous spectacle the whole crowd with a cry of horror, reeled and staggered back several yards."

From these descriptions one might be tempted to draw the conclusion that the British public at that time was becoming a bit more squeamish with regard to the barbarities which were being committed at executions. But in spite of the apparent revulsion on the minds of the onlookers the procedure still continued unaltered. In 1820 five of the Cato Street conspirators were hanged and beheaded in the same manner. The executioner on that occasion again wore a mask and his identity was kept closely secret. He was believed to be a surgeon owing to the professional efficiency with which he carried out his grisly duties.

I shall deal with the abolition of public executions in a following chapter.

During the past centuries, British judges as a body have been resolute believers in the efficacy of hanging as a punishment, and this irrespective of the age of the prisoner. In 1748 Chief Justice

Willis postponed the execution of a boy of 10, sentenced to death for murder, in order to consult his fellow judges as to whether it was proper to hang a child so young. The judges were unanimous in thinking that the punishment should be carried out, "for it would be a very dangerous consequence", they said, "to have it thought that children may commit such atrocious crimes with impunity . . .". They added that "the taking away of the life of a boy of ten years old may savour of cruelty, yet the example of this boy's punishment may be a means of deterring other children from the like offences".

In 1800 another boy was sentenced to death, this time for secreting bank notes at the Chelmsford Post Office. The trial judge, writing about the case a short while after it had taken place, said : "I therefore refused the application of his counsel to respite the judgment on the ground of his tender years, being satisfied that he knew perfectly what he was doing."

It would be easy to condemn the reactionary attitude of the judiciary throughout past ages on the subject of punishment generally. However, it is only fair to remember that the judges were merely reflecting the general sentiments of their times. The politicians, the writers, and the philosophers of a period have always dictated the current attitudes of thought, and the influence of the judges in this respect has usually been somewhat limited. It should also be borne in mind that the insensibility of the penal system was designed, in part at least, to compensate for the inefficiency and the inadequacy of the forces of law and order, and brutal sentences were regarded as providing a measure of protection to the public against the depredations of the criminal.

It would be extremely gratifying to scan the pages of British legal and social history and to find that the members of the judiciary were invariably in the forefront of the movements towards enlightenment, progress, and humanity. Unfortunately, until very recently, this has never been the case; in fact, it would be fair to say the judges have usually been amongst the principal opponents of penal reform. It may be that they were too far divided from the rest of the populace in the remoteness of their dignity, and too far removed in their standards of physical comfort and intellectual elegance. Perhaps if a number of them had personally investigated the pitiable squalor of the prisons, the depravity of the hulks, and the bestial cruelties on the scaffold, some at least might have been shocked into a public condemnation of the entire penal system. But, as it was, they preferred to remain either ignorant of or acquiescent to the aftermath of their judgments and of all the ensuing horrors which were being carried out in the name of the law.

Chapter Eight

Benefit of Clergy

ABOUT twelve years ago I listened to an impromptu discussion on capital punishment over the luncheon table in the Barristers' Mess at the Old Bailey. I happened to be sitting next to the Senior Medical Officer of Brixton Prison, who had himself given evidence at a large number of murder trials. Someone asked the doctor if he thought capital punishment would be abolished in the near future and he replied that in his opinion we were rapidly approaching the stage when British juries would be reluctant to convict in murder cases, merely so as to keep the defendants from the gallows. This was, of course, before the 1957 Homicide Act which divided murder charges into two classes—the one capital and the other non-capital.

There is nothing novel about the theory that the severity of criminal punishments can have the effect of influencing juries to acquit. Indeed, it was a view expressed by Jeremy Bentham over 150 years ago, and it was undoubtedly one of the factors which prompted Parliament during the course of the nineteenth century to curtail so drastically the number of offences which carried the penalty of death.

Throughout the history of our criminal law the judicial process has frequently been adapted, by means of recognised fictions and circumventions, for the purpose of mitigating the rigours and the inhumanities of punishment. Hence, at one time the defendant on a capital charge could obtain an acquittal merely because there had been some trivial technical defect in the wording of the indictment. For instance, in a murder trial if the surname of the person killed had been mis-spelt, or if one of his Christian names had been accidentally omitted—errors which today would be remedied very simply by a formal amendment—that might have resulted in a dismissal of the charge. One of the most important and the most commonly utilised of these legal fictions was the strange and ancient doctrine known as Benefit of Clergy.

Benefit of Clergy originated from the principle that only the ecclesiastical courts had the necessary criminal jurisdiction to deal with men who were clerks in holy orders. Henry de Bracton in his authoritative treatise on the English law, written about 1250, says :

> When a Clerk of whatever order or dignity is taken for the death of a man or for any other crime, and imprisoned, and an application is made for him in the Court Christian by the Ordinary . . . the prisoner must be immediately delivered up without making any inquisition. He must not, however, be set at liberty and allowed to wander about the country, but is to be safely kept, either in the bishop's prison, or in the King's prison if the Ordinary wishes, till he has duly purged himself from the accusation laid upon him, or has failed to purge himself, for which he ought to be degraded.

If a clerk in holy orders appeared before his bishop and a jury of his fellow clerks and he was convicted by them, the worst penalty he could suffer was to be downgraded in his ecclesiastical status or made to perform some religious penance.

Because of the great discrepancy between the punishments imposed by the lay courts and the ecclesiastical courts, a number of laymen took up some degree of minor orders or entered the service of an ecclesiastical dignitary simply to avoid the harsh sentences which otherwise might have been imposed on them if they were convicted of a crime.

In consequence of a statute in the year 1275 an accused person could only claim Benefit of Clergy after he had been formally indicted with an offence. A short while later the practice was again altered and prisoners were not permitted to make the claim unless and until they had actually been convicted.

Benefit never existed for all offences without exception. There were always some crimes for which the lay courts claimed to have a jurisdiction even over clerics. Hence the terms "clergyable felonies" came into being, covering offences for which Benefit existed, and "non-clergyable felonies" for offences for which it was not allowed.

In 1350 the privilege of Benefit was extended and was made available to the holders of a number of subsidiary ecclesiastical appointments, for instance doorkeepers and exorcists, whose connection with a clerkship in holy orders was somewhat remote. By a further sweeping extension Benefit was made available for all those defendants who were able to read, whether they were clerics or not. Thenceforth quite a considerable proportion of the population became immune from the penalties prescribed by the criminal law and were free to commit an unlimited number of crimes and always to avoid punishment by claiming Benefit. This ludicrous position was altered in 1487 when it was enacted that every person convicted of a clergyable felony was to be branded on the brawn of the thumb with the letter M if he had committed a murder, and with the letter T for any other offence. If the same person claimed Benefit of Clergy a second time, his plea was refused unless he could prove that he had actually been ordained.

The procedure for claiming Benefit was that the prisoner waited until he was asked if he had anything to say, just before the sentence of the court was passed on him. He would then fall on his knees in the dock and would read the first verse of the 51st Psalm, known as the "neck verse", which ran :

> Have mercy upon me, O God, according to thy
>   loving kindness;
> According to the multitude of thy tender mercies,
>   blot out my transgressions.

The strong tug-of-war between the desire to maintain public order and the wish to alleviate the undue severity of the criminal code continued unabated. The law-makers, very naturally, sought to exclude as many offences as possible from being clergyable felonies and they gradually whittled down the number of crimes for which Benefit was available. In 1496 a person who murdered his "lord, master or sovereign" was deprived of the privilege. In 1512 murders committed in churches or on highways were also made non-clergyable. In 1531 petty treason and robbery of holy places were added to the list, and, in 1536, all offences concerned with piracy. In subsequent years further crimes which were designated as non-clergyable included murder, highway robbery, rape, sacrilege, abduction, and certain forms of burglary and house-breaking.

But by and large Benefit of Clergy continued to play a predominant part in the administration of the criminal law for several centuries to come. In theory a prisoner who had made a successful claim was handed over to the ecclesiastical courts in order that he might be purged of his offence; in practice it seems very doubtful if this procedure was often followed as the clerical authorities had little or no facilities for dealing with ordinary criminals. In 1576 purgation was abolished by an Act of Parliament which required that from then on prisoners claiming Benefit should be branded with a hot iron on the brawn of the left thumb and should then be discharged from custody forthwith. Indeed, this had usually happened even before the Act, subject to the right of the trial judge to impose a sentence of one year's imprisonment if he chose to do so.

The position of women in respect of Benefit of Clergy was a strange and anomalous one. Women could not be ordained, and consequently it was considered for many years that they must be ineligible for the privilege of Benefit unless, up to the time of the Reformation, they happened to belong to one of the recognised orders of nunnery. However, when it came to be universally acknowledged that Benefit had developed into a legal fiction which bore little relationship to its historical origins, there remained no rational basis for the continued exclusion of the female sex. Accordingly, in the year 1622 women became partially eligible for the privilege, and in 1692 all the remaining distinctions were removed and they were placed on an identical footing with men.

Although the test of eligibility for Benefit of Clergy was in theory dependent upon the prisoner's ability to read, in fact many illiterate prisoners used to learn the text of the "neck verse" by heart and would then recite it from the dock with an open Prayer Book in their hands. In 1705 this subterfuge was granted official recognition and it was enacted that prisoners claiming Benefit would no longer be required to prove their capability of reading but should be permitted to memorise their lines.

By that time the criminal law had become divided into two distinct types of felony, those which were non-clergyable being punished with the utmost severity, and those which were clergyable only being punishable with a maximum of one year's imprisonment. Sir William Blackstone in his *Commentaries on the Laws of England,* first published in 1769, wrote : "Among the variety of actions which men are daily liable to commit no less than 160 have been declared by Act of Parliament to be felonies without Benefit of Clergy, or, in other words, worthy of instant death."

The incongruous situation in which a layman could only claim Benefit on one single occasion whereas a cleric might go on claiming the privilege indefinitely, thereby escaping serious punishment, was rectified to some extent in 1717 when clergyable offences became punishable with transportation for seven years in lieu of branding.

Benefit of Clergy was not finally abolished until 1827. The Act of abolition would have increased the number of executions to an appalling extent but for a section which provided that no one convicted of felony should suffer death unless his felony was one which had been formally excluded from Benefit, or had specifically been made a capital offence under statute. The new sentence for offences which had been clergyable was prescribed as seven years' transportation or two years' imprisonment, in addition to which male prisoners could be ordered a whipping.

It is interesting to note that in 1547 peers of the realm were granted a similar privilege to that allowed to clerks in holy orders, even though they were not able to read. They were, however, exempted from branding. It is said that due to a parliamentary oversight when Benefit of Clergy was abolished in 1827 the equivalent right allowed to peers was not rescinded. There is no recorded case, however, in which a peer is known to have claimed this unique privilege, and a short while later an Act passed in 1841 provided that peers who were convicted of felony should be liable to the same scale of penalties as commoners.

A strange relic of the doctrine of Benefit of Clergy persisted until very recently in our criminal procedure. At the close of a trial at Assizes or at Quarter Sessions the *allocutus* was put to all prisoners who had been convicted of a felony. The Clerk of the Court would say: "Prisoner at the Bar, have you anything to say before the sentence of the court is passed on you according to the law?" Historically, this was the moment at which the claim of Benefit had to be made. On 1 January 1968 the old distinction between felonies and misdemeanours came to an end and thus the last remaining relic of Benefit of Clergy vanished from our legal system.

Chapter Nine

The Ritual of Execution

THE historian G. M. Trevelyan in his *English Social History,* describing the public pastimes of the seventeenth century, says, "Single-stick, boxing and sword fighting, bull and bear baiting were watched with delight by a race that had not yet learned to dislike the sight of pain being inflicted. Indeed, the less sporting events of hanging and whipping were spectacles much relished."

Until the abolition of public executions in the year 1868 a hanging was regarded as a popular pageant by the British people and it was conducted in an atmosphere more consistent with a national carnival than a solemn ceremony. The underlying theory which lay behind public executions, in the words of the Select Committee on Capital Punishment in 1930, was that the "death penalty was the most effective deterrent and that, consequently, the more people who witnessed it the greater would be its salutary effect".

If this was indeed the reason and the justification for these sordid exhibitions, the response of the community could not have been more gratifying to the authorities, as the majority of hangings were attended by vast crowds drawn from every walk of life and from every age group, including very young children. In 1767 a record crowd, estimated at 80,000, watched a hanging in Moorfields, and in 1777 when Dr. Dodd was hanged at Tyburn there were about 30,000 spectators. On this occasion, we are told, every window and rooftop in the vicinity of the gallows was let out on hire and there were boxes specially erected for the gentry.

The crowds, on the whole, were rough and ill-disciplined, and it was not uncommon for onlookers to be injured or even killed by buffeting and trampling underfoot. Neither was it a rare occurrence for them to be robbed, for pickpockets usually abounded in the tight and jostling mass.

In his book *A History of Capital Punishment,* John Laurence has described the atmosphere which prevailed at a public hanging:

> Frightful scenes were witnessed at executions in those days [he wrote]; the crowd standing awestruck as it watched the convulsions of the strangling culprit. Every contortion of the limbs was hailed with a

cheer or a groan according to whether the sufferer was popular or not; appalling curses and execrations occasionally rent the air and rendered the last moments of the unfortunate criminal more odious; hawkers boldly sang the praises of their wares the while a fellow creature was being done to death. Rich and poor, thief and lord, gentle and simple attended "the hanging" and cracked jokes at the sufferer's expense.

The authorities did not only rely on public hanging to impress on the people the Nemesis which could overtake the law-breaker, but in addition the corpses of executed criminals were often exhibited for the benefit of sightseers, and if the sentence of death had entailed subsequent dissection of the body, this, too, was frequently carried out in public.

At that time there was no appeal against conviction or against sentence, and executions were usually carried out within a few days of the trial. By the Punishment of Murder Act, 1752, it was actually stipulated that any person who was convicted of murder was to be executed within two days of the sentence of death being passed. This Act also provided that between sentence and execution the condemned person was to be kept in a separate cell and served with a diet consisting only of bread and water.

The ritual of hanging evoked some of the best and some of the worst qualities in the British character at that period. On the one hand, brutality and morbid curiosity, and, on the other, compassion, independence of spirit, a preoccupation with "fair play" and a sensitivity for the atmosphere of an occasion. Even today, for all the cumulative refinement of two or three centuries of education and progress, the average crowd at a professional boxing contest will exhibit very similar tendencies to those which were displayed by their forebears at a public execution.

After sentence of death had been passed, the criminal was removed immediately to the condemned cell, which was usually small, bare, and ill-lit. G. T. Wilkinson, in *The Newgate Calendar*, published in 1816, relates how a number of prisoners "were struck with horror and shed tears, when they were brought to these dark and solitary abodes".

On the last night before execution the prisoner could order any food and drink he wanted for his supper. At one time his friends and his family were allowed to visit him in his cell, and sometimes the whole night was passed in ribaldry and carousing. The one amenity that he could not obtain was privacy, for it became the established practice of the gaoler to charge a fee to anyone who wished to enter the prison to peer at condemned criminals during their final hours of life.

On the day of the execution the prisoner was allowed more alcohol with his breakfast and, understandably enough, a large number of the condemned were in an advanced state of intoxication before they commenced the journey to the scaffold.

The procession to Tyburn was an important part of the pageant. It comprised the city marshal, the sheriffs and under-sheriffs, peace officers and constables, and the prisoners and their friends. The cortège wound its way slowly through packed streets. Well-to-do prisoners were allowed to travel in their own coaches with the hearse immediately behind them; the less fortunate actually travelled in the hearse itself, usually seated on the coffin. There were frequent halts, even, it is said, at taverns where all the participants, including the prisoner, could obtain refreshment.

Another important feature of the performance was the dying speech. This was made from the scaffold and a prisoner had an absolute right to say what he pleased. He could confess his guilt, maintain his innocence, or make an oration completely unconnected with the offence for which he was going to die. In some rather nebulous manner the dying speech was supposed to emphasise the Englishman's basic freedom of expression. Indeed, if the condemned person was inarticulate he was permitted to dictate his words beforehand and to have them read out for him.

The prisoner was the central figure of the occasion and the onlookers expected him to comport himself with courage and with dignity. Writing in 1640, a social historian remarked with evident pride : "In no place shall you see malefactors go more constantly, more assuredly, and with less lamentation to death, than in England."

The hangman was an official who also carried out floggings and the supervision of prisoners placed in the pillory. The customary payment he received was a guinea for an execution and half-a-crown for a flogging. Often, too, a prisoner handed him a sum of money immediately before his death, probably in the hope that the execution would be made more merciful.

It used to take at least a quarter of an hour to arrange the victim on the scaffold. During this time attempts were sometimes made to effect a rescue, and when a popular person was being hanged the military were turned out in force. On the other hand, if the crowds were hostile to the prisoner they might become impatient with waiting and pelt him with rubbish and stones while the ropes were being adjusted.

A foreign visitor to England has described the final moments at the execution of several men who were hanged together in 1725:

> When all the prisoners arrive at their destination they are made to mount on a very wide cart made expressly for the purpose and a cord is passed round their necks and the end fastened to a gibbet, which is not very high. The Chaplain who accompanied the condemned men is also in the cart; he makes them pray and sing a few verses of Psalms. The relatives are permitted to mount the cart and take farewell. When the time is up—about a quarter of an hour—the Chaplain and the relatives get off the cart, the executioner covers the eyes and faces of the prisoners with caps, lashes the horses that draw the cart, which slips from under the condemned men's feet, and in this way they remain hanging together.

The early gallows at Tyburn consisted of a wooden plank suspended between two trees with a series of ropes dangling below it. Later the gallows became a self-contained, movable structure which was specially erected for each execution.

By custom the prisoner was allowed to give the final signal to the executioner when he was ready to die. He usually did this by dropping a handkerchief. Sometimes, however, the stage management went a little awry. Once a woman collapsed while the rope was being fastened round her neck and was still unconscious when she was hanged. Another woman threw herself from the cart and broke her neck when the rope was in position and the hangman was awaiting her signal to lash the horses. Frequently the rope broke before a prisoner was dead and the executioner went through the gruesome process of fixing up a new noose and hanging him all over again. This happened to the notorious pirate Captain Kidd at his execution in 1701. Somewhat later, when a prisoner by the name of David Evans was being hanged, the rope broke whilst he was still completely conscious. When a new length of rope was produced Evans protested that the sentence had already been carried out, but the executioner argued that a hanging was not terminated until the prisoner was actually dead. The watching crowd became restive and cried out for Evans to be freed, but in spite of this he was hanged again, this time until he died.

Another macabre custom was for the friends of a prisoner, when he was first suspended, to drag at his legs in an effort to expedite the process of strangulation. Sometimes, too, the friends used to strike the hanging victim in the area of the heart with large stones to make him lose consciousness.

The clothes and the bodies of executed criminals were the property of the hangman, who was also permitted to sell the corpse to the relatives for burial, or to the surgeons for dissection.

The victim of a hanging remained suspended until the hangman decided that life had expired and allowed him to be cut down. This resulted, naturally enough, in considerable opportunities for bribery, as it was well known that any hangman who was disposed to do so could tie the noose in a special way so as to delay strangulation, and then deliberately cut down the prisoner while he was still alive. It is said that several partially strangled prisoners were rushed away by relatives and friends and restored to life in neighbouring houses. But the possibility of resuscitation under such circumstances was extremely doubtful as the dense crowds surrounding the scaffold made it very unlikely that the half-strangled prisoner could be removed with sufficient speed for the process of restoration to be commenced. However, there have been several recorded cases of surgeons who purchased "corpses" of hanged criminals for dissection and subsequently discovered them to be still alive.

There was always a possibility, too, that the hangman would cut down a victim too soon purely by inadvertence. This is known to have happened in 1736 when a prisoner named Reynold was hanged and cut down and was just being placed in his coffin when he suddenly commenced to struggle. The hangman on that occasion attempted to drag the semi-conscious man back to the scaffold with the intention of hanging him again, but he was prevented from doing so by the crowd, who removed Reynold to a nearby house, where he died a short while later.

On another occasion, in 1705, a prisoner named John Smith was granted an eleventh-hour reprieve. The message did not reach the executioner until Smith had been hanging for about fifteen minutes. He was immediately cut down and when he was examined it was found that he was still alive. Later he recovered from his ordeal.

The drop, as opposed to the slow strangulation method of hanging, was first used in 1760 for the execution of Earl Ferrers. It consisted of a collapsible platform standing only about a foot high with a small square of planking in the centre on which the condemned man was made to stand with the noose around his neck. This planking was supported by wooden props to which were attached lengths of rope. To carry out a hanging the executioner gave a sudden jerk on the ropes, collapsing the planking, to leave the prisoner suspended. This system was generally introduced in 1783. It was by no means foolproof, and when the primitive mechanism failed the victim was still subjected to death by the old form of slow strangulation. In 1828 a slight improvement was made in the efficiency of the drop when bolts were substituted for ropes to bring about the collapse of the planking.

Towards the close of the eighteenth century the authorities began to realise that these carnival executions instead of having a solemn, admonitory effect on the crowds were, in fact, only a source of demoralisation and debasement. It was then decided to discontinue the tragi-comedy of the ritual procession from the condemned cell to Tyburn, and from the year 1783 executions were carried out at an open space in front of Newgate Prison where the condemned prisoners had spent their final night in custody. It was once suggested that to add to the impressiveness of the occasion the scaffold should be draped in black and the prison bell should be tolled while the execution was taking place.

In general the new routine had the desired effect. At Newgate Prison the fete-like atmosphere was less apparent, and normally the crowds which attended the executions were less numerous (although there were close on 100,000 people at a hanging in 1824 and as recently as 1840 the interest was so great that windows overlooking the scaffold were being hired out for £2 each).

During the eighteenth and the early part of the nineteenth centuries public executions in England were accepted almost without question even amongst the most enlightened thinkers of the period. It is true that William Wilberforce (1759–1833), the great humanitarian, was opposed to capital punishment on principle and once expressed the view that "the barbarous system of hanging has been tried too long". On the other hand, Dr. Samuel Johnson (1709–84), a man of deep religious conviction, was able to defend the established practice. When it was suggested to him in a discussion that the abolition of the ritual procession to the gallows was a beneficial reform, the Doctor replied : "It is not an improvement; they object that the old method drew together a number of spectators. If they do not draw spectators, they don't answer their purpose. The old method was satisfactory to all parties; the public was gratified by a procession; a criminal was supported by it. Why is all this to be swept away?" Boswell, who has recounted this anecdote, added his own concurrence : "I perfectly agree with Dr. Johnson upon this head, and I am persuaded that executions, now the solemn procession being discontinued, have not nearly the effect which they formerly had."

The contemporary system met with very little criticism from the majority of the law reformers of the period. William Eden (1748–1814) thought that public executions were justified provided the scene was "solemn and affecting", but he was opposed to the public exhibition of the corpses of the prisoners. Jeremy Bentham (1748–1832) wished to heighten the drama and the solemnity of the occasion by a number of theatrical trappings. He suggested :

> A scaffold painted black, the livery of grief—the officers of justice dressed in crepe—the executioner covered with a mask which would serve at one to augment the terror of his appearance, and to shield him from illfounded indignation . . . whilst all the actors in this terrible drama might move in solemn procession—serious and religious music [would be played] preparing the hearts of the spectators for the important lesson they were about to receive.

One of the earliest opponents of public executions was Henry Fielding, the novelist (1707–54), who considered that the ghoulish and degrading scenes around the scaffold were detrimental to the proper dignity of justice. However, it was not until nearly a century after Fielding's death that a serious attempt was made to alter the existing practice when another celebrated novelist-reformer, Charles Dickens, who had started by opposing capital punishment completely, but later had modified his views, campaigned for prisoners to be hanged in private. Dickens had himself attended an execution in front of Horsemonger Lane Gaol in 1849 and had been so sickened and appalled by what he saw that he immediately wrote a series of letters to *The Times* newspaper stating his opinion that the spectators at a hanging were attracted solely by a depraved taste or a morbid curiosity. His views met with strenuous opposition from certain members of the Government and from the judiciary in general. The debate dragged on until 1868, when an Act was passed to the effect that all executions were thenceforth to take place inside the walls of a prison.

Under the new arrangements, hangings were usually carried out at 8 o'clock in the morning in the presence of the sheriff, the gaoler, the chaplain, the prison surgeon, and justices of the peace of the neighbourhood. The prisoner's relatives and members of the press were also allowed to attend. The death of the prisoner was certified by the surgeon and an inquest was held on the body by a coroner sitting with a jury. The prison bell, or the bell of a church in the immediate vicinity, was tolled for fifteen minutes before the execution and for fifteen minutes afterwards, and, until 1902, a black flag was hoisted on the prison masthead at the moment of death.

Immediately after the inquest the body of the executed prisoner was buried in quicklime inside the grounds of the gaol in which he had been hanged.

The peculiar fascination which surrounded a judicial execution was such that even after the public had been deprived of their ancient privilege of watching the actual killing of the prisoner, considerable crowds still used to gather outside the gates of a prison when a hanging was taking place. Some went there to protest, some out of sympathy, and some from religious motives, but there can be little doubt that the majority were drawn by the selfsame morbid curiosity which, in another age, used to attract the multitudes of spectators to Newgate and to Tyburn.

Chapter Ten

The Abolition of Hanging

I ATTENDED my first murder trial in 1951. I was at the time on circuit as a judge's marshal and in that capacity I was allowed to occupy a place on the bench alongside the judge, his clerk, the high sheriff, and the sheriff's chaplain.

In those days all murders were capital offences, whatever their circumstances, and one was conscious of the dark, sombre tension and the brittle stillness which overhung the courtroom even while the jury was being sworn in to try the case.

The defendant was a girl in her middle or late twenties. She would have been attractive, even beautiful, but her eyes were dulled with the shock of her predicament, and her pale face was ravaged with torment and hopelessness. For two and a half days she sat in the dock facing us, and I cannot remember during the whole of this period that she ever betrayed a vestige of feeling or comprehension of what was going on around her. She seemed to perceive, if she perceived at all, through a haze of unreality. She had drifted far off to that pinnacle of isolated detachment which so many people experience at those moments in their lives which are filled with exceptional stress or emotion.

After all these years I can picture her still. The dark hair, resting on her shoulders; the thin, drained face; the slight motionless body in a plain black dress, leaning slightly forward in the hard, upright chair and flanked on either side by two equally immobile uniformed women prison officers.

This girl was charged with the murder of her baby. Although she had pleaded "not guilty" there was little doubt from an early period in the trial that it was she who had done the killing. Her husband, whom the court never saw, had been away from home for many years serving a long prison sentence. During his absence the girl had become entangled with another man who had come to live with her at her house. He had been one of the principal prosecution witnesses and his evidence had supplied both the motive and the mitigation for the offence. He was a flashy young man of a particularly repulsive type. He admitted, without a vestige of shame, that during the whole period of his cohabitation with the defendant he had been entirely supported by her and had neither worked nor had he looked for employment. He also freely admitted that he was the father of the dead baby.

This situation might have continued a lot longer, but the defendant had received an unexpected letter from her husband saying that he was going to be released from prison very shortly and would be returning home. In his evidence the young man described the girl's consternation when she had received this news. Her husband was a man with a very violent disposition and was, in fact, serving a sentence for a wounding offence at that very time. There seemed to be little doubt what his reaction would be when he discovered his wife's infidelity while he had been in prison. The young man confessed that the prospect had so terrified him that he had decided to clear out before the husband returned. He had made his preparations in secret and one morning, when the defendant was out shopping, he had slipped away with all his belongings, leaving her a brief note merely telling her that she would never see him again.

In the evening of that same day someone had slipped upstairs to the room where the baby was sleeping and had killed it. All the evidence seemed to point almost conclusively to the girl; indeed, she had made a full confession in writing to the police, which she had later repudiated.

The counsel for the defence, who a few years later became a High Court judge, addressed the jury with an eloquence of despair, suggesting that anyone might have entered the bedroom on the fateful night and carried out the killing. Just before he closed his speech he invited the jury, even if they believed his client to have been responsible for the act, to find her guilty of manslaughter and not of murder.

The judge, in his summing-up, told the jury that there was no evidence before them on which they could possibly reach a verdict of manslaughter. The baby had been killed in such a way, he said, that it was extremely difficult, if not impossible, to believe that the act had not been carried out deliberately. The only question they had to decide, he went on, seemed to be whether it was the defendant or some other person who had performed the act.

The jury retired, the accused girl was taken back to the cells, and the judge adjourned to his room. That morning, before we had come to the court, the judge had told me that although he had presided at numerous murder trials before, he still found them a considerable strain. As well as that, he was himself wholeheartedly opposed to capital punishment and he found it a bitterly distasteful experience every time he was obliged to pass sentence of death. During the long vigil, whilst the jury were endeavouring to reach a decision, the judge sat in an armchair in his room, silent and pensive. The high sheriff and his chaplain, seated in an opposite corner, carried on a desultory conversation in hushed voices, and the judge's clerk and I spent our time carrying round endless cups of tea.

The judge's clerk was, perhaps, the only one of us who was not affected by some measure of emotional stress. He was an elderly man who had spent over sixty years in and out of the criminal courts and probably he had grown as accustomed to the grim, dispassionate recitation of the death sentence as a worker in an abattoir becomes acclimatised to the sight and the smell of blood. The clerk came up to me once while we were waiting and said, "Marshal, I'm a bit worried about the judge's black cap." I asked him why, and he told me that it was my duty, after the jury had returned a verdict of guilty, to go behind the judge's chair and place the black cap on his head before he repeated the words of the death sentence. I had lost the use of my right arm during the war and the judge's clerk was certain I would not be able to open out the cap with one hand. Eventually, he offered to prepare the cap himself and then to hand it over to me so that I could adjust it above the judge's wig. "Excuse me for mentioning this," he said, "but these formalities have to be carried out correctly."

An hour later we were back again in court and the clerk of the assize was asking the foreman of the jury for their verdict. The other jurors were either looking down in front of them or else had their eyes studiously fixed on a spot just below the bench. I glanced momentarily at the girl. She stood at the front of the dock, her hands clutching at the rail. On either side of her the two female prison officers had moved in so close that their bodies were touching hers and their inside arms were clasped inconspicuously around the back of her waist. It was obvious that they were adopting these positions not only to support the girl if she collapsed, but also as a mute expression of sympathy and consolation.

The foreman of the jury stood stiffly to attention, the sweat glistening on his forehead. The judge's clerk, sitting beside me, was frowning as he bent below his desk and struggled to open the black hat without making too much rustling.

The foreman cleared his throat and said slowly and precisely: "Not guilty of murder but guilty of manslaughter."

An audible sigh passed through the court. The girl in the dock staggered; then her head drooped forward, her body went limp, and the two prison officers closed up even more tightly on either side of her. The judge's clerk ceased his fumbling. The cap fell from his hands and subsided on to the floor in a black rectangular patch at his feet.

After that it was over very quickly. The judge sentenced the girl to a short term of imprisonment and the court rose.

In the passage outside the judge's clerk said to me: "That verdict would be very difficult to justify in law, wouldn't it, Marshal?" I agreed with him, but in my heart I was wondering if it was not the law itself which needed some justification.

A few years later, under the provisions of the Homicide Act, 1957, a verdict of manslaughter might have been legally justifiable in the circumstances of this particular case on the grounds of what became known as "diminished responsibility". The Act provided that if one person killed another while he was suffering from "such abnormality of mind . . . as substantially impaired his mental responsibility for his acts", the jury could return a verdict of manslaughter instead of murder. This opened the way, of course, to numerous cases of murder being reduced to the lesser homicidal offence solely because the jurors were sympathetic to the accused.

There would be very few people today who would deny that the Homicide Act, 1957, was a thoroughly unsatisfactory piece of legislation. It was moulded as an uneasy compromise between the total abolitionists and the total retentionists, and it set out to divide murder into two distinct categories—capital, which was punishable by hanging, and non-capital, punishable by life imprisonment.

The five categories of capital murder under the 1957 Act were:

1. A murder committed in "the course of furtherance of theft".
2. A murder committed by shooting or causing an explosion.
3. A murder committed in the course or "resisting or avoiding,

or preventing a lawful arrest, or effecting or assisting an escape or rescue from legal custody".

4. A murder of a police officer acting in the execution of his duty or of a person assisting a police officer so acting.
5. A murder by a prisoner of a prison officer acting in the execution of his duty or of a person assisting him.

Anyone who was convicted of murder and who had been convicted on a previous occasion of another murder committed in Great Britain was also liable to suffer the penalty of death.

Any attempt to devise a general formula by which murders can be divided up into "serious" and "not so serious" is almost certain to fail. The classification adopted by the Homicide Act led to numerous anomalies. For instance, murder by poisoning, always regarded as one of the most culpable forms of premeditated killing, became a non-capital offence. It was capital murder to shoot your victim, but non-capital if you hacked him to death with a pickaxe. Again, it was non-capital murder if one person strangled another, but if the killer helped himself to the least valuable item of his victim's possessions it automatically became a capital offence.

It would probably be true to say that one of the factors which hastened the abolition of capital punishment after 1957 was the appalling muddle into which the law of murder had fallen. The retentionists were faced with a position where they not only had to justify hanging as a punishment, but also to uphold the inconsistencies which had resulted from the Homicide Act.

There can be few issues which have divided the more thoughtful section of the British public so sharply as that of capital punishment. Sincere and reasoned arguments were advanced on both sides and it would be a gross error for anyone to imagine that the retentionists drew their principal support from the diehards, the blimps, and the reactionaries. In fact, many of those most wedded to the principle of retaining the punishment of hanging were radical, progressive, and humanitarian in their outlook.

All forms of punishment have two distinct components—the theory which lies behind them and the practical means by which they are carried out. Before one forms a definite view about the wisdom or unwisdom of any particular form of penalty it is advisable to consider it in relation to both of these separate aspects.

In the final era of capital punishment in this country the circumstances and the ritual of an execution were very different from those which had applied at Tyburn and Newgate. The Home Office, in their memorandum of evidence before the Royal Commission on Capital Punishment in 1949, gave a few details of a condemned person's last days. "Immediately a prisoner sentenced to death returns from Court", they stated, "he is placed in a cell and is watched day and night by two officers. Amenities such as cards, chess, dominoes, etc., are provided in the cell and the officers are encouraged to—and in fact invariably do—join the prisoner in these games. Newspapers and books are also provided." The prisoner was placed on hospital diet with such additions as the medical officer considered advisable. "A pint of beer or stout is supplied daily on request and ten cigarettes or half an ounce of pipe tobacco are allowed unless there are medical reasons to the contrary."

The *Sunday Times,* on 27 December 1964, published an account of an interview with Mr. Harry Allen, who had then been the chief executioner in Great Britain since 1956. Mr. Allen presented an intimate picture of the relationship of the prisoner with those around him at such a time. Speaking from his experience, based on the performance of over a hundred executions, Mr. Allen said : "Everyone feels very, very sorry for the man who's got to go. Especially the prison officers, the Chaplain and often the Governor. I've seen some very upset cases . . . there's nothing at all anyone can do about it—except to get it over as quickly as possible and forget about it."

It has been suggested that with the condemned cell so close to the execution shed—normally they adjoined each other—the prisoner could actually hear the hammering of the scaffold being prepared for his execution, but this has been officially denied.

There is considerable conflict of opinion regarding the condition of prisoners when they were finally taken to the gallows. In his book *Reflections on Hanging,* Arthur Koestler has said : "The truth is that some prisoners struggle both in the condemned cell and under the noose, that some have to be carried tied to a chair, others dragged to the trap, limp, bowels open, arms pinioned to the back, like animals; and that still other things happen which should happen only in nightmare dreams."

Mr. Allen was specifically asked about the reactions of condemned prisoners and he replied: "They seem more callous now than in the old days. Quite a few are pretty boastful—think they're heroes, I suppose. The other prisoners help this by chanting, and banging and kicking up a fuss. It's always surprised me a bit, but the concerned man often goes through the whole thing a lot calmer than those doing the job." Mr. Allen added: "From the moment we go in the cell it's all over in a minute at most. The man's dead in less than two seconds—he doesn't feel a thing."

From one's knowledge of human nature it is extremely difficult to accept that every condemned prisoner was docile when his final moments arrived. Indeed, the prison authorities always accepted that it was necessary to secure a man in an absolutely immobile position when he was about to receive corporal punishment, and there is no logical reason why a person who is going to be hanged should be any more complaisant.

We know that every effort was made to hurry through the last stages of the execution. The executioner had already prepared the scaffold and set the drop according to the height and the weight of the condemned prisoner. When the time came to remove the victim from his cell the executioner immediately rushed in and pinioned his arms behind his back.

Mr. Albert Pierrepoint, who was then our chief executioner, was questioned about this stage of the proceedings when he gave evidence before the Royal Commission on Capital Punishment in 1949.

"What happens if a prisoner faints at the last minute?"

"They carry him to the scaffold."

"What happens if he gets on to the scaffold and then faints?"

"He has to go just the same. They pull the lever and away he goes."

"Supposing he faints before you get him to the scaffold?"

"We would have to carry him there."

"And put the rope round his neck?"

"Yes. There is an officer on each plank holding him up. There's a rope for the officer to hold on to and he stands on the plank and holds him up."

Mr. H. N. Gedge, then Acting Under-Sheriff for the County of London, also gave evidence before the 1949 commission, and recalled the case of a prisoner who was hanged sitting on a chair because he had collapsed "and it was the only way of getting him on the drop".

Incidentally, Mr. Gedge and Mr. Pierrepoint gave conflicting evidence regarding the presence of women prison officers at the execution when a woman prisoner was being hanged. Mr. Gedge told the commission that they did, in fact, attend, but Mr. Pierrepoint said : "The women don't see the execution. The men take over out of the cell, just before the execution."

Arthur Koestler and C. H. Rolph, in their anti-capital punishment book *Hanged by the Neck,* state that a prisoner on the scaffold "often defecates, since people usually want to do this when they are frightened, and the shock to [the prisoner's] nervous system when the rope tightens removes the last vestige of self-control, together with the social need for it". The authors also quote a disclosure in the *Lancet* on 20 August 1955 that if the condemned prisoner is a woman "she is made to put on waterproof underwear on the morning of the execution".

The above paragraph is corroborated by a number of accounts which have appeared in the post-war period of the physical condition of the corpses when they were removed from Adolf Hitler's fiendish extermination gas chambers.

Mr. Pierrepoint was questioned by the 1949 commission about the adjustment of the noose.

"Have you ever known a case where you have not given exactly the right drop and have either decapitated [the prisoner] or strangled him instead of dislocating his neck?"

"I have never seen any signs."

"Never?"

"Never."

"The knot must always be under the angle of the left jaw?"

"Yes."

"That's very important, is it?"

"Very important."

"Why is it very important?"

"If you have the same knot on the right-hand side, it comes back behind the neck, and throws the neck forward, which would make a strangulation. If you put it on the left side it finishes up in front and throws the chin back and breaks the spinal cord."

In their memorandum of Evidence to the Commission the Home Office did not give the impression that our hanging system had always been so efficient. "In 1885", they said, "an unfortunate case occurred at Exeter Prison in which, owing to a defect in the apparatus, three attempts to execute a man named Lee were unsuccessful. His sentence was subsequently commuted. Cases had also occurred in which the effect of the hanging was that the prisoner was decapitated."

It is widely believed that prisoners were under the influence of drink or drugs when they were finally taken from the condemned cell to the execution shed. I once asked the principal medical officer of a prison if this was true and he told me that he had never seen any evidence of it himself. He added : "You couldn't possibly send a person to meet his Maker whilst under the influence of drink." One might well believe, on the other hand, that the Almighty would have considered this to be amongst the less objectionable features of the condemned prisoner's removal from this world to the next.

Whatever the general rule might have been, it was certainly waived on one occasion at least. When Ruth Ellis, a 28-year-old model, was hanged at Holloway Prison in 1955 for the murder of her erstwhile lover, the formal announcement of her execution was couched in a somewhat unusual form. It contained words to the effect that the doctor who had carried out the post-mortem examination on her body had noticed the smell of drink on her lips.

As soon as the Labour Government came into power in October 1964 the new Home Secretary made it clear that he intended to reprieve all murderers who were condemned to death pending the decision of Parliament on a Private Member's Bill to abolish the death penalty. This Bill was to be introduced by Mr. Sydney Silverman, the Labour member for Nelson and Colne, who had been for many years a staunch opponent of capital punishment.

From the day when the Homicide Act, 1957, received the Royal Assent until October 1964 there had been 29 executions, though during the three-year period 1962–4 the total had been only 7.

On 21 December 1964 Mr. Silverman moved the second reading of the Murder (Abolition of Death Penalty) Bill. This was a non-party measure and all three of the major political parties had decided to allow their members a free vote in the lobbies.

According to the parliamentary report in *The Times* newspaper on the following day, Mr. Silverman started his speech saying: "We are not concerned today with whether we should abolish or preserve the death penalty. That we have already done. The question before the House today—the only question remaining for Parliament to decide—is whether we shall abolish or retain, in the abolition of the death penalty, the exceptions to that abolition which were made in the Homicide Act, 1957."

Sir Peter Rawlinson, the Conservative member for Epsom and the Solicitor-General in the recently defeated Administration, was the first speaker against the Bill. "I do not believe", he said, "that you can deter the family murder, the crime of passion, the sexually perverted. But I do believe that you can deter the professional criminal who goes and fires his pistol, who goes out to rob as his occupation, weighing risk against risk."

Sir Peter continued: "I, personally, cannot take the risk with the lives of other innocent citizens; nor will I ignore the opinions of police officers. So, terrible and ugly as is this penalty, I believe there is a right and duty of the State to be able to say: do this deliberate act, then you will lose your life. I believe such a warning can and does deter the men who are needing to be deterred in this day and age."

One of the speakers who was listened to with the greatest attention in that debate was Mr. Henry Brooke, who, until a few months previously, had been the Conservative Home Secretary. He admitted he had once been in favour of capital punishment, but went on:

> By the end of my time at the Home Office I became convinced that the case for retaining the death penalty was no longer strong enough to justify its retention, and that we would come to the time when we ought to make a trial of abolition. The taking of a life is so grave a matter that the onus of proof must be upon those who sincerely believe that the death penalty should be retained. I do not share the view that taking a life by the State is contrary to moral principle. But I do believe that the death penalty can only be justified on the ground that it is a unique deterrent. If it is a unique deterrent, then there is justification for it. If there is not, I do not think the case for it can be upheld.

Mr. Brooke then quoted Home Office statistics which showed that during the last five years before the passing of the Homicide Act, 1957, a period when every murder was a capital offence, 14·4 per cent of all the murders committed would still have been capital after the Homicide Act had altered the law.

If the fear of the hangman's rope was as great a deterrent as the retentionists claimed, one might have expected to see a quite remarkable fall in this percentage figure immediately after the Homicide Act was passed. In fact, as Mr. Brooke disclosed, during the period from 1957 to 1964 the comparable figure was only reduced from 14·4 to 13·5 per cent.

Mr. Silverman's Bill was carried on its second reading by 355 votes to 170.

In his book *Crime and the Penal System,* Mr. Howard Jones, the senior lecturer in sociology at the University of Leicester, examined the argument that if capital punishment were abolished more criminals would carry weapons and there would be an increase in the number of murders. He says: "The evidence submitted to the Royal Commission on Capital Punishment [of 1949] by various European countries which have abolished the death penalty . . . fails to bear out these fears. Although in these countries, there seems usually to have been a wave of violence immediately after capital punishment was given up, this soon subsided and no unfavourable long-term effects can be discerned."

During the debate on the second reading of Mr. Silverman's Bill, several Members on both sides of the House expressed their concern at what would constitute a "life sentence" after hanging had been abolished. The Home Secretary, Sir Frank Soskice, answering this point, said that nine years was conventionally accepted as the period after which a life-sentence prisoner could expect to be released, but in certain circumstances a murderer might be detained for longer. Sir Frank stated that he himself would be reluctant to make it much longer because, "generally speaking, experience showed that nine or ten years or thereabouts was the maximum period of confinement that a normal human being could undergo without their personality decaying, their will going, and their becoming progressively less able to re-enter society and look after themselves and become useful citizens".

It was reported in *The Times* newspaper on 20 November 1964 that Miss Alice Bacon, Minister of State at the Home Office, whilst answering questions in the House of Commons the previous day, had said that prisoners who had been sentenced to death before the

Homicide Act, 1957, and had had their sentences commuted to life imprisonment had been detained "for nine years in an average case". She continued : "The period may well be longer for persons sentenced under the Act of 1957 to life imprisonment for non-capital murder in cases where there are no mitigating circumstances, but it is too early to give an estimate." In answer to a later question she disclosed that between 1959 and 1963 the duration of a "life sentence" had varied between four years and fourteen years.

It is interesting to learn that the rethinking on the use of capital punishment which has taken place here just recently has not remained entirely unobserved in other countries beyond the seas. Writing in *The Times* on 20 April 1965, a special correspondent in Florida said :

> The move towards the abolition of the death penalty in Britain has had a marked effect in the United States, increasing the tempo of a general debate on the subject which has been going on for some years. . . . No new arguments are being advanced for the abolition of the penalty. The case remains the same as it has been for many years— that to take life judicially is as bad as taking it in anger or with malice aforethought, that execution is brutalising and against the dignity and sanctity of human life. There have also been cases in America of innocent men being executed by judicial error.

Before Mr. Silverman's Murder (Abolition of Death Penalty) Bill finally became law, two important amendments were made to the original draft. The first provided that the Bill should expire in five years' time unless Parliament decreed otherwise—in other words, the death penalty was to be abolished for murder for a five-year trial period. The second enabled the trial judge to recommend to the Home Secretary the minimum period for which he considered that a murderer should be kept in prison before being released on licence.

The Lord Chancellor, Lord Gardiner, winding up the debate on the third reading of the Bill in the House of Lords on 26 October 1965, said : "I am sure that when the traps have been removed from the prisons we should not only be a safer country but a much saner and healthier one."

The death penalty still remains in Britain as the maximum sentence for the offences of piracy with violence and treason. For some reason these two offences were not included in the Act of abolition.

Chapter Eleven

Outlawry, Banishment, and Transportation

IT WOULD be difficult to specify with any degree of accuracy exactly when the system of outlawry originated in Britain, but it was certainly in use before the time of the Norman Conquest. When a person was officially declared to be an outlaw he immediately forfeited his land and all his other possessions. Henceforth he became a wandering fugitive with no more claim to life than a reptile or a wild beast. All law-abiding subjects could kill him with impunity; indeed, it was their bounden duty to do so.

At one stage the monarchs seem to have claimed the right to outlaw as their own exclusive privilege, which they exercised not only against genuine criminals but also to satisfy their personal fears and animosities. However, the Magna Carta in 1215, which has been described as "the keystone of English liberty", laid down that no freeman should be outlawed except by lawful judgment of his equals or else by the law of the land.

The old, draconian process was further ameliorated by a fourteenth-century statute which provided that a sheriff alone was entitled to put an outlaw to death and that any other person who did so would be guilty of murder except when the killing took place in the course of an attempted arrest.

Outlawry as a criminal sentence became obsolete in the Middle Ages, although it still remained as a civil procedure by which a party to a suit who absconded before his action was commenced could be declared an outlaw and as such was liable to the penalty forfeiture. Civil outlawry was ended in 1879 but criminal outlawry after centuries of disuse survived in theory until 1938, when it was finally abolished by the Administration of Justice (Miscellaneous Provisions) Act.

Banishment was another method of punishment of which the origins in Britain are rather obscure. In Blackstone's *Commentaries on the Laws of England,* first published between 1765 and 1770, he remarks that "no power on earth, except the authority of Parliament, can send any subject of England out of the land against his will; not even a criminal. For exile and transportation are punishments unknown to the common law."

There was, however, an ancient procedure known as "sanctuary and abjuration" which entailed a form of self-imposed banishment. It arose out of the doctrine that any criminal might claim sanctuary if he took refuge in a church or a churchyard. In the course of time about thirty churches, including Westminster Abbey, became recognised as regular criminal sanctuaries. Once the criminal had reached a sanctuary he was allowed forty days in which to confess his offence to a coroner and to take the oath of abjuration. He could then leave the kingdom unhindered provided he elected to undergo perpetual banishment in any foreign, Christian country. Sanctuary and abjuration was abolished in 1566.

The first statute to authorise banishment as a criminal punishment in Britain was passed in 1597, during the reign of Queen Elizabeth I. By its terms the courts were empowered to banish rogues and vagabonds to such places beyond the seas as should be chosen by the Privy Council. During the seventeenth century a number of other Acts of Parliament and Orders in Council extended the penalty to include dissolute persons, prisoners of war, petty thieves, fire-raisers, and Quakers. No official records are in existence showing the number of persons who were actually banished during this period, but a letter written by James I in 1619 mentions the fact that a hundred prisoners had been sent to the Colony of Virginia.

The term "transportation" was first used in a British Statute during the reign of Charles II. This Act provided that persons being convicted of certain offences might be pardoned on condition that they agreed to be transported overseas. The pardon was granted by the monarch, generally on the recommendation of the trial judge, and the duration of the transportation was normally for a term of years, but might even be for life. In a table of directions for justices of the peace, published in 1664, it is stated that "such prisoners as are reprieved with intent to be transported be not sent away as perpetual slaves, but upon indentures between them and particular masters to serve in our English plantations for seven years and the last three years thereof to have wages that they might have a stock when their time is expired, and that an account be given thereof and by whom they are sent and of their arrivals".

Readers of Daniel Defoe will recall that Moll Flanders having been sentenced to death for stealing lodged a "humble petition for transportation" from Newgate Gaol when she was awaiting her execution. The petition was successful and she was transported to Virginia but she returned to Britain years later when she had served her term. *Moll Flanders* was written by Defoe in 1683, at a time when the transportation of criminals to the American colonies was beginning to be adopted on a large scale. Formerly the colonial settlers had relied entirely upon Negro slave labour for the development of their plantations, but later on the supply of Negro slaves had not kept pace with the increasing demands of the settlers. Prisoners sentenced to transportation were usually handed over to special contractors in Britain who became responsible for their shipment to America. At one time the shortage of manpower in the colonies was so acute that the contractors frequently supplemented their official supply of criminals with young men whom they had kidnapped unofficially in and around the ports and had smuggled on to their ships a short while before they sailed on their transatlantic voyages.

During the first half of the eighteenth century transportation had come to be regarded as one of the principal features of the British penal system, but it was still used solely for prisoners who had been sentenced to death and reprieved. It must be remembered that in these days every felony was punishable by hanging, and a series of Acts passed in the reign of George I prescribed that, in general, those reprieved for a clergyable offence should be transported for seven years, those reprieved for a non-clergyable offence for fourteen years. In either case a prisoner who returned to Britain before the expiry of his sentence was likely to suffer instant death. After 1768 the judges were empowered to order the reprieve and the transportation of a prisoner without the matter being referred to the higher authority. The sentence could be for any duration which the judge considered appropriate, and if no period was mentioned transportation was automatically for a period of fourteen years.

Many people in England were of the opinion that convict labour, which had become a monopoly of the colonial settlers in America, might be employed more profitably at home. The matter came to a head in 1776 when the American colonies declared their independence and the regular flow of transportation was brought to an abrupt halt. Immediately an Act was hurried through Parliament providing that instead of being transported convicts could in future be sentenced to terms of hard labour in Britain. The task on which they were to be initially employed was the clearing out of soil and gravel from the beds of the Thames and a number of other navigable rivers. Whilst they were doing this the convicts were to be detained in special prison ships moored in the vicinity of their work. The shortage of prison accommodation was now desperate, and a commission was appointed to study the possibility of establishing penitentiary houses all over the country.

The first two prison ships under the new scheme, a frigate and an East Indiaman, were berthed at Woolwich. These and others which were instituted during the following years were known as "the hulks", and became notorious for their terrible conditions and for the brutal treatment suffered by the unfortunate wretches who were cooped up aboard them.

Even after the loss of the American colonies a strong view still persisted in England that the most effective method of disposing of criminals was either to hang them or else to remove them as far away as possible from their homes and their former associates. In consequence of this, before the penitentiary house project had been put into operation, it was superseded by a vast new plan for the use of British convict labour in developing the recently discovered lands of Australasia.

In the spring of 1787 a fleet consisting of two men-of-war and nine convict transports set sail for New South Wales and, after a voyage lasting for ten months, the human cargo was landed at Port Jackson in January 1788. Thereafter the convict ships sailed regularly to the antipodes. The Rev. Richard Johnson, the first Anglican Chaplain in New South Wales, has left a vivid account of the arrival of a flotilla of three convict transports at Port Jackson in June 1790. He notes that these ships had embarked 983 prisoners in England out of whom 273 had died on the voyage and a further 486 had been sick when they had landed. Mr. Johnson described the scene when he entered the hold of one of the ships before the convicts went ashore. "I beheld a sight", he says, "truly shocking to the feelings of humanity, a great number of them lying, some half and others nearly quite naked, without either bed or bedding, unable to turn or help themselves. Spoke to them as I passed along, but the smell was so offensive, I could scarcely bear it." The conditions on board another of the ships were so appalling that the Captain dissuaded Mr. Johnson from going down amongst the prisoners.

> Some of these unhappy people died after the ships came into harbour [Mr. Johnson goes on] before they could be taken ashore; part of these had been thrown into the harbour, and their dead bodies cast upon the shore, and were seen lying naked upon the rocks. . . . The landing of these people was truly affecting and shocking, great numbers were not able to walk, nor to move hand or foot. Some were slung over the ship's side in the same manner as they would sling a cask or box, or anything of that nature. Upon their being brought up to the open air, some fainted, some died upon the deck, and others in the boat before they reached the shore. When they came on shore, many were not able to walk, to stand, or to stir themselves in the least. Hence some were led by others, while some crept upon their hands and knees, and some were carried on the backs of others.

Johnson spoke to many of these convicts and found that:

> the usage they met with on board, according to their own story, was truly shocking. Sometimes for days, nay, for a considerable time together, they had been up to the middle in water, chained together, hand and leg—even the sick not exempted—nay, many died with the chains upon them. Promises, entreaties, were all in vain, and it was not till a very few days before they made the harbour, that they were released out of irons.

The first convicts to reach Australia were all employed by the authorities on the construction of public works such as harbours, roads, and bridges. Later on, however, convicts could be assigned to free colonists who thereby assumed liability for their maintenance under a similar system to that which had operated on plantations of Virginia in the earlier years of transportation.

Usually a period of assignment lasted for between eight and twelve years. When it was finished the convict was granted a ticket-of-leave, and although he remained under the supervision of the police he was permitted to find his own work and to live the remainder of his life in comparative freedom.

Chapter Twelve

The Later Development of Transportation

HERMAN MERIVALE, who lived at a time when transportation of convicts was at its zenith and who made a special study of its influence on colonisation, wrote: "There was general confidence in the favourite theory that the best method of punishing offenders was that which removed them from the scene of offence and temptation, cut them off by a great gulf of space from all their former connections, and gave them the opportunity of redeeming past crimes by becoming useful members of society."

It is interesting to observe from this quotation that in the early days of the nineteenth century the concept of the reformative value of punishment, as well as its retributive element, was already being canvassed among penologists. But when one studies the practical working of transportation one sees that, however admirable might have been the theory which lay behind the scheme, any notion that the convicts were encouraged to seek redemption is a complete and utter fallacy.

When convicts were ordered to be transported they were sent in the first place to the hulks to await shipment to Australasia. The plan of using these prison ships for sentences of hard labour at home had been abandoned and the hulks provided the only available accommodation whilst the fleets were being assembled to convey the prisoners to the antipodes. Both male and female convicts came on board the hulks in a pitiable condition. In 1822 a batch of women were described as arriving, "not merely handcuffed but with heavy irons on their legs, which occasioned considerable swelling, and in one instance, serious inflammation". And a year later Elizabeth Fry observed another party of women and girls being transferred from Newgate with "iron hooped round their legs and arms and chained to each other".

Life on board the hulks had eased off considerably from the ruthless discipline of former years. A House of Commons Committee reported in 1832 that the convicts were only made to work for comparatively short hours and were permitted to mix freely with their fellow prisoners and even to meet their friends from outside. Large quantities of alcohol and tobacco were regularly smuggled on board and at night the holds became the scene of drinking orgies, gambling, dancing, fighting, and debauchery. The House of Commons Committee remarked that: "Altogether the situation of the convicts cannot be considered penal; it is a state of restriction, but hardly of punishment."

From the demoralising atmosphere of the hulls the convicts next progressed to the second phase of their sentence, the lengthy and agonising sea voyage to Australia.

In the early days the convict settlement in New South Wales was far from successful. The establishment of a colony composed of a nebulous assortment of prison guards and conscript pioneers was shown to be a project beset with difficulties. It was essential that the colonists should become self-supporting, but the soil was unfruitful and few of the convicts had either experience of or aptitude for agricultural work. In consequence, they were forced to rely largely on food sent out from England, and when convoys were slow or spasmodic they were often faced with shortages amounting to famine.

The settlement at Sydney was ruled by a governor, usually a naval or a military officer, who exercised despotic powers. In 1803 the island of Van Dieman's Land, now Tasmania, was also occupied and became an auxiliary penal station under the control of the authorities in New South Wales.

It had been realised from the outset that a colony could not be populated and developed entirely by transported convicts, and it was hoped that there would also be a regular flow of free emigrants from Britain. But the number of voluntary pioneers to the new settlements remained disappointingly low and it was estimated in 1821 that the total population of the infant colony was 30,000 of which not less than three-quarters consisted of transported prisoners.

The life of the early convicts in New South Wales was devoid of comfort, mercy, or hope. The discipline was harsh and inhuman. Joseph Holt, who had been transported for a political offence in 1798, has described how he and a party of fellow prisoners were made to witness a flogging. They were marched to the scene of this barbaric spectacle and the victim, who was to receive 300 lashes, was placed with his arms around the trunk of a large tree and his chest squeezed up against it so that, as Holt put it, he had "no power to cringe or stir". When he was in this position the two floggers, one of whom was the hangman from Sydney, stood on either side of him and the chastisement commenced. At this point Holt endeavoured to look away but he was immediately ordered to watch by an angry warder. The flogging was carried out in the presence of a doctor whose duty it was to feel the prisoner's pulse from time to time in case he was growing too weak. Holt paid a grudging tribute to the skill of the floggers, one left-handed and one right-handed, who worked together in perfect unison. He himself was standing near to the tree-trunk and he says that "the flesh and skin" blew in his face as the flogging proceeded. At length, when the punishment was over, the victim was carried away in a cart.

The development of the new colony commenced in the coastal area and later reached back to the vast regions of the interior as the free settlers deployed to establish their sheep stations. This was when the system of assignment came into operation, most of the assigned convicts being allocated to settlers who were living in the more remote and widely scattered localities. But in the course of time some of the primitive encampments grew into settlements and some of the settlements became towns and a demand arose for assignees who could work as book-keepers, clerks, and handicrafts-men in general. It was found thereafter that the cleverer convicts, and the greater rogues, usually managed to secure themselves com-fortable and often profitable employment in a skilled or a semi-skilled capacity whereas the duller and the less cunning of their fellows were unable to evade the arduous and unremitting toil of the convict labour gangs.

Even though a convict had been assigned to a free settler he still remained, in theory at any rate, under the direct supervision of the police. In the isolated stations of the interior a strict standard of discipline was maintained. The master could either punish a convict himself or could summon the assistance of a police officer. More serious offences carried the death penalty, but lesser infringements of the regulations, such as drunkenness, idling, insubordination, or escaping, were handled by the police without recourse to higher authority and were usually punished with a severe flogging.

The convict assignees in the towns were in a vastly different position from those in the remote countryside. For the most part they lived in comparative freedom and were subject to little or no surveillance. A large proportion of their masters were totally unfitted to be in charge of prisoners, being themselves persons of dubious character or emancipated convicts who had stayed on in Australia on the expiration of their own sentences of transportation. The latter class frequently succeeded in arranging for their convict friends to be assigned to them. With such a population Sydney and the other large towns soon became hotbeds of low living and vice.

Not all the convicts, however, were lucky enough to be hired out on assignment. The less fortunate were constrained to serve their time in the road parties, the chain gangs, and the penal settlements. The road parties were usually based in the vicinity of the towns from which they were marched about the countryside to the places in which their labour was required. The work was hard and the hours long, but they were adequately fed and their general treatment was not over-severe. Indeed, their supervision was often somewhat lax and many of them managed to escape and to remain at large as wandering bushrangers. An absconder who was recaptured was usually hanged, or else he might be flogged and remitted to a chain gang.

The chain gangs operated from three centres—a hulk in Sydney harbour, a stockaded barracks in the interior, and a mobile prison caravan. Convicts could be sent to a chain gang for disciplinary offences or for being generally insubordinate or unmanageable. Escape was well-nigh impossible as every prisoner had to wear heavy leg-irons and they were watched day and night by armed, military guards. Punishment was administered freely, each gang having its own flogger who wielded his whip according to his personal discretion.

The convicts who were deemed to be unsuitable for any other form of detention were ordered to one of the four penal settlements, at Port Arthur, Moreton Bay, Norfolk Island, or Tasman's Peninsula in Van Dieman's Land. All these places stood at the very lowest rung of the penal ladder in regard to cruelty, depravity, and discomfort. A prisoner, speaking from his personal experiences, once made the comment: "The heart of a man who went to them was taken away from him and he was given that of a wild beast." From the accounts which survive it would be little exaggeration to say that the prisoners in a penal settlement were treated more like wild beasts than like human beings. The food was appalling and the hygiene almost non-existent in the squalid, overcrowded encampments where they lived. For the most part the warders were brutalised sadists who had instant recourse to the lash or the gallows at the slightest provocation. Indeed, it is said that many convicts preferred to escape, knowing that they would starve to death in the wilderness outside, rather than to continue such a savage and hopeless existence. Others chose deliberately to commit a capital offence so that the hangman's rope would end their suffering. This was a far cry from Herman Merivale's brave words about a system which would enable prisoners to become "useful members of society".

The authorities in Britain were by no means unaware of the completely unsatisfactory way in which transportation to Australia was taking shape. Nevertheless, they continued to make use of the scheme on an ever-increasing scale. Before 1824 a prisoner who had received a sentence of death might only be reprieved and transported with his consent; during that year the courts were empowered to impose transportation whether the prisoner agreed or not. Thereafter the flow was swelled considerably and the number of ships employed as convict transports went up from year to year. At one time, in 1833, there were 4367 prisoners in the hulks awaiting the formation of the next transportation convoy.

The end of the system was a direct result of a series of spontaneous protests which arose both in Britain and in New South Wales during the decade between 1830 and 1840. There was a growing feeling in Australia that the colony was destined for a barren future if it continued indefinitely to be used as a sump for the most vicious and the most dishonest types of British criminal. Further, the convicts, the warders, and the emancipists still far outnumbered the free emigrants, and in consequence of the prevalence of crime the general standards of morality were sinking to appallingly low levels. The situation degenerated to such an extent that in 1835 a Sydney judge vehemently condemned the entire transportation procedure. A few years later a new political party was formed in New South Wales with the primary object of bringing about the complete abandonment of the system.

In Britain itself the most cogent argument advanced against transportation was the expense. The cost of shipping convicts to

Australia and maintaining a prison colony there was estimated to be about £300,000 annual. In addition, at least £100,000 a year was being spent on the upkeep of military garrisons in New South Wales, whose main purpose was the supervision of the transported convicts. Apart from the financial aspect of the matter, it was generally acknowledged that the system was proving an unmitigated failure, not only as a settlement project but also from the penal standpoint. By then the convicts in the colony had divided up into two distinct classes. The one lived an easy and prosperous life with scant supervision and with plenty of opportunity to amass considerable fortunes in the rapidly expanding economy. The other existed in a state of fettered slavery and was subjected continuously to the most merciless forms of tyranny.

In 1837 a select committee, which had been set up in the House of Commons to report on the efficacy of the transportation system, came out wholly against the retention of this method of punishment and recommended in its stead imprisonment with hard labour, at home, or overseas, from periods of two to fifteen years. The Government, faced with the strong criticisms of its own committee and the mounting disquiet in Australia, suspended all further transportation to New South Wales in the spring of 1840. This created two major difficulties; what was to be done with convicts in the future, and what was to happen to the convicts who were at that moment in transit to the colony? The Government decided on a compromise. A new scheme was hurriedly prepared for making Van Dieman's Land a prison island for all the convicts transported from Britain. In addition, the whole transportation system was to be reorganised to rid it of the worst iniquities of the past. In the new procedure all convicts would be graded according to their characters and their records and they would be allocated to different types of settlement accordingly.

The prisoners in the reorganised Van Dieman's Land were divided up into five broad categories. The first, who were undergoing a life sentence or had been transported for the second time, served their sentence in maximum security and maximum discipline penal settlements, reputed to be almost as unpleasant and brutal as those of former years. The second category comprised the great majority of the unexceptional convicts. These worked in gangs, supervised by warders and by religious instructors who were supposed to teach them the "habits of industry and subordination". The remaining categories were progressive. In the third, the convicts were permitted to leave their encampments and to find employment outside. In the fourth, they were granted tickets-of-leave and were allowed complete freedom of movement within the island. And in the fifth, they were granted an absolute or a conditional pardon and stayed on in the island, through choice or from necessity, as free settlers.

In practice the new scheme proved to be as complete a failure as its predecessor. There were several reasons for this, the first being overcrowding. Instead of building up the facilities in Van Dieman's Land slowly and methodically, the Government poured in convicts as fast as ships were available to carry them. During the initial four years of the project no less than 17,638 prisoners were transported to the island from the shores of Britain. Further, the supervisors and the instructors who were in charge of discipline and training degenerated rapidly as they became tainted with the depravity and corruption which seemed to be endemic to this particular penal community.

Even the successive stages of liberation miscarried as the convicts who were released on pass or on ticket-of-leave discovered that they had little or no chance of obtaining outside employment. In truth, the proposed economic development of Van Dieman's Land had been based upon a conception which was both ill-founded and totally unrealistic. Since there was no trade or industry to support the ever-expanding population of the island, very little work which was either useful or productive existed for the vast conscript labour force. The net result was idleness, dissolution, and despair.

In 1846 the Government was forced to acknowledge that the scheme was heading for a complete breakdown and a decision was made to suspend transportation to Van Dieman's Land for two years whilst the matter could be further investigated. The decisions as to the future disposal of British convicts fell principally on Sir George Grey, the Home Secretary, but Mr. Gladstone, then the Under-Secretary of State for the Colonies, favoured a project for establishing an entirely new convict colony in North Australia. However, this idea was never seriously pursued.

Even after 1846 transportation to Australia was still continued, although on a lesser scale. The average number of convicts transported annually during the three-year period 1847–9 stood at about 1570. For the period from 1850 to 1852 the figure rose to an annual average of about 2480. Meanwhile Sir George Grey circulated an invitation to every colonial government, inquiring their views on the acceptance of transported British convicts. Only Western Australia expressed itself at all favourably to the suggestion.

The Penal Servitude Act, 1853, abolished transportation for periods of less than fourteen years, and for the ensuing ten years British convicts, ranging in number from 224 to 782 annually, were transported to settlements in Western Australia. Nevertheless, there was still a powerful element of opinion in favour of a massive return to the old system in spite of the fervent opposition from the colonies themselves. In 1856 a select committee, whilst condemning the use of the hulks, recommended that the minimum period of transportation should be reduced to ten years, thereby increasing the number of convicts to whom it applied. This proposal was never adopted, and the Penal Servitude Act of 1857 abolished transportation as a specific sentence although it provided that certain convicts serving terms of penal servitude might still be ordered overseas under conditions very similar to those of the former transportation scheme.

In fact the 1857 Act made very little immediate difference to the number of prisoners who were actually transported, and the feeling against the system in Australia continued to mount. Finally, in 1867 Western Australia closed its doors to any further convict emigrants and thus transportation as a feature of the British penal system was brought finally and irrevocably to an end.

Chapter Thirteen

Early Prisons

ALL contemporary penal systems rely to a large extent on an extensive prison system. Indeed, if at the present time any State was to close its prisons completely, it is difficult to imagine how the criminal courts could continue to fulfil their essential functions of maintaining law and order.

"Prisons as places of punishment are comparatively modern institutions", says R. S. E. Hinde in his study *The British Penal System (1773–1950)*. "As places of detention", he continues, "they are almost as old as man himself."

The dominant theme which runs through the history of English prisons is the ceaseless conflict between the attitudes of brutality and vengeance on the one side, and the slowly awakening instincts of compassion and humanity on the other.

The fact that the prison was recognised as an official institution soon after the Norman Conquest is witnessed by an enactment for the provision of gaols in the Assize of Clarendon in 1166. In those days the common gaols were situated, for the most part, in the vaults and dungeons of ancient castles. In addition, every court originally had its own prison, the most notorious of which were the Marshalsea, the gaol of the King's Bench, and the Fleet, which dated from Norman times and was used at a later stage as the gaol of the Star Chamber and Court of Chancery.

Prisons were conceived in the first place to provide temporary confinement for those who were about to be tried and for offenders awaiting the execution of their sentences. The idea of a fixed term of imprisonment is of fairly recent origin. In early times punishment was both immediate and severe; it took the form of death, chastisement, mutilation, banishment, or degradation in the pillory. The national purse was not expended in maintaining criminals in captivity for a day longer than was absolutely essential.

In the Feudal era imprisonment also served as an instrument of coercion by means of which the bishop and the baron were enabled to deal with the intransigence of their vassals. The subject, of course, had few rights and fewer remedies. He could be arbitrarily arrested and confined in the dungeon of his oppressor until such time as he either capitulated or expired. However, the concept of personal liberty was gradually taking root and by a series of charters, culminating in the Habeas Corpus Act of 1679, the British people established, on paper at least, their immunity from arbitrary arrest and unlawful captivity. But in spite of these safeguards the gaols were usually full, not only with criminals, but also with those who had been unfortunate enough to choose the losing side—the religious, political, and dynastic prisoners.

With the rise of commercialism in the eighteenth century a new category of prisoner began to swell the gaols. Men and women who could not meet their debts were divested of what remained of their money and possessions by their creditors and then, if the amount they owed was still unsatisfied, they could be condemned to prison as debtors. In the result the debtor was prevented from earning a living and unless a friend provided him with funds he was left to languish in gaol indefinitely. This system was strongly criticised by Dr. Samuel Johnson in 1758. "Scarcely the most zealous admirers of our institutions think that law wise", he said, "which, when men are capable of work, obliges them to beg; or just, which exposes the liberty of one to the passions of another."

A further hazard encountered by debtor prisoners, along with all the other inmates of the gaols, was the likelihood of being stricken down by disease. Gaol-fever, which was really typhus, periodically swept through a prison leaving a trail of death, misery, and suffering. These outbreaks were an inevitable result of the conditions under which the prisoners were existing. Absence of sanitation, dirt, verminous clothing, pitifully inadequate food, lack of light, fresh air, and washing facilities, all contributed to the spread of infection.

The organisation of the prisons and the lives of the prisoners were subject to no general regulations. Nor was there a national prison service from which the governors and the wardens could be drawn. The right to keep a prison depended on a franchise which was granted by the monarch, and the prison keeper, after his official appointment, was entitled to recruit his staff as and how he chose. No salary was paid to prison officials as the prison keeper was supposed to exact payment from his prisoners, a wretched system which gave rise to wholesale bribery and extortion.

It is probable that very few members of the general public would have either known or cared how the criminal element was being treated in prison. The primary consideration was complete security so that prisoners could be safely detained pending their trials and their eventual punishment. But the position of the debtors was altogether different, as they were imprisoned by way of commercial practice and not for any infringements of the criminal law. The sufferings imposed on the debtor came far closer to the respectable citizen than the agony of the felon. The permanent removal of one's bankrupt neighbour made a much deeper impression than the casual observance of some miserable pickpocket being strangled to death on a public gallows.

Accordingly, the country was awakened with a rude shock in 1729 to the true situation in the gaols—a situation which was equally applicable both to criminals and to debtor prisoners. The disclosures arose from a series of murder trials in which the defendants were John Huggins, Richard Corbett, and Thomas Bambridge, respectively Wardens and Tipstaff of Fleet Prison, and William Acton, the Keeper of Marshalsea.

The considerable effect produced by the trials can be judged from the fact that shortly after they had finished the House of Commons decided to appoint a special committee "to enquire into the state of the gaols of this Kingdom, so far as it relates to the cruel usage of the prisoners". Later on the committee reported its view that Thomas Bambridge, whilst a warden of Fleet, had "wilfully permitted several debtors to the Crown in great sums of money, as well as debtors to divers of his Majesty's subjects, to escape" from the prison. Further, that he had been guilty of "the most notorious breaches of trust, great extortions, and the highest crimes and misdemeanours" in the execution of his office. He had "arbitrarily and unlawfully loaded with irons, put into dungeons, and destroyed prisoners for debt under his charge, treating them in the most barbaric and cruel manner". The committee made similar findings against John Huggins.

This report is published in full in a volume of *State Trials* together with an account of the proceedings in the cases in question. It opens with a brief history of the management of Fleet Prison, which is of interest as it demonstrates the haphazard manner in which the prison system developed in its early stages. During the reign of Queen Elizabeth I, we are told, a table was drawn up stipulating the fees which were payable in the Fleet by various categories of prisoners, including archbishops, dukes, and marquises, in order to escape being shackled with irons. This scale was confirmed in the reign of Charles II and at about the same time the Warden of the Fleet rebuilt the gaol at his own expense in return for letters patent granting to him and his heirs the rentals from some shops and other premises in the vicinity. Making the wardenship of the gaol a perpetual, hereditary office was inevitably disastrous. The report states that from time to time the wardens were wholly unsuitable and the system "was the occasion of great abuses, and frequent complaints to Parliament, till at length the patent was set aside".

During the subsequent period the wardenship of Fleet was sold to the highest bidder for a specified duration of time. John Huggins had purchased the office for his own and his son's life for a payment of £5000, but his son being unwilling to succeed him he had eventually resold the prison to Thomas Bambridge.

Bambridge had carried out his management with incredible inefficiency. He confessed that he had never kept any lists or records of his prisoners, and when one of them was discharged the fact was never entered in an official register. On occasion, says the report, "Bambridge refused to admit new prisoners to the Fleet although they had been properly committed there". It is a most appalling reflection on the whole of the prison administration of that period that a warden was allowed to behave in such an inept manner without being reprimanded by some higher authority.

According to the committee, Bambridge had had a private door built through the walls of the prison. He had kept the keys to this himself and had once permitted a well-known smuggler to make use of it in order to effect his escape.

One of Bambridge's most notorious rackets was his "spunging house" just outside the precincts of the gaol. New prisoners were often forced to live in this place until their last penny had been extracted from them. The treatment they received was in direct ratio to the amount they were paying, "some being allowed a handsome room and bed to themselves", says the report, "some stowed in garrets, three to a bed, and some put in irons". When prisoners had come to the end of their own resources and could obtain no more financial assistance from their relatives or friends, they were transferred from the spunging house to the gaols, but even then Bambridge continued to press them for money.

The Fleet also had its own tenements. These belonged to the warden and were leased to tenants who could house prisoners in them. Needless to say, Bambridge charged extortionate rents and the tenants passed them on to the unfortunate prisoners.

The House of Commons committee examined a number of the prisoners who were then detained in the Fleet. One of them was a Portuguese named Solas who told the committee how Bambridge had suddenly ordered him to be seized and fettered for no apparent reason. Later he had been placed in the strong room, a dungeon which figured prominently in these murder trials. It was described by the committee as follows :

> This place is a vault like those in which the dead are interned, and wherein the bodies of persons dying in [the Fleet Prison] are usually deposited till the coroner's inquest hath passed upon them; it has no chimney nor fireplace, nor any light but what comes over the door, or through a hole of about eight inches square. It is neither paved nor boarded; and the rough bricks appear both on sides and top, being neither wainscotted nor plastered; what adds to the dampness and stench of the place is its being built over a common sewer and adjoining to the sink and the dung-hill where all the nastiness of the prison is cast.

Solas was kept in the strong room for two months, until eventually one of his acquaintances paid Bambridge a fee of 5 guineas to get him released. By then he was a mental if not a physical wreck.

The committee also cited the diabolical treatment meted out by Bambridge to Captain Mackpheadris, a debtor prisoner, in 1727. This man was at first allocated his own room but he was unwilling, or unable, to pay the heavy rent charged for it. Bambridge had stolen everything of value he possessed and ordered him thenceforth to sleep in the open prison yard. After a short time Bambridge discovered that Mackpheadris had built himself a makeshift shelter for protection from the weather. The shelter was promptly pulled down and Mackpheadris was severely beaten up for erecting it. He was rescued by some other prisoners and was hidden in a room in the gaol. The following day Bambridge found him there and ordered the guards to drag him away and to chain him up "with great irons". In fact, he was placed in a type of strait-jacket which was so tight that one of his legs was broken while he was being forced into it. Mackpheadris had protested that "By the law of England no man ought to be tortured", but Bambridge replied that "He would do it first, and answer for it afterwards".

When the irons were in place Mackpheadris was thrown into the dread strong room, where he remained for three weeks. During this time both his legs turned gangrenous and were dressed by a surgeon, but even then he was not released from the strait-jacket. As a result of this ghastly experience he was crippled for life and in addition he almost lost his sight.

Mackpheadris must have been a man of considerable courage and determination, for while he was still in the strong room he insisted on availing himself of his right to make a petition to the judges by way of appeal against the treatment he was receiving. It is a shocking reflection on the judiciary of the time that Bambridge had sufficient confidence in their reactions to allow this petition to go forward. After a full hearing, says the House of Commons report, the judges reprimanded Bambridge and Huggins and they went on to declare that "a gaoler could not answer the ironing of a man before he was found guilty of a crime, but it being out of term they could not give the prisoner any relief or satisfaction". The report continues: "Notwithstanding this opinion of the judges, the said Bambridge continued to keep the prisoner in irons till he had paid him six guineas."

It is apparent that a prisoner was completely at the mercy of his gaolers and any legal rights which existed in his favour were largely fictitious. Solicitors who wanted to interview their clients in prison were persistently refused admittance. On one occasion at the Fleet a debtor prisoner was detained in the strong room until he lost his memory and all his limbs became paralysed. Later when he tried to take legal action against the warden he was unable to prove his case because the majority of his witnesses were still prisoners in the Fleet and were refused permission to give evidence on his behalf.

But the cruelty and barbarism in the Fleet was not exceptional in those times. Probably almost similar conditions existed in most of the prisons in Britain. Certainly they occurred in another large London gaol, the Marshalsea in Southwark.

William Acton, the deputy-keeper and head turnkey of the Marshalsea, was tried at Kingston Assizes in 1729 for the murder of four of his prisoners. The first of his victims was a man who was caught when trying to escape. This unfortunate person was confined in the Marshalsea strong room for three weeks with an iron cap on his head, fetters on his legs, and his hands in thumb screws. At the trial the prosecuting counsel described the strong room to the jury. It was, he said, "A place so damp, in which there were so many noxious humours, that any one put there must be in danger of death, not only from the noxious vapours, but from the want of a due covering at top; and from its being so remote from the sun that it could have no influence upon it, and must for want of it grow noxious, even to infection."

The prisoner was kept in this rat-infested hole without any sort of bedding and was habitually subjected to the most sadistic beatings. Eventually he died, seemingly from sheer exhaustion.

Another of Acton's victims was a debtor prisoner, Captain Bromfield, who became fatally ill after only a few days in the strong room. A third man remained there for several weeks and then appealed to the judges, who ordered his immediate release. However, nobody ensured that this order was obeyed and Acton disregarded it completely, leaving the prisoner in the strong room until he died.

The fourth murdered man was a diabetic and evidence was given at the trial that Acton had kept him in a dungeon while he was dying and his face was being half-eaten away by rats. Not surprisingly, Acton had issued instructions for him to be buried within an hour or two of his death.

Although the trials of 1729 made a considerable impact on the country they did not bring about any immediate reform of the prison system. Indeed, forty-five years later, in 1774, John Howard conducted a personal survey of various gaols all over Britain and reported to Parliament that he had found the same terrible conditions everywhere he went. The prisoners, he said, were half-naked and half-starved; their bedding, which was never changed and never cleaned, consisted of foul and reeking straw. Men and women were heavily ironed both before and after trial. The prison buildings were dark, filthy-dirty, overcrowded, and under-ventilated.

The gaolers, according to Howard, for the most part were cruel and avaricious. They stripped a prisoner of his entire wealth by way of gaol fees and feeding costs. The discipline was harsh and arbitrary, beatings were frequent and severe, and other penalties consisted of torture and confinement in appalling subterranean dungeons.

In such circumstances viciousness, degradation, and disease ran rife. Men and women sank to the level of animals, and only a primeval instinct of survival enabled them to stay alive at all.

Chapter Fourteen

The Growth of the Prison System

THE declaration of independence by the American colonies in 1776 had a very far-reaching effect on British penal methods. Until that time long-term prisoners had been transported as a matter of course, and now, quite suddenly, the colonial convict settlements had ceased to exist.

The Government reacted to this new situation by appointing a Special Commission to consider the changed position and to make recommendations for the treatment of convicts in the future. This commission consisted of three men, one of whom was the knowledgeable reformer John Howard. Their proposals were embodied in an Act of Parliament, passed in 1778, which set out for the first time the basic principles which, however modified and developed, have lain at the very roots of our prison system ever since.

The Act of 1778 provided for the creation of a number of what were described as "Penitentiary Houses", the primary purpose of which was to teach the prisoner to lead an honest, industrious, and a Christian way of life. This was to be achieved by alternating periods of hard labour and solitary confinement. There would also be religious instruction and a course of training designed to inculcate an improved standard of sobriety, cleanliness, and hygiene. Detention in one of these institutions was to be for a specific period, thus introducing the conception of the fixed-term prison sentence to the range of punishments available to the British criminal courts.

In order to put these proposals into operation, the Government appointed three supervisors, including John Howard, to find a suitable place where the first penitentiary house could be built. The supervisors began work immediately and examined various sites in Limehouse and in Islington. It is believed that Howard was anxious that the location of the first of these institutions should be in the vicinity of London as this was to be the pilot venture of the new scheme and he thought it should be close enough to be kept under continual surveillance. Howard also suggested that the penitentiary houses should be built entirely by convict labour.

Before a satisfactory site had been found, Howard announced his resignation from the panel of supervisors. The reason for his decision was never disclosed, but it seems to be a safe assumption that it was the result of a difference of opinion, either with one of his colleagues or with some higher authority. He was promptly replaced and the work of the supervisors went on.

At this point the Government suddenly lost interest in the idea of the penitentiary houses and became obsessed with a vast new scheme for the colonisation and development of New South Wales by transported British convicts. The supervisors did not, in fact, ever carry out their project, but a small prison on the lines recommended by the 1776 commission was built at Gloucester and another was opened in Southwell a short time later. Both were said to be entirely satisfactory.

Howard's abiding interest in the future planning of prisons was continued by Jeremy Bentham, the writer on law and political economy. Bentham travelled extensively in Europe collecting information about penal methods and discussing various theories for the punishment of criminals. On his return to England he produced a book called *The Panopticon or Inspection House,* which was published in 1791, and in which he put forward his views on the ideal form of prison structure. His conception can best be summarised in his own words. He speaks of " a large circular building, an iron cage glazed, a glass lantern as large as Ranelagh with cells in the outer circumference". The prisoners were to be kept under constant observation from the centre of the circle. They would be forced to work but would be allowed to share in the profits of their labour.

Bentham believed, like Howard, that the object of a prison sentence was to reform the prisoner. He thought that this could be achieved by following a strict routine which would include a certain amount of religious instruction interspersed with long periods of solitary confinement. The faith in the reformatory value of solitude seems to have been based on the theory that if a criminal was isolated sufficiently with his own thoughts he would be almost certain to realise the wickedness of his ways. And with realisation would come repentance. This may be true in a number of cases, but certainly it cannot be accepted as a general principle, for it presupposes that there is a fundamental goodness in mankind which is continuously striving for ascendancy. Indeed, regarded from the standpoint of modern psychiatric knowledge, the effect would be somewhat similar to that produced by brain-washing. The prisoner's personality was to be destroyed by loneliness and the void was then to be filled by the instillation of a religious belief.

Bentham's ideas found considerable favour with the younger William Pitt, who was Prime Minister when his book was published, but they were viewed with deep mistrust by King George III, who regarded Bentham as a slightly dangerous radical. Notwithstanding the attitude of the monarch, the Treasury concluded an agreement with Bentham in 1794 by which he was to find a site and to build a prison for a thousand prisoners in accordance with his theories.

Bentham discovered the necessary site but the Treasury had had second thoughts on the matter and declined to produce the money for the new model prison.

Throughout the social history of Britain there can be few fields in which the reformers have had to wage a sterner struggle than that of penal administration. It may have been through ignorance; it may have been through fear; but the great majority of people in every age have been opposed to the amelioration or the humanisation of criminal penalties. When changes have eventually been brought about they have been lamentably overdue, since the public attitude towards penal reform has invariably trailed far behind the gradual advancement of civilised thought.

In 1811 a committee was set up to consider, once again, the future of the prison system. They reported that they considered that many offenders might be reclaimed by a form of imprisonment which entailed the safe custody of the person combined with the reformation and improvement of the mind. To achieve this they advocated "seclusion, employment and religious instruction".

In the following year James Nield, another who was interested in the cause of prison reform, conducted his own investigation into the gaols of Britain to discover if the disclosures made by John Howard about forty years before had resulted in any improvement. He found that, with the exception of the new prisons at Gloucester and Southwell, the changes for the better had always been short-lived and the gaols were then "relapsing into their former horrid state of privation, filthiness, severity and neglect".

Even if the views of Howard and Bentham had not gained immediate approval, as the years passed it became increasingly apparent that some drastic changes in the conditions of the prisons were inevitable. In 1813 the Government decided to act. They announced their decision to erect a large new reformatory gaol at Millbank on a site which had previously been acquired by Bentham for his abortive project in 1794. This massive building, to house a thousand prisoners, was completed in 1816 at a cost of half a million pounds. It was given a triumphant opening in the same year in the presence of a host of foreign dignatories. Towards the end of the nineteenth century the Millbank Penitentiary was found to be completely insanitary and was demolished. In 1892 the same site was used to commence the construction of the Tate Gallery.

In the light of afterknowledge, Millbank is generally considered to have been a costly failure, but it did, at least, mark a step forward in prison development as it incorporated a number of the progressive theories of the time.

By and large, however, the penal reformers were still encountering innumerable difficulties in having their proposals acted upon. A series of Bills were introduced in Parliament to combat some of the worst abuses of the prison system, but for one reason or another they never came into effect. These measures were concerned with administration, ventilation and cleanliness of cells, feeding, clothing, and bedding. Also, the abolition of gaol fees, the compulsory appointment of prison chaplains, and the complete segregation of male and female prisoners. It seemed that in neither the Lords nor the Commons was there a body of opinion sufficiently large or sufficiently influential to ensure that these and other reforms would be put into practice. Perhaps in the view of the majority the theories of men like Howard and Bentham were still suspect, or else regarded as the Utopian dreams of a handful of starry-eyed idealists.

It should be noted, too, that during this period of immense opportunity it was not the politicians, the prelates, or the judiciary who were providing the urge and the inspiration for the improvement of prison conditions. It was left to a small group of private individuals who by their determination and their singleness of purpose were endeavouring to shame the country into action.

It would be difficult to overestimate the influence of the Society of Friends in the field of penal reform. During the early years of the nineteenth century they formed their own Prison Discipline Society for the purpose of visiting gaols all over Britain and of giving the fullest publicity to the results of their investigations. The reports put in by members of the society were nearly always the same. It was the old story of filth, brutality, and degradation. Most of the prisons were shockingly overcrowded. By day the inmates thronged the barren yards; by night they were herded into the insanitary and grossly inadequate buildings. As a matter of general routine all prisoners were still kept in irons. If any were unable to buy food for themselves they had to subsist on a daily ration consisting of a quantity of dry bread.

The Quaker, Sir Thomas Buxton, a leading figure in the penal reform movement, gave the following description of the prisoners in a gaol at St. Albans in 1818: "All were in ill health; almost all were in rags; almost all were filthy in the extreme. The state of prison, the desperation of the prisoners, broadly hinted in their conversation and plainly expressed in their conduct, the uproar of oaths, complaints and obscenity, the indescribable stench, presented together a concentration of the utmost misery and the utmost guilt."

Another Quaker, Elizabeth Fry, at the same time was agitating about the state of the prisoners in Newgate, the gaol of the City of London. Mrs. Fry's tremendous achievements for the women in that prison will be referred to in a later chapter. It is sufficient for the moment to notice that Mrs. Fry's voice was added to the others who were pleading with the Government to intervene.

In the end, the courage and tenacity of the reformers was triumphant. Between the years 1820 and 1830 a series of Acts of Parliament wholly transformed the British prison system. The use of irons was forbidden unless it was absolutely necessary. The women prisoners were ordered to be kept in different buildings from the men and were to be supervised by a female staff. Every prisoner was to be provided with a separate bed and, whenever possible, a separate cell. The prison authorities were to be held responsible, not only for the safe custody of the prisoners, but also for their health and their moral welfare. Daily church services were made obligatory, as was the employment of schoolmasters and the arrangement of classes.

Above all, the inertia of prison existence was to be replaced by a programme of organised labour.

And so, in the space of one decade the old, draconian methods of prison treatment were replaced by a system which was, in theory at any rate, not only punitive but purposeful and reformatory at the same time.

But it was far easier to conceive these new-style prisons than to actually bring them into being. The majority of the wardens and keepers, on whom so much was going to depend, were too versed in the old methods to take kindly to the new routine. In addition, the necessary prison buildings did not exist, and the local authorities showed a marked reluctance to employ their funds for rebuilding or improving their present gaols.

Meanwhile, on the far side of the Atlantic many of the American prisons were being developed on the lines recommended by Howard and Bentham. Two distinguished Frenchmen, De Tocqueville and Beamont, after inspecting prisons both in England and America, commented on the superiority of the conditions in those of the latter country.

In 1831 a select committee was set up by the House of Commons to consider the immediate improvement of English prisons. The committee reported in favour of every prisoner having a separate cell, but they rejected the suggestion that prisoners might be classified and separated according to their crimes and their personalities, as they considered that this would be an impossible task to carry out. The Government, disappointed perhaps by the meagre results achieved by its select committee, decided to send a Mr. Crawfurd to America to carry out a special investigation of the prison system there.

Mr. Crawfurd's report was published in 1834. In view of his experience of American gaols he emphasised once again the desirability of separating prisoners in their own cells rather than keeping them together in communal wards. On this point he said, "So greatly does increasing experience prove the importance of solitude in the management of prisons that I could not, if circumstances admitted, too strongly advocate its application in Britain for every class of offender, as well as for persons before trial, under modifications which would divest seclusion of its harshest character."

When Mr. Crawfurd mentioned the advisability of divesting seclusion of its "harshest character" he was probably thinking of the experiences of the Auburn Prison in New York, one of the institutions he had visited in the preparation of his report. Auburn Prison had been opened in 1816 and had been specifically designed to operate on the principle of reformation by solitary confinement. The results had been disastrous. Many prisoners, unable to stand up to the prolonged isolation, had suffered hysteria, nervous breakdowns, and even complete insanity. There had also been several suicides or attempted suicides. Another American prison, Sing Sing, had originally embarked on similar methods of treatment but had been obliged to ameliorate the strictness of the routine so that, although the prisoners were isolated at night and at mealtimes, they were allowed to associate during working periods provided they held no conversation with each other.

It is thought that the belief in the mystical influence of solitary confinement in the reformation of criminals actually originated in America, where it was practised in the early Quaker prisons in the state of Pennsylvania.

Shortly after the publication of Mr. Crawfurd's report, a select committee of the House of Lords recommended that prisons should be standardised and that regular prison inspectors should be appointed by the Government. This proposal was adopted and in 1835 an Act was passed "for affecting greater uniformity of practice in the government of the several prisons in England and Wales; and for appointing Inspectors of prisons in Great Britain".

Transportation to New South Wales was suspended in 1840 and Britain once again faced the major problem of what to do with her convicts. At that time there was neither the organisation nor the accommodation to keep them all in the existing prisons in this country, for there had been far more talk than action in the new prison-building programme. The Millbank penitentiary was, of course, in full operation by then and another large gaol was under construction at Pentonville, but apart from these nothing much had been accomplished.

After a hasty consideration of the position the Government decided to cling to the policy of transportation and to embark on an extensive convict-colonisation of Van Dieman's Land. At the same time a scheme was started with the object of providing floating hulk prisons in Gibraltar and Bermuda, but these were never fully developed.

The home prison system was immediately reorganised to meet the altered circumstances. Millbank penitentiary became a general classification centre to which all newly sentenced convicts were sent to await their transfer to the hulks as a first stage in the process of transportation. After Pentonville Prison had been opened in 1843 a limited number of specially selected convicts were sent there for a course of remedial solitary confinement followed by release and freedom. Juvenile convicts were sifted from their elders at Millbank and were sent to prisons instead of the hulks.

As has been seen in an earlier chapter, the Van Dieman's Land project was short-lived and was suspended six years later, in 1846. The Government was then back again in the crisis of 1840 and this time there were no possible overseas penal settlements remaining. It was left to Sir George Grey, the Home Secretary, to find a solution. His proposals, whatever their defects, provided Britain with her first official reasoned scheme for the reformation and rehabilitation of the men and women in her prisons.

Sir George Grey's system was based on three progressive phases of imprisonment. In the first phase, as might be imagined, the prisoner was to pass through the panacea of reformation, a period of solitary confinement which was to be combined with a course of industrial and moral training. Millbank with 1000 separate cells, and Pentonville with 540, became the centres for this initial stage, and over fifty new prisons were built during the next few years to perform a similar role.

The duration of the solitary confinement was originally set at eighteen months, but later, in view of the adverse mental effects it was having on so many prisoners, the period was reduced to nine months. Even then some prisons unofficially lessened the extent of the loneliness by allowing prisoners to associate in silence for certain parts of the day.

The second phase of the scheme was a period of hard manual labour on public works either at home or overseas. It was considered that for prisoners to achieve the maximum benefit from this they must be made to appreciate that their work was for the ultimate good of the community as a whole. For a start it was decided to construct a harbour of refuge at Portland in Dorset, and 1500 convicts selected for this task were drafted to a specially built prison close at hand. New prisons were also opened in Portsmouth and

Chatham so that convict labour could be employed in the busy dockyards of both these towns. As a further enterprise the large prison building at Dartmoor was brought back into use. This had been established originally for French and American prisoners during the wars with these two countries a short while previously, but had lain idle since the wars had ended. It was now to be used to accommodate convicts who would form labour gangs on the wasteland in the vicinity of the prison.

Hard labour overseas presented a greater problem and was confined, in practice, to those prisoners serving sentences in the floating hulks at Bermuda and Gibraltar.

When the convict had passed through the first and second phases he was considered to have undergone the maximum possible reformatory treatment. He would not be fitted, even then, to resume his life as a free citizen in Britain, but was to be released on a conditional pardon provided he was willing to emigrate and to spend the rest of his days in one of the British colonial possessions.

When he planned this third phase Sir George Grey was assuming that the British colonies would assent to the scheme, mainly on the ground that it would keep them supplied with a steady stream of conscripted settlers. However, when inquiries were made it was discovered that only Western Australia was agreeable to give the arrangement a trial. Therefore it was apparent that the final phase of the programme would have to be completely rethought.

There were many people at that time who clung to the old belief that a criminal could never be wholly redeemed. There was also a general antipathy to any suggestion that a number of partly reformed ex-convicts should be set at large in Britain. However, the only two alternatives remaining seemed to be either to keep the convict in some form of perpetual detention or to accept that having expiated his offence he should be gradually returned to a life of freedom in his own country.

Eventually, in spite of all opposition, the Government adopted the more merciful procedure and the third phase of Sir George Grey's scheme was altered from compulsory emigration to a period of penal servitude in a British prison followed by release on ticket-of-leave.

By the middle of the nineteenth century no serious effort had been made to bring about any uniform standard in prison conditions throughout the country. Each prison was virtually free to adopt its own methods of treatment and naturally enough they varied enormously from place to place. The food in some was adequate, and in others almost inedible. The minimum size of a cell was not laid down, nor was the daily routine of the convict's life. Sometimes "hard labour" consisted of long, monotonous spells at the treadmill or the crank, sometimes the comparative normality of manufacturing work. The discipline in certain prisons was harsh and onerous, in others it was moderate, or even lax.

In 1850 the House of Commons set up a select committee to investigate the inconsistencies of the prison system. The committee reported that the numerous variations of treatment could not be justified. Further, they considered that the only way of establishing a uniform standard would be to entrust all matters of discipline and routine to some central authority.

After thirteen more years of governmental lassitude another select committee was set up to review the situation in 1863. Once again they commented on the great disparities between the conditions of various prisons. These were, said the report, "leading to an inequality, uncertainty and inefficiency of punishment, productive of the most prejudicial results".

At long last the Government decided to act. In 1865 a measure was introduced in Parliament to consolidate all the previous legislation on the subject of prison discipline and to set out a series of regulations for the uniform management of every prison in Britain. To ensure that these regulations were enforced a team of visiting prison inspectors was to be appointed forthwith.

Sir George Grey's three-phased programme for convicts had by then been in operation for over twenty years and was meeting with increasing disapproval. Many people were saying that the whole scheme ought to be abandoned and that a return should be made to transportation. The public, in general, were not particularly interested in the theory which lay behind Grey's system of progressive imprisonment. What concerned them far more was the eventual release into their midst of so many nominally reformed criminals. It was believed that, far from being cured of their anti-social tendencies, the majority of the ticket-of-leave prisoners were speedily relapsing into their old criminal habits.

In addition, the second and third phases of the scheme were being strongly criticised on another ground. It had been discovered that, following the 1865 Act, most prisoners were working far shorter hours and were much better fed than the average free employee of the same period. The rate of prison payment was also excessive, so much so that a convict on his release might draw as large a sum as £80 in accumulated wages. Bearing in mind the value of money at the time, that amount must have appeared to be astronomical.

With the advent of reform, the discipline in a number of prisons had greatly deteriorated. "Penal servitude", commented a judge, "was hardly calculated to produce on the mind of the criminal that salutary dread of the recurrence of the punishment which may be the means of deterring him, and through his example others, from the commission of crime."

In the face of so much public misgiving the Government gave way and drastically altered Sir George Grey's scheme.

The new procedure was still to be divided into a three-phased progression. The first, as before, was the inevitable spell of separate confinement, and from this the convict graduated to a period of hard labour during which he was allotted marks by the prison staff for the diligence and industry he showed at his work. The convict remained in the second phase until he had gained sufficient marks to qualify him to enter the third, which was a release on licence to complete his sentence in comparative freedom in one of the British colonies.

But once again when the colonies were asked to co-operate in the scheme only Western Australia expressed a willingness to do so, and in 1867 even she declined to receive any further convict emigrants.

Reluctantly the British Government was forced to accept the proposition that there was no longer any possibility of dumping all her ex-convicts in her colonial possessions. Phase three of the prison scheme was then amended so that prisoners who had totted up the necessary marks during their hard labour would be released on licence at home.

The Act of 1865, which had been designed to bring about a general uniformity in prison standards, failed completely to achieve its object. This was principally due to the fact that individual prisons were still the responsibility of the local authorities and were financed entirely out of local rates. In consequence, the recently formed panel of visiting prison inspectors found themselves relatively powerless to see that their recommendations were ever implemented. To remedy this unsatisfactory position the Government, in 1877, vested control of all British prisons in a new statutory authority to be known as the Prison Commissioners. These officials were appointed by and solely responsible to the Home Secretary. They were authorised to make regulations affecting every aspect of prison discipline and routine. Further, they were placed in charge of the building and the distribution of all new prisons and were authorised to transfer prisoners from one area to another according to the accommodation available.

After 1877 very few people can have seriously believed that transportation would ever again be a feasible proposition, and an increasing study was made of the best use of the British prison system. As a result, in the years that followed, the lives of the prisoners were gradually brought under a very much stricter control. Sentences became longer, food became more plain, and discipline more stringent. There was also a general tightening up in the supervision of convict labour.

On the more progressive side, a start was made at segregating the hardened criminal from both the novice in crime and the prisoner who showed a reasonable prospect of reformation.

The Prison Commissioners succeeded where the visiting prison inspectors had failed in bringing about a common standard in the state of the prisons.

It is interesting today to look back at the conditions of imprisonment which existed in this country as recently as the early 1890's— just over seventy years ago.

At that time there were two types of penal detention—an ordinary prison sentence which could last up to two years, and a sentence of penal servitude which could be for any period from five years to life.

Every prison sentence commenced with a spell of separate confinement. This went on for a minimum of one month and continued thereafter until the prisoner had accumulated a sufficient number of good conduct marks to graduate to the next phase. During the period of separate confinement every male prisoner, with the exception of boys under 16 and men over 60, had to sleep at night on a plank bed without a mattress.

The second, third, and fourth phases of imprisonment all entailed very slight progressive privileges. For instance, in the second phase the food was slightly better than in the first and the male prisoner was allowed a mattress on two nights each week. In the third phase the prisoner had a mattress every night and in the fourth he could receive a letter and a visit from a relative or a friend.

Each of the four phases lasted for at least a month, and having passed through all of them the prisoner settled down into the drab routine of normal prison existence.

The labour for ordinary prisoners consisted of a daily stint of 8640 feet at the treadmill, which was used to pump water and to grind corn for the prison. Alternatively, they might be made to perform six hours of drudgery at the crank, or a monotonous period of oakum beating or mat making. Later on, if a prisoner had given satisfaction in his general behaviour, he might qualify for industrial work, usually tailoring, shoe and basket making, bookbinding, or printing, for each of which he would receive a small rate of remuneration.

The procedure for a prisoner serving a sentence of penal servitude was altogether different. This commenced with a period of nine months in separate confinement during which time both male and female convicts had to work in isolation in their cells and were only permitted to see, but not to talk to, their fellow prisoners during exercise or on visits to the prison chapel. Next followed a long period of hard labour on public works, the convicts being allowed to associate together, but once again being forbidden to converse with each other.

From the start of a sentence of penal servitude prisoners could earn marks for good conduct which would entitled them to a varying amount of remission at the end of their sentences. The final stage was, in fact, release on licence, or ticket-of-leave, until the full period of the sentence had expired. Whilst on ticket-of-leave a convict had to report to the police at regular intervals and was liable to be recalled to prison for any infringement of the conditions of the licence.

A good idea of the effects of prison life at this time on a sensitive individual can be gained from Oscar Wilde's very moving account of his own experiences in his book *De Profundis*. He tells us:

> The paralysing immobility of a life, every circumstance of which is regulated after an unchangeable pattern, so that we eat and drink and

lie down and pray, or kneel at least for prayer, according to the inflexible laws of an iron formula: this immobile quality that makes each dreadful day in the minutest detail like its brother, seems to communicate itself to those external forces, the very essence of whose existence is ceaseless change. Of seed-time or harvest, or the reapers bending over the corn, or the grape gatherers threading through the vines, or the grass in the orchard made white with broken blossoms or strewn with fallen fruit: of these we know nothing and can know nothing. For us there is only one season, the season of sorrow.

A social historian must frequently encounter the greatest difficulty in forming an assessment of the forces which have been paramount in causing a sweeping change in the general outlook towards some established feature of a nation's life. Without speculating on the causes, one can say with certainty that during the closing years of the nineteenth century and the opening years of the twentieth the mood of the British people was moving swiftly towards a more merciful and a more tolerant attitude in regard to the punishment of criminal offenders.

In 1895 Mr. Herbert Asquith, the Home Secretary, appointed a departmental committee to review the condition of the prisons. The committee's report was revealing and purposeful. They had come to the conclusion, they said, that the system was achieving almost nothing from a moral standpoint, for "few inmates left prison better than they came in". A blind faith in the employment of more prison chaplains and more prison schoolmasters would not provide a solution, they continued, but far more emphasis must be placed on reformation, especially in the case of those prisoners who were most likely to respond. The committee felt that increased attention should be paid to the segregation of juveniles and first offenders from confirmed criminals. They commented on the very useful work which was being performed by a handful of voluntary societies in looking after discharged prisoners and they recommended that this particular work should be greatly expanded.

About this time the Prison Commissioners were beginning to have second thoughts about the efficacy of solitary confinement as a universal means of reforming the criminal. In 1899 the initial period of isolation for prisoners undergoing penal servitude was reduced to six months, and for those serving ordinary prison sentences it was virtually abolished.

There were few features of prison life which remained untouched by the winds of reform around the turn of the century. As regards prison labour, the crank and the treadmill were being replaced by the industrial workshop. Prison diet was improving and the strictness of the rules relating to the receipt of letters and to visits from friends and relations was gradually being relaxed. Sentences were becoming shorter and attention was being paid to the development of prison libraries and the opportunities for the education and training of the prisoners.

Although a great deal still remained to be done, within the span of a few decades the breath of humanity had entered the British prison system.

Chapter Fifteen

The Young Offender

It seems scarcely credible today to reflect that until a little over a hundred years ago the British penal system made little or no distinction between the punishment of adult and juvenile offenders.

At the beginning of the nineteenth century children were not completely exempt from hanging on account of age alone unless they were under 7. Between the ages of 7 and 14 they could be hanged provided their cases showed strong evidence of malice, but if they were over 14 they were entitled to no special consideration whatsoever.

Children of both sexes were liable to be sentenced to transportation and, irrespective of age, they were forced to endure the full horrors of the hulks and the transports, to say nothing of the compulsory banishment from their families and their homes. In 1756 the harshness of this procedure was to some extent mitigated when a voluntary reformatory institution was opened by the Philanthropic Society. Later another was opened by the Marine Society.

This measure was far too minor, of course, to have any real effect on the treatment of juvenile offenders in general, and the courts continued to deal with them in a manner which paid little or no regard to their youth. Apart altogether from the cruelties of the system, it was administered without any thought being given to the consequences upon the character and outlook of a youngster who was thrown indiscriminately into the company of hardened criminals. This defect was recognised by a Committee on Prisons which reported in 1811 : "It is highly inadvisable to expose young persons of twelve and thirteen years of age to the instruction of those who can initiate them into all the mysteries of fraud and villainy." The obvious logic of this statement seems to have evoked no immediate response from the legislature.

Charles Dickens has described how he stood outside a court, probably around the year 1830, and watched the convicted offenders being led off to prison. Amongst others, he mentions, were "boys of ten, as hardened in vice as men of fifty". Dickens has also written of a visit he paid to Newgate about the same period. He was taken to the portion of the prison set apart for boys under 14 years of age and the youthful prisoners there were lined up for his inspection.

> There were fourteen of them in all [he says], some with shoes, some without; some in pinafores without jackets, others in jackets without pinafores, and one in scarce anything at all. The whole number, without exception, we believe, had been committed for trial on charges of pocket-picking; and fourteen such terrible little faces we never beheld. There was not one redeeming feature among them—not a glance of honesty—not a wink expressive of anything but the gallows and the hulks in the whole collection. As to anything like shame or contrition, that was entirely out of the question . . . we had never looked upon a more disagreeable sight, because we never saw fourteen such helpless creatures of neglect before.

It was not until 1835 that a House of Lords committee recommended the setting up of a special type of penitentiary for young offenders. Two years later, in 1837, the first official reformatory was opened at Parkhurst Prison in the Isle of Wight. Boys and youths who had been sentenced to transportation were sent there for disciplinary training combined with academic, religious, and industrial instruction. They remained until they were moved to ordinary prisons, en route for Australia, or else to wait until they were released under pardon and placed in the care of some recognised charitable organisation.

Even after the opening of Parkhurst reformatory a distinctive form of sentence for juveniles was not available to the courts. And yet the country was slowly becoming aware of the fact that the age groups of criminals might bear some significance in the general pattern of crime. A census carried out in 1841 revealed that "Juveniles aged over fifteen years and under twenty, form not quite one-tenth of the population, but they are guilty of nearly one-fourth of its crime".

About the middle of the nineteenth century there seems to have been some real awakening of a national awareness regarding the methods in which young offenders were being treated. In 1846 a Member of Parliament, Mr. Monckton Milnes (afterwards Lord Houghton), introduced a Bill in the House of Commons for the purpose of setting up an official reformatory in which a juvenile could remain for the duration of his sentence instead of being sent to one of the ordinary prisons. This wise and humane measure was rejected out of hand by a legislature which, in the field of penal reform, must have been one of the more barren and reactionary repositories of the public conscience which has ever existed.

However, Mr. Milnes's Bill was not entirely devoid of effect, for it focused attention on the appalling treatment of young offenders. A select committee of the House of Lords reporting in 1847 on the punishment of juveniles said that they were "disposed to recommend the adoption, by way of trial, of reformatory asylums, together with a moderate use of corporal punishment". They went on to make the general observation : "It may be safely affirmed that the duty of all rulers is both to prevent, as far as may be possible, the necessity of punishing, and where they do inflict punishment to attempt reformation."

A voluntary conference was held in Birmingham in 1851 to look into the subject more fully. As a direct consequence of this new interest the House of Commons decided to form a committee to study the whole problem of juvenile delinquency and the punishment of young offenders.

Meanwhile a number of voluntary organisations were opening their own private reformatories based on those run by the Marine and Philanthropic Societies, and more and more young offenders were being sent to them under a conditional pardon instead of being imprisoned or transported.

Three years later Mr. Adderly, M.P., carried through Parliament the Youthful Offenders Act, 1854, which provided that :

> Whenever any person under the age of 16 years shall be convicted of any offence, it shall be lawful for any court, in addition to the sentence passed as a punishment for his offence, to direct such an offender to be sent at the expiration of his sentence to one of the Reformatory Schools and to be detained there for not less than two and not exceeding five years, provided that the sentence passed shall be one of imprisonment for fourteen days at the least.

At first sight this Act might seem to be regressive as it made the reformatory school additional to the child's ordinary prison sentence, but, in fact, it was intended to give the courts the opportunity of keeping a sentence of imprisonment down to the minimum by ordering that the child should be sent on to a reformatory at its conclusion.

Another type of institution for the compulsory detention of the young at this period was the Industrial School. Children could be ordered to these establishments provided that they were under 14, but they could not be kept at them when they had passed the age of 16. Industrial schools were intended for children who had not yet committed a criminal offence but whose background and environment were such that they seemed likely to drift into a life of crime if they remained at liberty. The procedure was similar in a way to the modern jurisdiction by which the courts can order a child to a home as "being in need of care and protection".

The industrial school differed from the reformatory in that its origins had no connection with the prison system.

At the beginning of the nineteenth century a Portsmouth shoe-maker named John Pounds set up a number of what he called "Ragged Schools" in order to meet the needs of the vast number of destitute children in the neighbourhood. This experiment was so successful that it was followed by other philanthropists in different parts of the country.

Although industrial schools were conceived as private and charitable enterprises, as the years passed they achieved a growing importance in combating juvenile delinquency. In 1854 the industrial schools in Scotland were placed on an official footing, and in 1857 those in England were incorporated into the authorised penal system by an Act of Parliament which officially accepted for the first time that there might be a method of dealing with the very young other than by sending them to ordinary adult prisons. This Act only applied to vagrant children below the age of 14. If they had not yet committed an offence the courts could order them to be taken to an industrial school for one week only, but if they had been convicted they could be sent for a longer period of training or could be handed back to their parents provided that the latter undertook responsibility for their behaviour for any duration up to twelve months.

Another Act, in 1861, extended the categories of children who might be sent to industrial schools. The new list included boys and girls of less than 14 who had been found wandering abroad without visible means of support, or begging, or keeping company with reputed thieves. Also, any child below the age of 12 who had been convicted of a serious criminal offence could be committed to one of these institutions instead of being sent to prison.

The system of training at reformatories and industrial schools was very similar. Great emphasis was placed on religious instruction, and also on industrial training, physical culture and the inculcation of a spirit of obedience and discipline. The aim of both types of institution was principally to mould the inmates into a prescribed pattern and little or no deference was paid to the various individualities of temperament.

The style of living was spartan in the extreme. The rules were strict and the routine arduous.

The principal of Redhill reformatory described his own methods of enforcing discipline.

> Confinement in a cell [he said] with bread and water diet, for periods varying from a few hours to a few days, will be found in general a sufficient punishment, provided always that the cell is not warm and fitted up as comfortably as a fashionable boudoir, but gives the inmate just as much cold and privation and discomfort as proper regard to health, cleanliness and the making of a kindly impression on the offender will allow for. Cases may arise when the cell fails or is inappropriate, and in which a good whipping will do the culprit far more good.

As has been seen, the 1854 Act which created reformatory schools specifically stated that they were to be used as an additional form of sentence after the expiry of a term of imprisonment. Another Act, in 1866, preserved the same principle but modified the position slightly by making it possible for any court which sentenced a child under 16 to a term of imprisonment lasting ten days or more (and not fourteen days or more as hitherto) to order a period in a reformatory at the conclusion of the sentence. The possible length of the reformatory sentence remained at between two and five years. A child under 10 could only be sent to a reformatory school if he had previously been convicted of an offence punishable with imprisonment or penal servitude.

The most important change introduced by the 1866 Act was a provision that children who had served a minimum of eighteen months of their sentences at reformatories were eligible for release on licence to live with any "trustworthy and respectable persons" who were willing to take charge of them.

Looking back at the penal system during the second half of the last century it is difficult to imagine why the realisation that reformatories might be used as an alternative to imprisonment for children under 16 was so slow in taking root. In fact, it was not until 1893 that the courts were empowered to send children to them direct, without an intervening period in an ordinary prison. Even then the court had an absolute discretion whether or not the child was to be made to serve a preliminary sentence of imprisonment. Six years later, in 1899, it was provided that no person should be sentenced to both prison and reformatory, but simply to one or the other.

In 1900 there was a total of 48 reformatory schools in Britain, at which there were 4953 boys and 658 girls. Industrial schools had a wider use. There were 142 of these in the country, some under Protestant and some under Roman Catholic direction, to which children could be committed according to their religious denomination.

Some effort was being made to fit children for the future at both types of institution. Accordingly, two of the reformatories and eight of the industrial schools were in reality training ships, and many others specialised in agricultural and dairy farming.

The Gladstone Committee, which met in 1894 and 1895, heard a number of witnesses who believed that it was inadvisable for juveniles to be sent to ordinary adult prisons. The view was not always put forward from the dictates of humanity. For instance, the Governor of Pentonville said in his evidence: "I think that most people dread a prison until once they have been in it; but once they have been in it a good deal of that dread is gone, particularly amongst juveniles." For that reason, he thought, children should be kept out of prison altogether.

But whatever the motives which prompted the suggestion, the committee remained unconvinced and rejected it in their report as being neither "practicable nor desirable". However, they did recommend that youthful offenders should be completely segregated from other prisoners.

One of the many beneficial results of the Gladstone Committee's report was the passing of the Youthful Offenders Act, 1901, which allowed the courts, in certain circumstances, to remand a young defendant to the care of a "suitable person" instead of sending him to prison. The Act also enlarged the categories of children who could be sent to an industrial school.

Perhaps the greatest achievement of the Gladstone Committee, certainly in their recommendations affecting young offenders, was the proposal that Britain should adopt the system of juvenile–adult reformatories which had been tried out so successfully in the United States of America, in particular at Elmira in the State of New York. This reformatory had been opened in 1876 and accommodated specially selected prisoners ranging in age from 15 to 35. The main emphasis of the routine there was placed on moral regeneration rather than on punishment as such. The inmates, in general, were sentenced to an indefinite period of detention and underwent various courses of progressive training until they were deemed to be fit for release.

It will be remembered that the top age limit for sentence to a British reformatory was 16, but the Prison Commissioners took up the Gladstone Committee's recommendation in their report for 1901–2 in which they said:

> Figures . . . have testified that the age between 16 and 21 is essentially the criminal age and that from criminals of this age the professional criminal of later years is generated. It is also known to students of human nature that this age is a particularly plastic age and that the habits which may lead to crime or virtue cannot be said to be fully formed before the age of 21.

The Commissioners went on to propose that certain youths between 16 and 21 years of age might be sent to a new type of prison for a period of six months and that they should undergo there "a special form of disciplinary and reformatory treatment". An essential condition of this scheme, they said, would be that the youths should be adequately supervised after they had been discharged.

The Government decided to give this idea a trial, and in 1902 the whole of Rochester Prison in Kent was taken over for the experiment. It happened that this prison was situated a little distance from the town in the tiny village of Borstal, and consequently the new scheme became known as the "Borstal system".

A few years later Lincoln Prison was also converted into a special prison for boys, and from then on more Borstal institutions were opened in various other parts of the country.

The daily routine at the early Borstals was little different from that at the adult prisons, although, according to the first Borstal rules, particular attention was to be given to "special instruction, useful trades and physical drill". Writing about the initial development of the project in his book *The English Prison System*, Sir E. Ruggles-Brise, one of the founders of the Borstal scheme, said:

> Experience showed that the system should be one of stern and exact discipline, tempered only by such rewards and privileges as good conduct, with industry, might earn: and resting on the physical side on the basis of hard manual labour and skilled trades, and on its moral and intellectual side on the combined efforts of the chaplain and the schoolmaster.

The 1901–2 report of the Prison Commissioners was also followed with regard to their suggestion that adequate facilities for supervision should be available when a youth had been discharged from Borstal. This aftercare work was performed by an organisation which was principally supported by voluntary subscription.

The Prison Commissioners, who had the utmost confidence in the new scheme, suggested in their report for 1905–6 that the courts should be enabled to pass specific sentences of Borstal detention. Up to that time Borstal institutions merely ranked as a special type of prison and the selection of youths to attend them was carried out as an administration arrangement by the prison authorities.

Once again the Government adopted the Prison Commissioners' proposal. The Prevention of Crime Act, 1908, introduced a new type of sentence, one of Borstal training, which could be passed as an alternative to imprisonment on youths between 16 and 21 for a period of two or three years.

Another measure of far-reaching importance, passed in 1908, was the Children's Act. This set up special Juvenile Courts to deal with cases against offenders who were under 16 years of age. Until then every offender, whatever his age, had been tried in the ordinary criminal courts. This Act also provided that children between 14 and 16 were only to be sent to prison if the court certified that they were "so unruly and depraved" that they could not be treated in any other way. A child under 14 could not be sent to prison at all.

The legislation of 1908 may properly be regarded as the dividing line between the old and the new methods of dealing with youthful offenders. Since then the criminal law has gradually edged forward to a more and more enlightened policy in its attitude towards the young.

Borstal institutions suffered at first from the fact that they were administering no preconceived system of training. They were being managed, too, by men whose principal experience had been derived from their work in prisons, and who found it difficult, as a result, to visualise any form of penal detention which was too dissimilar from ordinary imprisonment. This condition persisted until the year 1922, when Sir Alexander Paterson was appointed Prison Commissioner.

Describing the change which Paterson brought into the Borstal scheme, Winifred Elkin, in her study *The English Penal System,* says : "It is largely due to the late Sir Alexander Paterson that the Governors and housemasters came to include so many men with a high moral purpose and a love of humanity, based generally on a deep religious sense."

Paterson has given his own views on the way in which a youth should be handled at a Borstal institution. "The task is not to break or knead him into shape", he said, "but to stimulate some power within to regulate conduct aright, to insinuate a preference for the good and the clean, to make him want to use his life well, so that he himself and not others will save him from waste."

In 1933 several changes were made both in the law and in the procedure applicable to the trial and punishment of young offenders. The minimum age for imprisonment was raised from 16 to 17, with the proviso that children between 14 and 17 could still be imprisoned if they were certified as being sufficiently unruly and depraved. The minimum age for any person to suffer the death penalty was set at 18. Further, the jurisdiction of the juvenile courts was increased to take in children under 17 instead of under 16 as before.

The industrial school has now vanished from the British penal system. Since 1933 there has been established in its stead a new type of institution called an Approved School, to which children may be sent if either their past records, or their home circumstances, make it desirable for them to undergo a period of supervision and treatment in custody. The schools, which are all approved by the Home Office, are managed by local education authorities, philanthropic societies, or religious bodies.

Two further methods of punishing the young were introduced in 1948. The Detention Centre, which takes offenders between the ages of 14 and 21, aims at administering a short but rigorous course of discipline and training lasting from three to six months. The system calls for a high standard of physical fitness in the first place, so that the number of boys who could benefit from it is somewhat restricted. There is also at the moment one detention centre in England for girls. The other innovation in 1948 was the Attendance Centre, at which young people between 12 and 21 may be ordered to spend a prescribed number of hours of their spare time.

With the setting up of detention and attendance centres, Parliament raised the age below which no person could be sent to prison from 14 to 15, and further provided that no one under 21 might be imprisoned unless the court was of the opinion that no other method of dealing with him (or her) was appropriate.

In 1961 the minimum age for a sentence of imprisonment was raised from 15 to 17.

In spite of the great and manifold reforms that have taken place in the law affecting young persons in recent years, it seems that we are now standing on the brink of some of the most sweeping changes ever contemplated in this field.

In August 1965 the Government issued a white paper outlining its intention to abolish juvenile courts completely, and to substitute Family Councils and Family Courts in their stead. Defendants between the ages of 16 and 21 would have their own Young Offenders Courts. Borstals would become Youth Training Centres, and for those in the 16 to 21 age group who are in need of a longer period in custody there would be a new type of establishment known as the Young Offenders Institution.

The proposals have already come in for much criticism from probation officers, magistrates, and others with a vast experience of the juvenile courts and of the young delinquent. It is certain that they will arouse a considerable amount of controversy before they are finally implemented.

Chapter Sixteen

Fines and Probation

UNTIL 1 January 1968 the British law had always divided criminal offences into two broad categories—felonies and misdemeanours. This distinction had long ceased to have any logical merit and was over-due for removal.

Offences might have been felonies at common law or they might have been specifically designated as such by an Act of Parliament. Theoretically, the more serious crimes were supposed to be classified as felonies and the less serious as misdemeanours. In consequence, the former usually carried a heavier scale of penalties than the latter.

Many of the offences which ranked as misdemeanours were, in fact, amongst the most serious in the criminal calendar. For instance, conspiracy to murder, perjury, incest, using a firearm with intent to resist arrest, and an indecent assault on a girl between the ages of 13 and 16.

On the other hand, many other offences which were of a comparatively trifling nature were classed as felonies. Amongst these were the abduction of an heiress, the larceny of a tree, and the stealing by a lodger of property worth under £5.

I have mentioned the distinction between the two types of crime at this point because it played an important role in the historical development of punishment by the imposition of fines.

During the Feudal era any person who was convicted of a felony was made to forfeit his lands and all his possessions as a matter of course. At a later period the felon suffered execution in addition to forfeiture. An historical aftermath of this practice had been that until 1948 felonies were very rarely punishable by fines on the basis that a felon, directly he had been convicted, would be stripped of his entire substance automatically.

As regards misdemeanours, however, the courts always had jurisdiction to impose fines at common law, the amounts being wholly discretionary with no prescribed maxima. The only restriction on the courts' powers in this respect were prescribed by the Magna Carta (1215) and the Bill of Rights (1688), both of which forbade the levying of fines which were excessive and unreasonable. On the other hand, statutory misdemeanours laid down a maximum fine which could not under any circumstances be exceeded.

Anyone who has sat on the bench at a criminal court would probably agree that one of the most difficult tasks when imposing fines is the assessment of the defendant's means from the scant and frequently misleading information available. In past generations a large number of men and women were committed to prison solely because they had been ordered to pay fines which were wholly beyond their resources.

Until the year 1879 a fine became payable the moment it was imposed, otherwise the defendant had to remain in prison until the amount had been settled in full. This meant, of course, that unless his friends could lend him the money, or he could raise it in some other way, he would be constrained to indefinite imprisonment.

The position was fundamentally changed by the provisions of the Summary Jurisdiction Act, 1879, which granted magistrates' courts the power to allow defendants a period of time in which a fine could be paid, or else to make an order that it was to be payable by regular instalments. The Act also laid down the maximum periods of imprisonment, proportionate to the size of the fine, for which a defendant could be committed to prison as an alternative to payment. Since the same periods were preserved by later enactments, and were still applicable until the end of 1967, it might be of interest to enumerate them. They were:

Amount of fine	Alternative imprisonment
Up to 10s.	7 days
10s. to £1	14 days
£1–£5	1 month
£5–£20	2 months
Over £20	3 months

In recent years the majority of courts never specified an alternative period of imprisonment, when imposing a fine, without adequate grounds for believing that the defendant would refuse to pay unless they did so. On 1 January 1968, by a section of the latest Criminal

Justice Act, magistrates were virtually deprived of this power to order alternative sentences.

The 1879 provision had an immediate and beneficial result. A census taken for the year 1889 showed that about 46,000 people, who would formerly have suffered immediate imprisonment, had been granted time in which to pay their fines and had succeeded in retaining their liberty.

Apart from a few minor modifications, the law regarding time for payment of fines remained unaltered for almost ninety years. In 1914 it was provided that when a young person was allowed time to pay he should be given not less than seven clear days in the absence of good reason to the contrary. In 1935 an Act was passed requiring all magistrates' courts to inquire into the means of an offender who had failed to pay his fine in the time allowed before committing him to prison in default.

The centuries-old legal fiction that felons were devoid of any worldly wealth was finally abandoned in 1948 when the criminal courts were given jurisdiction to impose fines on defendants who had been convicted of felony.

The Advisory Council on the Treatment of Offenders submitted a report to the Home Secretary in 1957 in which they commented :

> A number of witnesses have pointed out to us that fines of an amount higher than now imposed might be used in some cases where the courts at present feel that they must impose imprisonment. The representatives of the police were firmly of the opinion that the deterrent value of the fine is under-rated by the courts and that fines are more appropriate for many acquisitive and personal offences than the courts apparently think, although they warned that in unsuitable cases a heavy fine would serve only as an inducement to commit further offences.

In fact, the proportion of offenders who were dealt with by fining has grown steadily throughout the past ten or fifteen years. In 1962 of all those persons convicted for non-indictable (i.e. less serious) offences, about 98 per cent, and of all those convicted of indictable (i.e. more serious) offences, about 34 per cent, were punished by the imposition of fines.

I have deliberately coupled fines and probation in the same chapter because they seem to me to have in common a more humane and civilised approach to punishment than many other of the penal methods we have inherited from the past.

The introduction of a Probation Service has proved without doubt to be the most notable improvement in our penal system during the last hundred or so years. It might be said, with evident truth, that the start of probation signified the real turning point in the public attitude towards the punishment of offenders. Formerly there had prevailed the unyielding view that a criminal, once caught, must be treated in such a manner as would by its sheer horror deter others from acting in a like manner. If this objective could only be achieved by the complete destruction of the individual, then he must be completely destroyed.

But the system of probation entailed the acceptance of a doctrine that the criminal, no matter how evil had been his crime, was still a human being. Further, it was based on the recognition that environment and circumstances had sometimes played a considerable part in forming an offender's disposition, and that given the necessary guidance he might yet be transformed into a useful and law-abiding citizen.

The first attempt to formulate a probation system took place in the American state of Massachusetts during the seventeenth century, but it is very doubtful if this experiment attracted much attention in Britain. At any rate, even if it was noted, it certainly was not imitated.

Even so, as the years wore on, a few of those who bore the responsibility of sentencing in the inferior courts were probably aware of the wholly nihilistic effects of the available penal methods. In the early nineteenth century the magistrates in Warwickshire evolved their own unofficial procedure by which they used to sentence certain young offenders to a day's imprisonment and then release them on an undertaking from their parents or schoolmasters to be responsible for their good behaviour in the future. Another unorthodox arrangement was started by the Recorder of Birmingham in 1841 when he requested the police to report to him on the subsequent careers of some of the offenders who had been sentenced in his court.

But these were mere antennae probing out towards a more merciful policy. The really important development in the origins of the probation system came in 1876 when Frederick Rainer, a printer in Hertford, suggested to the Church of England Temperance Society that something should be done to "arrest the downward career" of the offender who, following his first conviction, was destined to spend the rest of his life in serving one prison sentence after another. The Society considered Mr. Rainer's proposal very carefully and decided to appoint their own agent in the Metropolitan police courts of London. This agent had no official status whatsoever and simply attended the court in a private capacity to be available to the magistrates if they wished him to make inquiries about a defendant or, indeed, to render any other assistance which was necessary. The Metropolitan magistrates might have reacted with a curt refusal to accept the uninvited help of the Temperance Society's agent. It is pleasing to relate, however, that they gave their immediate blessing to the new scheme and after a short while they declared themselves immensely satisfied with it. This will not be altogether surprising to anyone who has borne the heavy responsibility of passing sentence and who is aware of the tremendous gulf which seems to separate the dock from the bench at the moment of judgment.

After a year the Church of England Temperance Society decided to appoint a second agent to the Metropolitan courts, and others to the courts in Greenwich and Birmingham. These initial agents, who were all appointed on an unofficial basis, were known as Police Court Missionaries. The scheme expanded rapidly and by 1880 there were six missionaries in the London courts and five more in other parts of the country. A few years later the total number had risen to twenty-three.

At first sight it may appear strange that what was virtually a probation service should have been managed by a temperance society, but it must be remembered that at this period drunkenness was one of the major social vices in Britain, and it was the root cause of a great many people appearing before the courts.

The judicial statistics show that during the decade between 1872 and 1882 an average of over 7 persons per 1000 of the population of England and Wales were charged annually with some offence relating to drunkenness. These defendants were drawn from both the sexes, about 24 per cent of them being women. They also comprised both adults and juveniles. During the year 1877 no fewer than 707 children between the ages of 10 and 14 were charged before the Liverpool courts with being drunk and incapable.

The number of deaths attributable to alcohol almost doubled between 1880 and 1900, and an investigation carried out during that period suggested that excessive drinking of spirits was one of the principal causes of suicide in the country as a whole.

This was the era of the gin-palace and also of the increasing popularity of what Lord Randolph Churchill once called the "fatal facility of the public house".

Charles Dickens had visited a gin shop in Tottenham Court Road some years earlier and he has left us his description. He says of the locality :

> The filthy and miserable appearance of this part of London can hardly be imagined by those (and there be many such) who have not witnessed it. Wretched houses with broken windows patched with rag and paper; every room let out to a different family, and in many cases to two or even three . . . filth everywhere—a gutter before the houses, and a drain behind—clothes drying, and slops emptying from the windows; girls of fourteen or fifteen with matted hair walking about barefoot, and in white great coats, almost their only covering; boys of all ages, in coats of all sizes and no coats at all; men and women in every variety of scanty and dirty apparel, lounging, scolding, smoking, squabbling, fighting, and swearing.

And in contrast to all this was the fascination of the gin-shops :

> All is light and brilliancy . . . the gay building with the fantastically ornamented parapet, the illuminated clock, the plate glass windows, surrounded by stucco rosettes, and its profusion of gaslights in richly-gilt burners, is perfectly dazzling. . . . The interior is even gayer than the exterior. A bar of French-polished mahogany, elegantly carved, extends the whole width of the place and there are two side-aisles of great casks, painted green and gold, enclosed within a light brass rail.

Dickens concludes by saying :

> Gin-drinking is a great vice in England, but wretchedness and dirt are a greater; and until you improve the homes of the poor, or persuade a half-famished wretch not to seek in the temporary oblivion of his own misery, with the pittance which, divided among his family, would furnish a morsel of bread for each, gin-shops will increase in number and splendour.

It was in this type of setting that the police court missionaries began to carry out their work.

The modern conception of probation entails two essential factors : firstly, a period of supervision and guidance, and, secondly, the suspension of punishment conditional upon the future good conduct of the probationer. The British system derives in the latter respect from the Summary Jurisdiction Act, 1879, which provided that a court, having convicted a defendant, might proceed to discharge him conditionally "on his giving security, with or without sureties, to appear for sentence when called upon, or to be of good behaviour".

This was followed in 1887 by the passing of the Probation of First Offenders Act. The new enactment authorised the courts in certain circumstances, when they had convicted a first offender, to release him and to direct that he should appear for sentence if called upon to do so, but that in the meantime he should be of good behaviour and keep the peace. This jurisdiction was only permissible if an offence was punishable with less than two years' imprisonment and also having regard to "the youth, character, and antecedents of the offender, to the trivial nature of the offence or to any extenuating circumstances under which the offence was committed".

It was specified that the probationer must have a fixed address where he would reside for the whole of his term of probation. At first this created an almost insoluble difficulty as a large proportion of the offenders most likely to benefit from the new system were, in fact, homeless vagrants. However, the police court mission immediately began to set up hostels in London and in the provinces which would provide the accommodation necessary under the requirements of the Act.

Apart from the fact that this initial form of probation could only be applied to such a restricted range of offenders, it did not entail any form of supervision or guidance. The probationer was merely granted a conditional release and thereafter he was left to work out his own salvation. Nevertheless, the criminal courts made extensive use of their new jurisdiction from the start. During 1893, five years after the introduction of the system, it was estimated that about 5000 offenders were released on probation.

Meanwhile the dedicated band of police court missionaries continued to increase numerically. There were 51 of them in 1892, 112 in 1900, and 144 in 1907. Moreover, it was soon realised that theirs was a task for both sexes and a number of female missionaries were appointed to labour alongside their male colleagues. These voluntary workers covered a vast field of work which at the present time is the concern of many thousands of highly trained probation officers and social welfare workers. Amongst other things they interviewed defendants and visited their homes; they helped the wives and families of men in prison; they assisted newly discharged prisoners and endeavoured to find them accommodation and employment; above all, they offered sympathy and understanding to people who were passing through some of the bitterest moments of their lives and who might otherwise have felt that the hand of everyone was against them.

The unofficial probation officer continued until the passing of the Probation of Offenders Act in 1907. During the previous year the Liberal Party had swept into power, obtaining a majority of 354 over their Conservative opponents in the House of Commons. The new administration was pledged to carry out a programme of social and legal reform and the Home Secretary, Mr. Herbert Samuel (later to become Viscount Samuel), turned his attention almost immediately to the founding of an official, full-time, probation service. In his memoirs Lord Samuel told how this came about.

> When I came to the Home Office [he said] I was impressed by the success—particularly with children and young persons—of a system of Probation of Offenders that was coming into use in America. As is now well known, this consists of attaching to the Courts men or women Probation Officers, to whose care offenders may be committed. . . . We had nothing of this kind in this country; except that in London and a few other places, a voluntary organisation maintained Police Court Missionaries who attended the sittings, without legal status or authority, but were often asked by the magistrates to keep a friendly watch on offenders "discharged with a caution".

Speaking of his scheme, Lord Samuel said :

> My Bill gave general powers to all courts of criminal jurisdiction to appoint Probation Officers, men or women, and to make Probation Orders in every class of case, whether of juveniles or adults and whether first offenders or not. I drafted the Bill in the widest terms, as I was convinced that the courts would know better than the legislator in what circumstances this course would be proper. A new alternative was added to the fine, imprisonment or discharge, which had been from time immemorial the only choice.

The Probation of Offenders Act, 1907 completely repealed the Probation of First Offenders Act, 1887. The new system was restricted to cases in which the court considered that, owing to such matters as the age, background, health or mental condition of the defendant, or to the triviality of the offence, or the extenuating circumstances under which it was committed, it became unnecessary to punish at all or, at most, unnecessary to impose anything more than a nominal punishment.

Having decided to proceed under the Act, a court was given three alternative methods of dealing with the defendant. Firstly, and somewhat illogically, they could dismiss the charge, even though they had previously recorded a conviction. Secondly, they could make an order by which the defendant was discharged conditionally "on his entering into a recognizance, with or without sureties, to be of good behaviour and to appear for conviction and sentence when called on at any time during such period, not exceeding three years, as may be specified in the order". And, thirdly, the defendant could be made to enter into a similar sort of recognizance with the added requirement that he should be placed under the supervision of some nominated person for the duration of the order.

This third alternative laid the basis of our present probation system. It also gave official recognition to the valuable work which was being accomplished by the police court missionaries. But there was, in fact, no authorised probation service in existence to carry out the task of supervision, so the Act provided that every petty sessional division would be allowed to appoint and to pay its own probation officers, who could be either men or women. This power of appointment was permissive rather than mandatory, and one can only assume that Lord Samuel must have been reasonably confident that the new scheme would receive universal support. In reality, a number of courts were extremely reluctant to avail themselves of the opportunity of employing the new form of official. Even as late as 1922 a departmental committee reported : "It is very disappointing to find that fourteen years after the principal Act* was passed, out of 1034 courts of Summary Jurisdiction in England and Wales, no less than 215 have taken no steps to appoint a Probation Officer."

Under Lord Samuel's scheme the duties of probation officers were laid down as being :

(a)   to visit or receive reports from persons under supervision;
(b)   to see that such persons observed the condition of their recognizances;

* The Probation of Offenders Act, 1907.

(c)   to report to the court on their behaviour; and
(d)   to advise, assist, and befriend them, and, when necessary, to endeavour to find them suitable employment.

A probationer who failed to comply with the conditions of his order was to be brought back before the court which had made it and was to be punished for his original offence.

Although the passage of the Probation of Offenders Act, 1907 marked a tremendous new development in the British penal system, the event was virtually unnoticed at the time. Lord Samuel has written : "The Bill attracted very little attention, either in Parliament or outside, and passed all its stages almost without discussion."

Naturally enough, the first probation officers were largely recruited from the police court missionaries, who were already experienced in this sort of work. Their new official status proved to be beneficial from the outset. In 1909, two years after the system had been introduced, a departmental committee reported : "All the Probation Officers who had had experience of both methods were emphatic in declaring that the probation order under the Act of 1907 gave them a much stronger hold over the offender than the recognizance that was previously the rule."

The report went on to mildly criticise some magistrates for failing to make sufficient use of the system on the ground that they regarded "the visits of a Probation Officer to an offender as an intrusion, causing him to be marked by the neighbours and to become a subject of gossip". The committee believed that these fears were unwarranted. Of the probation officers themselves the report said :

> The value of probation must necessarily depend on the efficiency of the Probation Officer. It is a system in which rules are comparatively unimportant and personality everything. The Probation Officer must be a picked man or woman, endowed not only with intelligence and zeal, but, in a high degree, with sympathy, and tact and firmness. Probation is what the officer makes it.

The law which governed the machinery of the probation system remained unchanged for seven years until it was slightly modified by the Criminal Justice Administration Act, 1914. This Act gave a court the right to impose a much wider range of conditions in a probation order, as it enacted that "a recognizance may contain such additional conditions with respect to residence, abstention from intoxicating liquor and any other matters, as the court may, having regard to the particular circumstances of the case, consider necessary for preventing a repetition of the same offence or the commission of other offences". The courts were also given the power, during the period of a probation order, to vary its provisions, or to shorten, extend, or abbreviate its duration, although it was specified that the whole term must not last for longer than three years in all.

The 1922 Departmental Committee surveyed the entire results of the probation system during the first fourteen years of its operation. They said:

> Experience has proved beyond doubt that the ordinary methods available to judicial authorities for dealing with offenders, such as fine and imprisonment, too often fail either as reformative or preventive agencies. On the other hand, probation, when applied in suitable cases, has frequently proved successful in producing a real change in the moral attitude of persons brought before the courts, restoring their self-respect, and enabling them to take their places as decent and law-abiding citizens.

It was largely as a result of the comments and suggestions contained in this report that various improvements in the probation system were incorporated into the Criminal Justice Act of 1925. In the first place, every court was placed in a specified probation area which was to be controlled by a probation committee made up from local justices of the peace. The probation committees would be responsible for the appointment of all probation officers and for the general supervision of their work. Further, the courts were no longer to be allowed a discretion as to whether or not they employed probation officers, for the Act laid down that "one or more Probation Officers" must be appointed for every probation area.

Another modification in the scheme was that: "Where circumstances permit the Court shall appoint a Probation Officer who is a woman to supervise an offender who is a woman and an officer experienced in dealing with children or young persons to supervise an offender who is under the age of 16 years."

It was left for the Criminal Justice Act of 1948 to tidy up the remaining loose ends in the probation procedure. This Act abolished the anomalous situation which had existed since 1907 whereby a convicted person might still be technically unconvicted if the court exercised their jurisdiction to dismiss the charge. Also it was now provided that a probation order might be made whenever a court was of the opinion that "having regard to the circumstances, including the nature of the offence or the character of the offender", it was expedient to take such a course. At first sight this new formula might not appear to add very much to the elaborately stated, governing condition for a probation order under the 1907 Act. In fact, it extended the availability of the system to those cases in which there was virtually no aspect of the circumstances of the offence, or of the character or background of the offender, which would have merited a lenient sentence, but, nevertheless, the court felt justified in taking a chance—albeit a gamble—in making a probation order in the hope of plucking a defendant from a life of crime in the future. Such instances are by no means rare today and sometimes this course can prove surprisingly successful.

A probation order must now be for a minimum period of one year, but the old maximum of three years still remains. The order may contain any requirements which may be considered necessary "for securing the good conduct of the offender or for preventing a repetition by him of the same offence or the commission of other offences".

The 1948 Act introduced a process for the provision of medical treatment during a term of probation. When the court has received evidence from a doctor that the mental condition of an offender is such that he requires and would be susceptible to treatment, either as a resident or as a non-resident patient, a condition can be attached to the probation order that the probationer should attend a named hospital or clinic for any period up to twelve months. This method is not used for offenders who are actually certifiable, but merely for those whose conduct has been influenced to some extent by a transient mental or emotional disturbance.

Although they do not fall under the heading of probation, it should be mentioned, for the sake of completeness, that the 1948 Act added two new types of sentence which could be employed by courts when they wished to dispose of offenders without inflicting any, or any immediate, punishment upon them. These are known as the absolute and the conditional discharge. When a defendant is granted an absolute discharge, that is the end of the matter and he suffers no penalty whatsoever. A conditional discharge, on the other hand, can be made for any period up to twelve* months, and if, during that time, the defendant is convicted of a further offence, he becomes liable for sentence, not only for the new offence, but for the original one as well.

The size of the probation service (and the extent to which the probation system is employed) is growing year by year. In modern times a humane penal system without a large, trusted and efficient probation service is almost impossible to imagine. In a report published in 1952 the Economic and Social Council of the United Nations aptly described probation as "one of the most important aspects of the development of a rational and social criminal policy", and went on to say that it formed "a major instrument of policy in the field of the prevention of crime and the treatment of offenders".

* The maximum was extended to three years by the Criminal Justice Act, 1967.

Chapter Seventeen

Witches

A DIGRESSION with the subject of witchcraft might seem, at first sight, to be rather out of place in a study of the history of punishment. In fact, the attitude of the courts towards those who were suspected of being witches provides a very interesting sidelight on the treatment of offenders in general.

At the outset it might be useful to define a few of the terms which were used in demonology, several of which even found their way into the English Statute Book during the Middle Ages.

In his fascinating essay on witchcraft, Dr. Hutchinson, one-time Bishop of Down and Connor, explained that conjurers were people who, "by force of magic words endeavoured to raise the Devil and compel him to execute their commands". Witches, on the other hand, were those who, "by way of friendly conference are said to bargain with an evil spirit to do what they desire of him". Sorcerers or charmers, Hutchinson tells us, "by the use of certain superstitious forms of words, or by means of images, or other odd representations of persons or things, etc., are said to produce strange effects above the ordinary course of nature".

A belief in witchcraft has existed throughout the world since time immemorial. The Old Testament contains many allusions to the subject, including what is probably the best known of all, the exhortation in the 22nd chapter of the Book of Exodus: "Thou shalt not suffer a witch to live." This biblical precept was used amongst Christian nations as a justification for a great deal of the cruelty which they meted out to supposed witches.

The practice of sorcery was viewed with suspicion by the Romans, and the performance of certain types of magic was made a criminal offence. Thus, in the year A.D. 150, Lucius Apuleius, the writer and philosopher, was indicted on a charge of gaining the affections of a rich widow by the use of magic. He managed to prove his innocence, although his own belief in the existence of such supernatural power is borne out by a "true" story he told later in life about a witch who, in order to kill her enemies, conjured up "a woman of hideous aspect, marked by guilt and extreme sorrow, whose haggard face was sallow as boxwood".

In early English law witchcraft and sorcery were regarded as crimes against God, and they therefore lay within the jurisdiction of the ecclesiastical and not the secular courts. A number of cases featuring the alleged use of witchcraft are cited in ancient legal volumes, the majority being no more serious than the employment of magical assistance in affairs of the heart. For example, in 1482 a girl named Joan Beverley was charged with entreating witches to help her win the affections of two lovers; and eight years later a man was tried for telling a widow that by the use of magic he could find her a husband worth £1000. Other cases were concerned with the employment of magic to locate lost or stolen property, or for the curing of illnesses in animals and human beings.

The ecclesiastical courts punished these trivial offenders by fines or by ordering simple penances such as an instruction that the defendant must walk barefoot before the procession of the Cross. According to Sir Edward Coke, however, when a witchcraft offence was of sufficient gravity to rank as a heresy, punishment was usually handed over to the secular courts and many offenders were burned alive by the king's writ.

It was only in later centuries that the public conception of the witch reached such a pitch of loathing and horror that she came to be regarded as the very personification of evil. Exactly how this thought process developed must be a matter of conjecture. It is a fact that amongst immature civilisations the belief is widely held that all harm and suffering are inflicted deliberately by some super-natural agency, and it seems an easy progression from this view to the idea that the forces of evil are accustomed to work through mortal agents. The historian William Lecky puts forward the interesting theory that the Church was indirectly responsible for the upsurgence of anti-witch mania by generating so much religious excitement which centred attention on "the other world".

The earliest ordinances in Britain against the use of witchcraft and other forms of magic are probably those appearing in the Codes of Ethelred and Canute. These were the forerunners of a line of statutes which marked the mounting intensity of the campaign against witches. King Henry VIII passed an Act in 1541 which made it a felony, and consequently triable by the secular courts, to practise various kind of conjurations, witchcraft and sorcery; also, "to consume any person in his body, members, or goods; or to provoke any person to unlawful love". A defendant convicted under this Act could not claim Benefit of Clergy, so the penalty was immediate death. In fact, as far as is known, the Act was never invoked against either witches or sorcerers, and it was repealed in its entirety soon after the death of Henry VIII.

No further laws were passed against witches or sorcerers until the year 1562, when Queen Elizabeth I revived and amended her father's 1541 Act on the ground that since its repeal there had been an increase in the practice of witchcraft. By this new enactment the use of sorceries, enchantments, charms, and witchcrafts, by means of which the victim was killed, were punishable by death. However, if the victim was only "wasted, consumed or harmed in his body or member", or his goods and chattels were "destroyed, wasted, or impaired", the penalty was reduced to six hours in the pillory and a year's imprisonment for the first offence, and death for the second. Even when the sorcery or witchcraft had been used for some other purpose, e.g. to provoke unlawful love, and no person had suffered any physical harm thereby, it was still an offence punishable by the pillory and imprisonment if a first conviction, and by death for a second.

The legal case records for this period of history are spasmodic and inadequate, but at least five trials are known to have taken place under Queen Elizabeth's Act, in one of which eighteen or nineteen women were condemned at one sitting.

Although witches are known to have been burnt to death during the latter part of the sixteenth century, it was in the seventeenth century that witchcraft trials reached the highest level, both in their frequency and also in the hysterical absurdities of the charges which were made, and the hideous cruelties to which the prisoners were submitted.

King James I had made a detailed study of witchcraft long before he ascended the English throne. While he was still in his early twenties he had taken part in the examination of several witches, and later he had published a study of demonology in the foreword of which he explained that he was "moved to write that work by the fearful abounding at this time in this country of those detestable slaves of the devil, the witches and enchanters".

It was not surprising in view of his feelings on the matter that James I should waste no time after he became king in putting his principles into practice. In 1603, during the first year of his reign, a new statute was passed against witches and sorcerers. The language of this enactment affords a startling insight into the standard of enlightenment which existed at that period.

> It shall be an offence [says the Act] if any person or persons shall use, practise, or exercise any invocation or conjuration of any evil or wicked spirit, or shall consult, covenant with, entertain, employ, feed or reward any evil and wicked spirit to or for any intent or purpose, or take up any dead man, woman or child out of his, her or their grave or other place where the dead body resteth, or the skin, bone, or any part of any dead person, to be employed or used in any manner of witchcraft, sorcery, charm, or enchantment, or shall use, practise or exercise any witchcraft, enchantment, charm or sorcery, whereby any person shall be killed, destroyed, wasted, consumed, pined or lamed in his or her body or any part thereof.

The reason why James I included in this catalogue of crimes the offences of removing dead bodies, or parts of dead bodies from graves, was probably due to the confession he had heard of a witch named Agnes Simpson to the effect that graves had been opened and the fingers, toes, and noses of dead people had been taken away for use in charms. Belief that such practices existed was at one time widespread. It will be remembered that Shakespeare makes his three witches in *Macbeth* describe their boiling cauldron as containing, amongst its revolting assortment, the "liver of blaspheming Jew", the "nose of Turk and Tartar's lips", and the "finger of birth-strangled babe".

Although the British system of law has always vaunted the complete absence of torture from its judicial processes, the trials for witchcraft throughout the seventeenth century were conducted with the utmost brutality, and torture was consistently employed to induce the alleged witches to confess. The methods used were unusually callous even for the period. This was partly due to the universal and quite fanatical detestation in which witches were held, partly to the unfathomable terror with which a backward people regarded the interventions of an unnatural power of evil, and partly to the fact that witches were not really considered as human and it followed that they must be largely incapable of experiencing ordinary human suffering. Further, there was a popular belief that the Devil granted them protection against ordinary methods of inflicting pain.

The favourite instrument of torture was known as the witch's bridle. It consisted of an iron collar complete with a metal gag which was clamped round the woman's neck and jaw and could be slowly tightened. However, alternative methods were also used. Bulstrode Whitelocke, writing in the year 1652, described the treatment of some suspected witches in Scotland. "These women", he says, "had been tortured to make them confess, by tying their thumbs behind them, and then hanging them up by their thumbs, while two Highlanders whipped them; after which they set lighted candles to the soles of their feet and between their toes, then burned them by putting lighted candles in their mouths and then burning them in the head." He goes on to say that out of six accused, no less than four died from torture. "Another woman being accused for witch", writes Whitelocke, "was kept 28 days with only bread and water and stripped naked and laid upon a cold stone, with only hair-cloth over her. . . . Other witches", he says, "had hair shirts dipped in vinegar put over them, to fetch off the skin."

Apart from torturing witches in an effort to make them confess their guilt, there were other incidents of a witchcraft trial which must have inflicted extreme mental and physical suffering on the accused woman. It was thought that somewhere on a witch's body was an insensible spot called a devil's mark. In the course of her examination she was held down naked while a witch-pricker systematically thrust pins in every part of her flesh to see if he could locate the painless place. A witch was also supposed to have an abnormality known as a tett or teat. This term seems to have covered every conceivable blemish or malformation on the skin and might be found anywhere at all on her body. In consequence, she was forced to submit to a far-reaching and intimate search by a specially appointed panel of investigators. Almost invariably they succeeded in finding what they were looking for. Dr. Hutchinson, in his *Historical Essay concerning Witchcraft,* which was published in 1718, commented: "Some said the credulity was such that a flea bite would pass for a tett or a devil's mark."

Another ordeal a suspected witch might have to undergo was being thrown into a pond to see whether or not she would sink. There was a belief that if she was really a witch she would float on the surface.

If a woman was convicted of witchcraft, every person who had played a part in her condemnation would probably insist on drawing off some of her blood as this was supposed to be a method of freeing himself from her power. That is why in Shakespeare's *King Henry VI* when Talbot is fighting with Joan La Pucelle, he says to her, "Devil, or devil's dam. I'll conjure thee. Blood will I draw on thee, thou art a witch."

It is difficult to say how many witches were convicted in Britain during the seventeenth century. The author James Howell, in a letter written in 1648, said :

> We have likewise multitudes of witches among us, for in Essex and Suffolk there were above 200 indicted within these two years, and above half of them executed: more, I may well say, than ever this island bred since the creation, I speak it with horror. God guard us from the Devil, for I think he was never so busy upon any part of the earth that was enlightened with the beams of Christianity.

As the witch-hunting cult developed, there sprang up a host of professional witch-finders and witch-prickers. A man in England named Hopkins, and Kincaid, his counterpart in Scotland, built up such reputations that their accusations alone were usually considered sufficient evidence to justify the conviction of a woman.

Hutchinson describes some of the methods which were employed by the man Hopkins to discover witches. "Hopkins", he says, "searched for teats, set some upon stools or tables cross-legged, and kept them 24 hours without meat or drink, within which time it was said their imps would come and suck; others he tried by swimming them."

No woman was entirely safe from the accusation of witchcraft. Many churches in Scotland actually encouraged the making of such charges by keeping special boxes in which the written allegations could be placed. A large proportion of those who were accused eventually succumbed to torture and made full confessions of their guilt. This was probably due partly to the ferocity of the tortures employed and partly to the fact that the victims were fully aware that, even if they refused to submit and managed to secure acquittals, they would never cleanse themselves from the taint of witchcraft and the consequent abomination which would stigmatise them for the rest of their unhappy lives.

Most of the confessions followed a set pattern. The woman would describe how she had made a pact with the Devil, the king of elf-land, or some other evil spirit. The terms of the bargain were usually that the embryonic witch exchanged her soul for the offer of wealth and happiness. Thereafter, at night-time in a church or at a deserted place in the open, she had sworn to worship the Devil and had received from him certain supernatural powers. This was usually followed by various ritualistic ceremonies consisting of blasphemous parodies and wild sexual orgies. An example of the former is given in a contemporary account of the confessions of a number of witches who were jointly accused in 1678: "They declared and confessed the first thing the Devil caused them to do was to renounce their baptism; and by laying their hand on the top of their head, and the other on the sole of their foot, to renounce all betwixt the two to his service."

The witches, in their confessions, frequently admitted that they had had sexual intercourse with the Devil, presumably to signify the complete consummation of their union with him. Such acts, apparently, created no physiological difficulties. Hutchinson has remarked that the Egyptians used to believe that a male spirit could indulge in sexual intercourse with a mortal woman, but a female spirit enjoyed no similar ability with a mortal male. On the other hand, in Greek mythology it seems that both gods and goddesses suffered no restrictions whether they wished to make love to mortals or to each other.

Every witch was supposed to have her quota of imps or familiars, and most of the women described them with childlike simplicity in their confessions. Joan Cooper, at her examination in the year 1645, admitted that she had "three familiars, two like mouses, and the third like a frog; the names of the two like mouses are Jack, and the other Prickeare, and the name of the third, like a frog, is Frog". Another witch at the same trial said she had "four familiars, which she had from her mother about two and twenty years since, and that the names of the said imps are James, Prickeare, Robin and Sparrow; and that three of these imps are like mouses, and the fourth like a sparrow, which she called Sparrow".

Several of the trials for witchcraft are reported in various volumes of *State Trials,* the earliest in point of time being that of Marie Smith who was condemned and executed in 1616. The general introduction to the report demonstrates the flimsiness of the evidence that could be capable of substantiating the charge. "Marie wife of Henry Smith, glover," it reads, "possessed of wrathful indignation against some of her neighbours in regard that they made gaine out of their buying and selling cheese which shee (using the same trade) could not do . . . oftentimes cursed them."

Having been cursed by Marie Smith, several of her neighbours developed pains and mysterious, wasting illnesses, which was adjudged sufficient to put Mrs. Smith on trial for being a witch.

If a woman was accused of witchcraft it was never very difficult to discover in her neighbourhood a number of calamities, sicknesses, and other mysterious happenings which could be attributed to her evil machinations. No doubt once the word was circulated that a witch had been at large a great many people examined their recent experiences to discover whether or not they had ever fallen under her influence. Fear and superstition in most cases distorted and embellished their memories, and it was then comparatively simple for the prosecution's case to be moulded into the pattern which everybody had learned to expect.

In 1645, at Chelmsford, a number of women and girls were tried, condemned, and executed in what became known as the "Trial of the Essex Witches". The proceedings, which were probably fairly typical of a seventeenth-century witchcraft trial, have been preserved for posterity in one of the volumes of the *State Trials*.

The account of the trial commences with details of the matters which brought the witchcraft to light. One day the wife of a certain John Rivet, who lived at Manningtree, "was taken sick and lame with such violent fits that [John Rivet] verily conceived her sickness was something more than merely natural". Mr. Rivet thereupon decided to consult "a cunning woman", who told him that his wife was labouring under a curse imposed on her by two of her female neighbours. Moreover, the cunning woman was able to identify the houses in which the two witches were living.

It then transpired that various other people in the neighbourhood had also been affected by evil spells. Robert Tayler, a shopkeeper, recalled that after he had refused to serve one of the witches with cheese she had gone away muttering and mumbling to herself and within a short while his horse had been stricken with a mysterious illness and had wasted to death. Prudence Hart, who had recently suffered a miscarriage, disclosed that "one night when she was in bed a short while before, something fell down upon her right side, but being dark she cannot tell in what shape it was : and presently she was taken lame on that side with extraordinary pains and burning, but she recovered again after a few days". Robert Edwards told how on one occasion he had just driven his cattle past one of the witches' houses when a perfectly healthy cow inexplicably fell ill and died.

There were many others who related similar happenings.

In view of all this, the notorious witch-finder Mathew Hopkins was summoned to Manningtree to carry out some investigations. Mr. Hopkins's evidence at the trial did not describe his methods, but only told of his remarkable successes in obtaining confessions from the suspected witches. The first woman he examined admitted "she had had carnal with the Devil six or seven years". She went on to say that Satan visited her three or four times a week "in the shape of a proper gentleman, with a laced hand . . . and would say to her, 'Besse, I must lye with you', and she never did deny him". The alleged witch willingly supplied Mr. Hopkins with a description of her two imps. One, she said, was called Jarman and was "like to a dog which was white with some sandy spots, and seemed to be very fat and plumpe, with very short legges". The other, called Vinegar Tom, was "in the shape of a greyhound with long legges".

As happened so often in witchcraft examinations at that period, the first two women gave Mathew Hopkins the names of many others whom they alleged to be operating as witches in that immediate locality. The process continued until a whole network of witchcraft was revealed. One girl, the report does not mention her age, confessed that she was a witch and incriminated five more women, including her own mother.

The editor of this account in the *State Trials* describes how, as a result of Mr. Hopkins's inquiry, "several murders and devilish witchcrafts committed on the bodies of men, women and children and divers cattle were fully discovered". He adds the reassurance that all the witches, "according to their demerits, and according to the lawes of God, have received their just reward".

The *State Trials* also contain a report of the proceedings against two widows who were indicted for witchcraft at Bury St. Edmunds

Assizes in the year 1665. The evidence in that case was principally based on the startling behaviour of three children who were said to have been placed under an evil spell. These children were produced in the court, where they dutifully threw fits, "closing their fists", we are told, "in such a manner as the strongest man in the court could not force them open; yet by the least touch of one of these supposed witches, Rose Cullender by name, they would suddenly shriek out opening their hands, which accident would not happen at the touch of any other person".

There was someone in the court, however, who was not impressed by these experiments. In the report he is described as "an ingenious person", without his name or his status being disclosed. He objected, apparently, on the ground that the children might be putting on a deliberate and calculated act. The judge, who happened to be the eminent lawyer, Chief Baron Hale, decided to carry out a simple test. He instructed some gentlemen in court to cover up one of the children's eyes with an apron and to observe whether she reacted any differently if she was touched by one of the defendants or by another person. As might have been expected, the blindfold child's reactions were exactly the same whoever touched her, "whereupon the gentlemen returned, openly protesting that they did believe the whole transaction of this business was a mere imposture".

Even the disclosure of the child's fraudulent behaviour did not influence the course of the trial. Chief Baron Hale decided to hear the rest of the prosecution's case, and evidence was given that in view of the two widows' persistent denials of witchcraft, a justice's warrant had been obtained to have them physically examined for witches' marks. In the case of one of the women the court was not told of the result of the examination—presumably because it proved to be negative. In the case of the other, she had been stripped naked and examined in her own home by six accredited persons. "In the lower part of her belly", says the report, "they found a thing like a teat of an inch long. They questioned her about it and she said that she had got a strain by carrying of water which caused that excrescence."

Chief Baron Hale summed up to the jury in the briefest possible manner by telling them that "he would not repeat the evidence unto them, lest by doing so he should wrong the evidence on the one side or on the other. Only this acquainted them, that they had two things to inquire after. First, whether or no these children were bewitched? Secondly, whether the prisoners at the bar were guilty of it?"

The judge then left the facts of the case and proceeded to express a few personal opinions about witchcraft. "That there were such creatures as witches", he said, "he had no doubt at all. For first, the scriptures had affirmed as much. Secondly, the wisdom of all nations had provided laws against such persons, which is an argument for their confidence of such."

The Chief Baron concluded his words to the jury by imploring "the great God of heaven to direct their hearts in this weighty thing they had in hand". He reminded them that "to condemn the innocent and to let the guilty go free, were both an abomination to the Lord".

There was little fear that a jury at that time would run the slightest risk of letting any reputed witch go free, and after a retirement of only half an hour they returned with verdicts of "guilty" against both women, who were hanged a few days later, protesting their innocence to the end.

The terror of witchcraft in Britain began to abate towards the end of the seventeenth century. By then the anti-witch hysteria was largely working itself out. Also, the teachings of such philosophers as Descartes, Spinoza, and Leibniz were introducing the intelligentsia to the concepts of a new theological rationalism which discounted the theory of arbitrary supernatural intervention of everyday human affairs.

Dr. Hutchinson relates how even Mathew Hopkins, the ace witch-finder, eventually came to grief when certain indignant gentlemen "caused him to be seized, and his hands and feet being tied, to be thrown into the water, where fortunately for him he was proved to be a witch or wizard himself, by his swimming or floating on the water". Dr. Hutchinson comments : "The country was cleared of him, and some lamented that the experiment had not been made sooner."

It is impossible to ascertain how many women were convicted wholly or partially on the evidence of Mathew Hopkins. It is said that in one year alone he was directly responsible for the execution of no less than sixty reputed witches.

Between 1694 and 1701 Lord Chief Justice Holt presided at eleven trials for witchcraft, all resulting in acquittals, which provides a fair indication of the changing attitude of the public towards this particular offence. On the other hand, the old fear and superstitious belief was not entirely dead, for in 1697, at a trial in Scotland, seven women were executed as witches entirely on the testimony of one 11-year-old girl.

The last trial for witchcraft which took place in England is generally believed to have been at Hertford in the year 1712. On that occasion Jane Wenham was convicted of being a witch and condemned to death, but for some reason the sentence was never carried out. There is, however, an old report of an execution at Huntingdon in 1716 when a Mrs. Hicks and her 9-year-old daughter were both hanged as witches. They were accused of "selling souls to the devil, tormenting and destroying their neighbours by making them vomit pins", and of "raising a storm so that a ship at sea was almost lost".

The last known hanging for witchcraft was in Scotland, and took place in the year 1722.

The statutes against witchcraft were finally repealed in 1736. But even then the terror of witches was not wholly eliminated, for Dr. Nash, in his *History of Worcestershire,* tells how, many years later, "a poor woman who happened to be very ugly was almost drowned in the neighbourhood of Worcester upon a supposition of witchcraft; and had not Mr. Lygon, a gentleman of singular humanity and influence, interfered on her behalf, she would certainly have been drowned, upon a presumption that a witch could not sink".

It was not until the nineteenth and the twentieth centuries that the civilised world was able to relegate the image of witchcraft to the realms of fantasy, folklore, and fairy tale. The brutality and the suffering of the past were then forgotten and the witch became a pantomime figure, obnoxious rather than terrifying—the hag on a broomstick casting spells on all her enemies and eventually succumbing to the forces of purity and goodness.

There may be quite a simple psychological explanation for this development. When man begins to jest about his former fears and prejudices, his underlying emotion is often, in reality, a deep, unrecognised sense of shame.

Chapter Eighteen

Prostitutes

THE practice of sexual prostitution is probably even more ancient than belief in witchcraft, although allusions to both occur in various books of the Old Testament. Chapter 23 of Deuteronomy contains the warning, "There shall be no whore of the daughters of Israel", and in Chapter 19 of Leviticus, Jewish fathers are told: "Do not prostitute thy daughter, to cause her to become a whore; lest the land fall into whoredom, and the land become full of wickedness."

Certainly prostitutes have plied their trade in most, if not all, civilised countries from the earliest times, and any attempts to eliminate their existence have invariably ended in failure.

The British have never really been able to decide on a general or a specific attitude towards prostitution. This uncertainty of mind has been reflected in our law on the subject. Stephen, in his *History of Criminal Law,* says that the doing of "any grossly indecent act in any open and public place in the presence of more persons than one" has always been treated as a common law misdemeanour. But merely to solicit for the purpose of prostitution has never been a common law offence in this country. This was authoritatively stated in a case as far back as 1705 when it was held that "solicitation of chastity . . . is a spiritual offence and not inquirable or punishable at Common Law".

Throughout the Middle Ages prostitution was a flourishing profession in Britain, as it was on the whole of the continent of Europe. For the most part the Church was concentrating its efforts on endeavouring to reform the prostitutes rather than attempting to condemn them. At the beginning of the thirteenth century Pope Innocent III expressed the view that it was praiseworthy for any man to marry a prostitute. A few years later Pope Gregory IX, in a letter to brothel-keepers, told them to "urge bachelors to marry repentant girls, or induce the latter to enter the cloister".

In Britain at this period there were officially licensed brothels. A number of such premises, in the vicinity of London Bridge, were reputed to be owned by the bishops of Winchester, and evidence exists that in 1383 the Lord Mayor of London was controlling some others on behalf of his corporation. Licensed brothels continued here until 1546, when they were abolished by Henry VIII.

The hardening in the public attitude towards prostitution was probably due to the sterner moral climate which ensued from the Reformation, and also to the growing awareness of the nature of venereal disease. Throughout the seventeenth century a series of repressive measures were enacted throughout the entire continent of Europe. In Germany brothels were demolished and harlots were expelled from the towns where they had operated. In France pimps were condemned to the galleys for life and prostitutes were whipped, their heads were shaved, and they were banished from their homeland indefinitely.

In England legislation was not directed at the harlots personally as much as against the brothel-keepers and the others who were living indirectly from the trade of prostitution. It was an offence for a prostitute to behave indecently in the public view, but soliciting and harlotry were not, in themselves, against the law. It is true that for a short period during the Cromwellian Protectorate the act of fornication became a criminal offence, punishable by three months' imprisonment, and convicted bawds were liable to be whipped, pilloried, branded, and imprisoned for three years for a first offence, and to be hanged for a second. However, these were merely incidents of the widespread puritanical purge which was taking place throughout the country at that time.

After the seventeenth century there was a general relaxation in the laws against prostitution on the Continent. A number of countries reverted to the customs of Imperial Rome and instituted a system of officially licensed brothels with registered harlots who were subjected to periodic medical examinations.

At this stage Britain parted company with many of her cross-Channel neighbours and embarked on a somewhat vacillating policy of her own. In the eyes of the legislature there was, apparently, a sharp moral distinction to be drawn between brothels, places at which two or more prostitutes were working together, and the individual prostitute who was operating on her own. Three successive Acts, passed in 1752, 1754, and 1763, were all designed, as stated in the preamble of one of them, "for encouraging prosecutions against the keepers of bawdy houses". But the law continued to treat the prostitute herself as a public nuisance rather than as a criminal.

Nevertheless, there was a great deal of concern about the presence of so many harlots soliciting in the streets of London and of other large cities.

Bernard Mandeville, the philosopher and satirist, writing in the year 1725, suggested that the evil of prostitution could be best eradicated by treating it as "a profession conducted according to strict rules". He thought that prostitutes should only be allowed to operate in certain places, and that in London there should be "about a hundred houses in a convenient quarter of the city with a Matron in charge of each, to whom certain quantities of liquor should be allowed custom-free".

Mandeville's lax proposals were not shared by the majority of his contemporaries. About the same time an anonymous pamphleteer was advocating that prostitutes should be punished by whipping and transportation, and in 1748 it was seriously proposed that "all lewd and disorderly persons known to be common street-walkers or persons conversing with them should be rounded up and punished as vagrants". Saunders Welch, a Westminster magistrate, proposed in 1758 that prostitution would be curbed if any person had the right to apprehend, and hand over to a constable, a woman he found "plying in the public streets or other public places". The harlot would then be committed to prison and later she would be sent to a special hospital "whose governors would have discretionary powers of inflicting penalties".

In spite of these and numerous other suggestions, Parliament took no active measures which seriously interfered with the prostitute's trade. A woman who practised singly in her own house remained inside the law. But, in fact, there were many harlots who earned their fee in shop doorways, side areas, and open spaces, and thereby ran the risk of a prosecution for indecent behaviour.

Until the Metropolitan Police Force was established in London in 1829 and more police forces were set up in other parts of the country in the years that followed, the duties of maintaining law and order were carried out by parish constables, special constables, and town watchmen. The latter had their own beats to patrol at night-time and it was the general custom, in London at any rate, for a watchman to levy contributions on every prostitute in his area in return for a guarantee of immunity from arrest. It was said that some night-watchmen were receiving regular payments from as many as twenty different women.

In the early part of the nineteenth century prostitution in large English cities was on the increase. In London many of the harlots solicited in the streets and others were starting to frequent some of the disreputable taverns and coffee houses. They also patronised the unsalubrious establishments which were coming into vogue at that period and were known as "flash houses". A flash house was not simply a brothel—in fact, the majority of such places catered for an assortment of vices. A report published at the time described them as "obscure resorts opened for the entertainment of thieves, notorious gamblers and prostitutes, which are usually kept without licence and never in conformity with the provisions of the law".

In 1817 a special committee inquired into the prevalence of prostitution in London. "The streets are crowded every night", they said, "by women of the most abandoned and profligate characters who . . . by their interference and riotous conduct are the principal cause of the disturbances and brawls that nightly disgrace the Metropolis." A few years afterwards, the Vagrancy Act, 1824 made it an offence for a common prostitute to wander in public streets or on public highways or in any place of public resort and to behave there in a riotous or indecent manner. Again, a prostitute was enabled to continue soliciting in the streets provided she did not conduct herself in an unruly fashion. One woman was convicted under the terms of the 1824 Act, the evidence showing that she had accosted a man in public and walked beside him, forcing her arm into his. She appealed successfully on the ground that her action had not constituted either riotous or indecent behaviour.

On 6 December 1827 *The Times* newspaper declared in a leading article : "The state of our streets as to abandoned women is scandalous. What a disgrace to the city is Temple Bar on the Eastern side every night !"

Eventually in 1839 it became an offence in London for a common prostitute to solicit or to loiter in a public place for the purpose of prostitution "to the annoyance of passers-by or inhabitants". Other towns subsequently introduced their own bye-laws in similar terms. The 1839 Act created two different offences—soliciting prostitution and loitering for the purpose of prostitution. In both cases it was necessary in law for the prosecution to show that some passer-by, or some local inhabitant, had been annoyed by the prostitute's behaviour.

The law against prostitutes remained virtually unchanged from that time until 1957.

One of the most serious aspects of prostitution was the comparative ease with which a very young girl could drift into the trade. Even during the nineteenth century there were no social services and few accredited societies to provide for the guidance and the protection of youth. For the most part the only work which was available to women of the less-privileged classes entailed the acceptance of incredibly long hours, a paltry rate of payment, and a rigorous code of personal discipline. In consequence, the temptations offered by the life of the street-walker were all too obvious.

On one occasion in the 1830's Charles Dickens stood outside the old Bow Street Police Office, very near the site of the present Bow Street Magistrates' Court. He was watching a group of prisoners being conducted from the building and placed in a waiting prison van. Among them he saw two prostitutes.

> There were a couple of girls [he says] of whom the elder could not be more than sixteen, and the younger of whom had certainly not attained her fourteenth year. That they were sisters was evident, from the resemblance which still subsisted between them, though two additional years of depravity had fixed their brand upon the elder girl's features as legibly as if a red-hot iron had seared them. They were both gaudily dressed, the younger one especially; and, although there was a strong similarity between them in both respects, which was rendered the more obvious by their being handcuffed together, it is impossible to conceive a greater contrast than the demeanour of the two presented. The younger girl was weeping bitterly—not for display, or in the hope of producing effect, but from very shame; her face was buried in her handkerchief; and her whole manner was but too expressive of bitter and unavailing sorrow. . . . What the younger girl was then, the elder had been once; and what the elder then was, the younger must soon become.

Dickens goes on to criticise the negative official and public attitude to the situation. "These things pass before our eyes, day after day, and hour after hour—they have become such matters of course, that they are utterly disregarded."

The maximum penalty for soliciting or loitering for the purpose of prostitution under the Metropolitan Police Act, 1839, and under most of the bye-laws which followed it, was a fine of forty shillings.

As the years passed and the value of money was utterly transformed this penalty remained unaltered, until the time arrived when it had become scarcely a penalty at all to a reasonably successful prostitute who was probably paying no tax whatsoever on her earnings. Basically, the mischief against which these laws were aimed was the causing of annoyance to other users of the streets or to people living near by. But the vast majority of prostitutes were prepared to plead "guilty" and to pay a fine without putting the prosecution to the trouble of proving that any person had, in fact, suffered annoyance.

In the magistrates' courts of the West End of London before the legislation of 1959 the scene was always the same. A score of prostitutes trooped into the dock one after another and almost invariably pleaded "guilty". Usually they offered no excuses but hurried from the courtroom to pay their trivial fines and to catch a taxi home. This procedure was a regular incident—troublesome, but not unduly onerous—in the life of a London prostitute.

In the years immediately following the end of the Second World War the number of prostitutes in the large English towns increased considerably. In the West End of London there was a locality, respectable enough in the daytime, which by night had become the recognised haunt of the streetwalker. A man could not pass along some streets without encountering a succession of muted invitations from the slow, slinking figures on the inner sides of the pavements, or from the solitary forms, dimly visible in the glow of a cigarette, standing in the doorways of shops and offices. At that time a new evil had insinuated itself into the shadowy world of the London prostitute, for the large-scale ponses were gradually and systematically moving into the trade. These people apportioned out the vice area of the West End amongst themselves, and the prostitutes in their employment were allocated to clearly defined beats. Any woman who attempted to solicit on her own account in one of the prescribed streets ran the risk of violence and disfigurement from the squads of thugs who were on constant vigil for this very purpose. The majority of prostitutes were left with three alternatives. They could offer their services to one of the vice-magnates and become percentage employees; they could move out to less central and less lucrative districts; or they could find themselves new jobs.

The fact that so many prostitutes withdrew from the "night-life" locality of central London and began to solicit in the outlying residential areas was one of the causes of the outcry which led to the passage of the Street Offences Act, 1957. By and large, people had grown accustomed to the presence of the harlot in the vicinity of Piccadilly and in the side streets of Soho, and it was unrealistic to imagine that she was causing undue annoyance to the sort of people who frequented these places by night. But it was a different matter for the inhabitants of flats and houses in hitherto respectable districts when the prostitute not only solicited from their doorsteps but frequently left her discarded contraceptives in the basements and the areas surrounding their homes.

The 1957 Act made it an offence for a common prostitute to "loiter or solicit in a street or public place for the purpose of prostitution". It was no longer necessary for the prosecution to show that anyone had been annoyed by the prostitute's behaviour, and, further, a new scale of penalties included increased fines and a possible term of imprisonment. For her first conviction the prostitute was now liable to a fine of £10, for a second conviction to a fine of £25, and for a third conviction to a fine of £25 and/or to three months in prison.

If Parliament's principal purpose in passing the Street Offences Act was to clear the prostitutes from the streets, the measure was highly successful. A large number of women were deterred by the prospect of a prison sentence and abandoned the trade. Others became "call girls" or found their way into offshoots of prostitution which would not lay them open to a conviction under the new Act.

But the roots of vice are deep and are almost indestructible. In place of the prostitute, the streets of Soho were rapidly filled with male and female touts for clip-joints, strip-tease clubs, and depraved film shows. Behind all this, it was said, lay a network of degradation, corruption, and violence, backed by some of the most sinister and vicious characters in the underworld of London.

Chapter Nineteen

The Discharged Prisoner

IT HAS often been remarked that the discharged prisoner faces the hardest part of his sentence when the prison gates have closed behind him.

Considering the rather dismal record of the legislature in the field of penal reform over the last 200 years, it is rather surprising to discover that throughout this period various Acts of Parliament have sought to provide financial and other assistance to newly discharged prisoners. Whether the official motive was a genuine philanthropy or an appreciation of the dangers inherent in allowing destitute criminals to wander at large must be a matter of considerable doubt.

The first enactment for this purpose was passed as early as 1776. It laid down that men and women on release from prison were to be given a sum of money "not being less than forty shillings, nor more than five pounds, together with decent clothing". In those days, of course, forty shillings was a substantial amount of money and £5, to some prisoners, must have seemed a veritable fortune. However, another Act three years later cut down the scale of these payments to a minimum of twenty shillings and a maximum of £3.

Prison records of the period, such as they are, fail to disclose to what extent these payments were ever made, but it is thought that these provisions were seldom, if ever, acted upon.

At the beginning of the nineteenth century a local prison was controlled by the justices of the peace for the area in which it was situated.

The Prison Act of 1824 gave the visiting justices authority to recommend that certain prisoners should have their sentences reduced. If the reductions were granted, the justices were given statutory power to supply the discharged prisoner clothing and money, "so as such sum shall not exceed twenty shillings nor be less than five shillings". At that time many prisoners were serving their sentences in the new central prisons a long way from their homes, and the 1824 Act also authorised the justices "to direct that such moderate sum of money shall be given and paid to any and every such prisoner so discharged who shall not have the means of returning to his or her family or place of settlement or resorting to any place of employment".

Naturally, it was one thing to give a prisoner clothing and money and then to leave him to his fate, and another to take a genuine interest in his welfare during the difficult period while he was seeking to readjust himself to a life of freedom. In the late eighteenth and the early nineteenth centuries a number of voluntary charitable organisations were founded with the object of assisting the discharged prisoner through the process of returning to normality. These bodies, mostly attached to the local city and county jails, were supported entirely by private donations and attracted as their workers the finest types of Christian philanthropists and humanitarian idealists.

Thus the position towards the middle of the nineteenth century was that a prisoner on release had two entirely separate methods of assistance available to him. First, the official offering of clothing and money under the auspices of the visiting justices and, second, the financial and rehabilitative aid organised by the voluntary discharged prisoners' aid societies.

Both these forms of help were amalgamated in 1862 under the provisions of the Discharged Prisoners' Aid Act. Voluntary organisations were thenceforth enabled to apply to their local justices to be certified as "approved" societies. Further, the official money grant to a discharged prisoner could be made payable through the approved society which happened to be supervising his welfare.

In 1877, when control of local prisons was transferred from the justices to the Home Secretary, the same system of after-care was still continued. The Act which brought about this shift of authority stated that :

> When any prisoner is discharged from prison, the Prison Commissioners may, on the recommendation of the Visiting Committee, order a sum of money not exceeding two pounds, to be paid by the gaoler to the prisoner himself or to the treasurer of a certified prisoners' aid society on the gaoler receiving from such society an undertaking in writing to apply the same for the benefit of the prisoner.

To anyone accustomed to the ordered and all-providing security of a modern welfare state it is extremely difficult to visualise the uncertainty and helplessness which must have confronted the newly discharged prisoner during the eighteenth and nineteenth centuries. At that time there were no official systems of national assistance, sickness benefit, or unemployment relief payments. There was no general social service scheme and no universal public acceptance of the principle that the more fortunate section of the community owed any duty whatsoever to the more needy.

It was easy enough for Sir William Blackstone to write in 1765, from his position of sheltered privilege: "There is no man so indigent or wretched but he may demand a supply sufficient for all the necessaries of life from the more opulent part of the community by means of several statutes enacted for the relief of the poor." Actually, any charitable arrangements made by the authorities on behalf of the destitute were usually as inadequate as they were harshly administered.

Parliament and the law, until a comparatively recent era, have always treated the homeless pauper as something of a cross between a criminal and a scavenger. As a class they were variously described in statutes as "rogues", "vagabonds", and "idle and disorderly persons". In the Tudor period they were driven from village to village with frequent floggings to help them on their way. It was true that there was a duty imposed on all parishes to look after those they considered to be genuinely in need, but the administration was purely local and every parish interpreted its obligations in a different way. If pauperism was one of the greatest pestilences of the sixteenth and seventeenth centuries in Britain, the Industrial Revolution considerably worsened the situation by spreading unemployment wholesale and reducing large numbers of the working class to a state of complete and utter privation.

Admittedly, in addition to the involuntary paupers there were many vagrants by choice. Writing in 1700, John Cary commented: "Beggary is now become an art of mystery to which children are brought up from their cradles. Anything that may move compassion is made a livelihood, a sore leg or arm, or for want thereof a pretended one."

Poor Law relief was managed unevenly and inefficiently. In 1753 Henry Fielding complained bitterly, "the poor are a very great burden and even a nuisance to the kingdom. . . . Every person who hath any property must feel the weight of that tax which is levied for the use of the poor." Fielding was criticising the application of the system rather than the necessity for having it, and he went on : "The sufferings indeed of the poor are less known than their misdeeds. They starve, and freeze, and rot among themselves, but they beg, and steal, and rob among their betters. There is not a parish in the Liberty of Westminster which doth not swarm all day with beggars and all night with thieves."

A less sympathetic view was expounded by Dr. Burn, writing on the same problem eleven years later. "There is an infallible way to put an end to all this", he said, "and the easiest way in the world, which consists merely of a non-feasance. Give them nothing. If none were to give, none would beg; and the whole mystery and craft would end in a fortnight."

The Government, however, had another solution to the problem. It was believed that if the paupers could be collected together and isolated the situation might be brought under stricter control. So, in 1783 the first workhouses were set up. An Act of Parliament was passed which provided that these new institutions would have responsibility for aiding paupers, and that any persons refusing to go into them would be entitled to no form of authorised relief. This stipulation was unnecessarily severe, and in 1795 an amending Act was passed by which relief could be obtained by "industrious persons at their homes under certain circumstances of temporary illness or distress".

The conditions in the early workhouses were deplorable. Food was scarce, comfort non-existent, and discipline rigorous. Right up to 1816 the workhouse master had power to chain up or manacle his residents for minor breaches of the regulations. In addition, all classes of "pauper" were mixed up with no attempt being made to classify or to segregate them. Thus, tramps, young children, the aged, the insane, deserted wives, unmarried mothers, disabled soldiers, and down-and-out criminals were all herded together under a single roof. Most workhouses more than justified the cynical nickname of "Bastilles" by which they were generally known.

In 1832 a commission was set up to inquire into "the practical operation of the laws for the relief of the poor in England and Wales". The commission reported two years later and severely censored both the maladministration in running of workhouses and the abuses which abounded in the system of home relief.

As a result of this inquiry a new body called the Poor Law

Commissioners was instituted to control the whole of the relief organisation, and an immediate attempt was made to separate the various categories of inmate which were comprised in the workhouse population. Some effort was made, too, in respect of the appalling inadequacy of medical facilities which existed in the average workhouse and for the provision of medical attention, at the expense of the parish, for the very poor in their own homes.

Even after these reforms the welfare services remained patchy, inhuman, and grossly insufficient. Until the Education Act of 1870 the children of paupers continued to be locked up in workhouses as though they had done something deserving of punishment, and at the close of the nineteenth century an authoritative writer could still describe the regular workhouse population as being "sunk in helpless, irretrievable poverty".

The official attitude towards unemployment and pauperism was partly defeatist and partly *laissez-faire*. As the population increased, so did both the number of workhouses and the total figure of those receiving poor relief.

In 1849 there were 590 workhouses in England and Wales. By 1877 the figure had risen to 650.

The statistics for the period between 1851 and 1871 tell their own story :

Year	Residents in workhouses	Others on public relief	Total on public relief	Total population
1851	110,565	750,328	860,893	17,927,609
1861	130,961	759,462	890,423	20,066,224
1871	165,289	916,637	1,081,926	22,712,266

This, then, was the Britain which greeted the discharged prisoner at the end of his sentence. It was a Britain which tended to regard destitution as if it were some form of repulsive, self-induced, contagious disease.

Although both before and after the 1877 Act, which brought all prisons under the control of the Home Secretary, the maximum sum payable to a discharged prisoner was £2, the authorities concerned appear to have administered this form of assistance in a rather niggardly manner. The records show that for the years

1875–8 a total of £11,000 was paid to over 370,000 discharged prisoners, an average of only about 7*d.* per person.

The official assistance which was bestowed on released prisoners by way of boots, clothing, and a pittance in their pockets could not possibly qualify for the description of "after-care". The social rehabilitation of the ex-prisoner was left entirely to the voluntary societies, the number of which was growing rapidly and most of which received a very small annual subsidy from the Treasury.

One of the principal weaknesses developing in the system was that each of the societies was using its own methods and granting assistance according to its own standards. There was no liaison, no mutual planning, and no overall co-ordination of their efforts. The Prison Commissioners endeavoured to correct this failing in 1883 when they issued a memorandum to all the prisoners' aid societies laying down a set policy for them to follow. Although this move had a definite beneficial effect it did not achieve the uniformity which had been intended.

At this time every prisoner was released on licence or ticket-of-leave towards the end of his sentence and was obliged to report to the police at regular intervals until his period of licence had expired. He was liable to be recalled for the smallest act of misbehaviour or the slightest infringement of the regulations.

It was customary for the prisoners' aid society to interview a male prisoner at their offices immediately after his release. He would then be questioned about his intentions and an assessment would be made of his capabilities. Next he would be given some clothes to change into, as most prisoners were more than eager to divest themselves of the rough, ill-fitting "liberty clothing" with which they had been issued in prison. Finally, he would be given some pocket money and placed in a selected lodging-house until a job could be found for him.

With female prisoners the position was slightly different as they usually spent the last nine months of their sentences, prior to their conditional release, at an institution known as a "Refuge". These refuges were described as being "more like homes than prisons". There were, in fact, only two of them, one for Protestant women in Streatham and one for Roman Catholics in Finchley. The routine at both was supposed to train the women for their return to freedom. They would be visited there by voluntary workers from the prisoners' aid societies who would offer them help and advice about finding employment when the time came.

In 1894 the Gladstone Committee brought out their report which, as has been seen in a previous chapter, marked a turning point in the official view of the function of the prison system. The committee also emphasised the need for an efficient system of after-care.

> Prisoners have been treated too much as a hopeless and worthless element of the community [they said], and the moral as well as the legal responsibility of the prison authorities has been held to cease when they pass outside the prison gates. We think that the system should be made more elastic, more capable of being adapted to the special cases of individual prisoners; that prison discipline and treatment should be more effectively designed to maintain, stimulate, or awaken the higher susceptibilities of prisoners, to develop their moral instincts, to train them in orderly and industrial habits, and, whenever possible, to turn them out of prison better men and women physically and morally than when they came in.

The report went on to praise the work of the voluntary prisoners' aid societies but commented on the lack of uniformity in their methods. It was suggested that there should be a central organisation to supervise and to co-ordinate the activities of all the various societies and that a representative conference might be held in London to study this possibility.

A few years after the Gladstone Committee had published their far-reaching report, the Prison Commissioners set up a special inquiry under the Rev. G. P. Merrick, Chaplain of Holloway Prison, to investigate the methods being used by the prisoners' aid societies. Mr. Merrick recommended that every society should be registered with the Home Office and should be required to hold a certificate of efficiency from the Home Secretary. He also suggested a uniform code of duties for the societies' agents. They should interview prisoners before and after their discharge; they should meet them immediately on release and should be prepared to help them in obtaining board and lodging, railway tickets, clothing, and employment. Subsequently, the agents should exercise a friendly supervision over the prisoners and should submit periodic reports on their welfare.

Mr. Merrick's suggestion that aid societies should be registered was put into effect soon afterwards, when it became necessary for every recognised society to possess a certificate of efficiency granted by the Home Secretary.

After-care commenced as a humanitarian function performed by a number of philanthropic organisations. The original project envisaged an entirely voluntary association between the ex-prisoners and those who desired to help them, and it was designed essentially for the purposes of rehabilitation. The officially administered ticket-of-leave system, on the other hand, offered no help or guidance to the ex-prisoner, but only ensured that he should consistently report his whereabouts to facilitate his recall to prison should it become necessary.

A completely new conception of after-care was introduced in Britain at the beginning of the present century by the Prevention of Crime Act, 1908. This statute provided that a sentence of preventive detention or of confinement in a Borstal institution should be followed by a compulsory period of supervision under the aegis of a specially selected organisation.

Sir Evelyn Ruggles-Brise, one of the innovators of the Borstal system, had started up his own Association of Visitors to call on Borstal detainees and to offer them friendship and advice. This society, which was formed largely from Sir Evelyn's own friends, now became known as the Borstal Association and was given responsibility for the supervision of the youths on the completion of their sentences. At a later date the compulsory after-care of female prisoners, both Borstal detainees and adult offenders, was handed over to a society called the Aylesbury Association.

The question remained which organisation was to be allocated the task of providing compulsory after-care for the adult male prisoner after his discharge from preventive detention. These sentences were invariably served, like those of penal servitude, in one of the centralised convict prisons. The aid societies, whose functions had been associated with the local prisons, had never dealt with this class of offender. In 1910 the Home Secretary, Mr. Winston Churchill, decided to form a new body to take charge of this all-important work, and he established the Central Association for the Aid of Discharged Convicts. The new organisation was financed entirely out of public funds and was controlled by a General Council of which the Home Secretary himself was the *ex officio* president, and various voluntary societies were represented by members. In practice, the management was in the hands of a permanent director. The objects of the Central Association, as laid down by its constitution, were: "to combine into one organised effort all agents and persons engaged in the work of assisting discharged convicts; to effect economies in working and prevent overlapping; to strengthen the hands of those assisting convicts, and to render their position more forcible and effective".

It should be emphasised that the Central Association was only concerned with the discharged prisoners who had completed sentences of preventive detention. The voluntary aid societies remained in charge of the prisoners released from the local prisons.

In 1918 the aid societies formed their own organisation called the Central Discharged Prisoners' Aid Society. In spite of the similarity of name, this had no connection with the body which had been set up by Mr. Churchill in 1910. The objects of the latest body were to promote co-ordination among the localised discharged prisoners' aid societies and to provide for an interchange of information. The society was to be, in fact, a representative body of the aid societies with a central executive in London.

The peculiar division of responsibility between the paid official and the unpaid social worker, and between the dual systems of compulsory and voluntary after-care, never proved to be very satisfactory. It had always been felt that the dedicated philanthropist was an essential component of any successful after-care scheme, but obvious difficulties arose in deciding such matters as how much control should be exercised over the prisoners' aid societies by the Prison Commissioners and to what extent they should be reimbursed for their out-of-pocket expenditure from public funds. Having accepted the fundamental necessity for an organised system of after-care it would have been simple for the Government to set up a service of full-time, salaried officials to carry out the necessary work. However, it was appreciated that in the sensitive relationship between the supervisor and the ex-prisoner some added advantage would accrue if the former happened to be a voluntary, unpaid agent.

The report of the Salmon Committee, published in 1935, brought to a head the difficulties which were latent in the dual control system. A departmental committee had been appointed three years earlier under the chairmanship of Major (later Sir) Isidore Salmon to study the question of the employment of prisoners during their sentences and the assistance which might be given to them to find work when they were released. Although it was scarcely within their terms of reference, the committee decided to make a series of recommendations affecting the functioning of the prisoners' aid societies, culminating with the proposal that their work should be controlled by a National Council with a chairman appointed by the Home Secretary.

The prisoners' aid societies saw in these recommendations a veiled attempt to bring them completely under government control. They immediately organised a conference at which they set up a committee under Mr. Frank Whitbread, the chairman of the Central Discharged Prisoners' Aid Society, "to inquire into the present position from the inside of our movement, and to report what reforms, if any, are desirable and necessary".

The report of the Whitbread Committee advocated the continued independence of the voluntary societies and their freedom from strict governmental control. On the other hand, the committee thought that the central society should adopt a more active policy in the future and should be "re-modelled and strengthened so as to meet the new requirements".

Anyone with experience of the extremely delicate task of controlling a voluntary organisation will sympathise with the position of the authorities in this matter. To encourage, with the right amount of persuasion; to guide, with the right amount of tact; and to dictate, with the right amount of deference. These are the essential attributes in handling a body of philanthropic workers.

In 1936 the aid societies resolved, as their official announcement put it, "to abandon their strict independence and join together in common cause, not only with each other, but in full co-operation with the prison authorities". Their purpose, they said, was that "a way should be found for the free adjustment of [their] organisation so that they could meet the needs of the inevitable developments desired by the authorities in their prison administration". With this in mind, the name of their association was changed from the Central Discharged Prisoners' Aid Society to the National Association of Discharged Prisoners' Aid Societies. It is by no means rare for a charity to change its name when it is seeking to revitalise itself after a long period of inertia.

This new formation, known as NADPAS, was entirely responsible for voluntary after-care throughout the whole of Britain. It was really an experimental merger between an official and an unofficial organisation and was financed chiefly from public funds but partly by private donation. Although the staff were appointed and paid by the Home Office, the ultimate control was vested in an unpaid elective committee.

Meanwhile, compulsory after-care still remained the concern of the Central Association for the Aid of Discharged Prisoners, the Borstal Association, and the Aylesbury Association. Later on these three societies were incorporated into a single body known as the Central After-care Association.

The enormous importance of compulsory supervision as a means of rehabilitating ex-prisoners had become very apparent in the years that followed the introduction of the scheme in 1908. A further extension was brought about by the Criminal Justice Act of 1948 which provided for a period of compulsory after-care for every prisoner who had been released from the new punishments of corrective training and preventive detention, and also for every prisoner who was still under the age of 21 at the date of his conviction.

During the period of the 1939–45 war, and in the years immediately afterwards, the voluntary societies were finding it increasingly difficult to raise the amounts they were expected to donate to their parent organisation, NADPAS. This caused certain administrative difficulties, and in 1950 the Home Secretary set up a committee under the chairmanship of Sir Charles Maxwell to conduct a thorough review of their functions.

In their report the Maxwell Committee traced the origin and the growth of the aid societies and commented on the fact that they had been started at a time when there was no organised form of assistance for the discharged prisoner other than what was bestowed on him by private charity. The committee were extremely critical about the method of liaison between the prison officials, on the one hand, and the voluntary workers, who were going to supervise the discharged prisoners, on the other. The existing system was that the prisoner due for release would be interviewed by a case committee composed of members of the prison staff and of part-time welfare officers, who then sent a totally inadequate dossier on his case to the society which would be supervising him. There was a need, in the opinion of the Maxwell Committee, for the setting up of a service of full-time, professional prison welfare officers to become acquainted with the prisoners during their sentences and to compile constructive proposals for the best forms of assistance they should receive on their discharge. This was, indeed, a system which was already being applied in some Continental and Scandinavian countries.

A pilot scheme on these lines was started in a few of the larger prisons in 1955. The innovation of full-time prison welfare officers was an immediate success, and it was decided to spread the idea gradually throughout the whole prison system. After the scheme had been in operation for eight years the Advisory Council on the Treatment of Offenders reported :

> The system is new, its personnel has been rapidly recruited, training still needs to be developed; and the establishment of relationships, both with members of the staff inside the prison and with allied social workers tence, and to encourage him to discuss any personal problems.

The Council went on :

> The social worker should have an unhurried initial interview with a prisoner as soon as possible after reception, to relieve the anxiety that is inevitable when domestic ties are disrupted, and to find out what urgently needs to be done. He should then take steps to solve any social problems left behind and to preserve family ties. Thenceforth he should be available to advise, assist and befriend the prisoner during his sentence, and to encourage him to discuss any personal problems.

By the end of the year 1962 every local prison in England and Wales had its own welfare officer, and several of the larger prisons had more than one of them. The Council of the Central After-care Association, in its 1963 report, published an extract from an account of his early days at Parkhurst Prison by one of the prison welfare officers there. "Almost as soon as I arrived", he said, "individual officers began to telephone through to my office to say that a particular prisoner needed help and often the censor would bring me an incoming letter containing bad news." Referring to his contact with the men, he went on :

> It quickly became apparent that the most satisfactory place to talk to prisoners is in their cells. To arrange for an officer to collect a man with some half a dozen others, and to require them to wait outside a

door until it is their turn, creates an unfavourable atmosphere at any interview. The method I have adopted is to go and find the man I want in his cell at a time when I know he is there. Sometimes I talk to them in the dining hall, in the association room or while they are at work. Almost always, when walking round the prison when men are not at work, someone will approach me for a short talk and these informal contacts are invaluable.

Even for those of us who have never had the misfortune to serve a prison sentence it is very easy to understand how the advent of the prison welfare officer must have brought a glimmer of hope, humanity, and warmth into a cheerless, impersonal world of stone walls, barred windows, heavy footsteps, and jangling keys.

In 1957 the Home Secretary asked the Advisory Council on the Treatment of Offenders to consider whether compulsory after-care should be extended. At that time the system affected only a comparatively small proportion of the prison population, and the Council reported that they were very much in favour of its being broadened so as to take in various other categories of prisoners. Their recommendations were followed in the Criminal Justice Act, 1961, when the Home Secretary was granted wide powers enabling him to extend the scheme to new classes of offenders in the future.

Speaking in the debate on the Criminal Justice Bill in 1961, the Home Secretary admitted that the extension of compulsory after-care would create new problems of organisation and would materially affect the existing voluntary after-care scheme. But whatever the future of the voluntary aid societies in Britain, there can be no denying that they have been the pioneers of this country's after-care system, and no praise could be too high for a little band of men and women who worked so selflessly and so tirelessly for the welfare of the discharged prisoner.

Chapter Twenty

Changing Attitudes on Punishment

THE early penal systems were devised for two purposes—to exact vengeance on the wrongdoer and to deter other potential offenders. With these objectives the penalties had to be brutal and they had to be widely observed, the only limiting factor being the tolerance of the community.

In 1764 a wholly new conception was propounded by Cesare Beccaria in his *Treatise on Crimes and Punishments.* Beccaria, an Italian writer on moral and political philosophy, completed this work at the age of 26. The views he expressed were far in advance of his own time, but they aroused so much comment and controversy that his great treatise is said to have been translated into twenty-two different languages, and, after his death, Beccaria was described by Voltaire as "the benefactor of all Europe".

Beccaria had little doubt of the fundamental right of the State to inflict punishment, as he accepted Rousseau's doctrine of *The Social Contract,* the unwritten agreement by which the rulers and the ruled are bound together by a series of mutual obligations. The contract comes into existence, according to Rousseau, because individuals are unable to maintain themselves in independence and find it necessary to form a society. In this society each person alienates his personal rights to the whole community. "The sovereign", said Rousseau, "is the sole judge of what is useful or useless to the community. . . . Each of us puts his person and all his power in common under the supreme direction of the general will."

Beccaria was utterly opposed to the idea of capital punishment because he did not accept that man had a right to take away the life of his fellow human beings. In any case, he considered that execution was a far less effective deterrent than the continuing example of the criminal working out the expiation of his wrongdoing in a state of perpetual slavery.

A penalty could not undo a crime, said Beccaria. "The end of punishment is no other than to prevent the criminal from doing further injury to society and to prevent others from committing the like offence." A punishment ought not to involve violence, for ferocious penalties breed ferocious crimes. It was the paramount duty of the State to provide the greatest happiness for the greatest number of its subjects, and the imposition of punishment should be regulated according to such a doctrine.

Although Beccaria favoured moderate penalties he also laid great stress on the fundamental importance of the certainty and the promptitude of punishment. He felt that there should be some analogy between the penalty and the offence. For instance, a simple theft should be punished by a fine, and a robbery with violence, a fine and a whipping. But he believed that the principal factor in bringing about a reduction of the crime rate in the future was going to be the spread of enlightenment and education rather than the increased efficiency of penal methods.

Beccaria's *Treatise* was the first reasoned exposition in favour of a positive and humanitarian system of punishment. The most remarkable aspect of the work is that written more than two centuries ago. Without a doubt it exercised a profound influence on the penal developments in nearly every country in Europe.

The eminent British jurist Sir William Blackstone published the first volume of his *Commentaries on the Laws of England* in 1765, a year after the initial publication of Beccaria's *Treatise*. Blackstone was only concerned incidentally in his massive work with the punishment of criminals. His views on the subject were coloured by his belief that all laws, whether civil or criminal, should be based on the fundamental tenets of Christianity. "No human laws are of any validity", he says, "if contrary to this." Blackstone considered that the purposes of punishment were threefold. Firstly, to deter, secondly, to deprive the criminal of the opportunity for further wrongdoing, and, thirdly, to bring about his reformation.

William Eden (Lord Auckland), a diplomatist and politician, made the first serious attempt at reforming the penal system in England. His ideas were inspired by the views of Beccaria and also by those of Montesquieu, another advocate of less brutal methods of punishment. Eden set out his suggestions in his book *Principles of Penal Law,* which was published in 1771. He considered that the main object of punishment was deterrence, but he thought that severity must always be tempered by what he called "natural justice" or "public utility". Barbarous penalties, in his view, were detrimental to society. "When the rights of human nature are not respected", he wrote, "those of the citizen are gradually disregarded." Eden favoured the banishment of criminals, but he was critical of the efficacy of prison sentences. "Imprisonment inflicted by law as a punishment", he said, "is not according to the principles of wise legislation. It sinks useful subjects into burthens on the community and has a bad effect on their morals. Nor can it communicate the benefit of example, being of its nature secluded from the eye of the people."

The most effective form of punishment, in Eden's opinion, was one which was widely observed and which produced a sense of shame in the criminal. Accordingly, he favoured public floggings and a far greater use of the pillory.

It is a strange historical coincidence that four great advocates of penal reform—Beccaria, Eden, Romilly, and Bentham—were all born within a span of seventeen years. It would be true to say that although they were individually fired by the same ideals, they varied considerably in their opinions as to how these could best be effected.

Sir Samuel Romilly, who was a contemporary of William Eden in the House of Commons, devoted the whole of his public life to attempting to mitigate the severity of the penal code. In doing this his purpose was not only humanitarian, but also he believed that brutal penalties had a tendency to increase the incidence of crime. Romilly agreed with Blackstone that the objects of punishment were to deter the criminal, to control him, and to achieve his ultimate reformation. When he was the Solicitor-General, Romilly succeeded in bringing about a considerable reduction in the number of offences which were punishable by hanging.

It is probable that the views of Jeremy Bentham have made a greater impact in this country than those of any other penal reformer. When Bentham was 80, and within a few years of the end of his long life, Lord Brougham said of him, "the age of Law Reform and the age of Jeremy Bentham are one and the same".

Bentham lived from 1748 to 1832. Although he became involved with the practical aspect of punishment, it is difficult not to regard his opinions as those of theoretician. In his own day he was considered to be a great humanitarian, but some of the penalties which he advocated for criminals must strike us at the present time as being harsh to the extent of brutality.

Like Beccaria, Bentham believed that a system of law should be formulated so as to bring "the greatest happiness to the greatest number". The objects of punishment, he thought, were to prevent crimes from being committed and to achieve the moral reformation of the criminal. He was opposed to the use of torture, and he believed that the certainty of punishment was a more effective deterrent than the severity of the penalties imposed. Moreover, severe penalties induced juries to acquit and thereby diminished the certainty of punishment.

The prevention of crime, according to Bentham, could best be attained by depriving the criminal of his liberty. He set out his own views on the ideal form of prison in 1791 in his book *The Panopticon or Inspection House*. The prisoners were to live in limited seclusion, but they would be fully employed and would be allowed to share in the profits of their labour. The essential purpose of prison existence was to reform the criminal. This, said Bentham, could only be achieved by making him repent his wickedness, and as there could be no repentance without pain, the prisoners would have to pass their days in solitude, darkness, and discomfort until they had developed an aversion to crime and a respect for the law.

Bentham accepted the ineradicable presence of a criminal element in any organised society, but he had an interesting theory that punishment should be adapted so as to minimise the gravity of the general run of criminal offences. Certain crimes, he said, could be committed either in a more harmful or in a less harmful way. For instance, a theft from the person might be perpetrated with or without the use of violence. The penalties imposed by the courts should reflect such a marked distinction, according to how the offence had been carried out, that criminals would be tempted to commit their crimes in the less serious manner.

It was essential, in Bentham's opinion, that criminals must not be allowed to derive any profit from their wrongdoing and consequently the courts should be given jurisdiction to order them to pay full compensation to their victims.

For the rest, Bentham held that the sentences of the courts should be variable, equable, and commensurate with the offences for which they were passed. He also thought that the punishment for a crime should be as analogous as possible to the crime itself.

Bentham believed that every State had the fundamental right to inflict capital punishment, but he considered that this penalty should only be employed very sparingly. In fact, he would have confined its use to those offences which outrage the public sentiment—for instance, murders committed with aggravating circumstances.

John Howard, undoubtedly the best known of the British penal reformers, was born in 1726, so chronologically he should have been considered before Jeremy Bentham. I have interposed them, however, because Howard differs from the other reformers I have so far dealt with inasmuch as he was neither a visionary nor a theorist, but a person whose radical views on punishment emanated from his personal observation of the state of the prisons.

Howard's close concern with prison conditions commenced when he was appointed High Sheriff of Bedford in 1773. During the assizes there he decided to visit the gaol in which both the condemned prisoners and those awaiting trial were being detained. He witnessed, as he said, "the distress of which there are few who have not some imperfect idea". What shocked him particularly was that so many defendants who had previously been acquitted were still kept in custody because they had been unable to pay the gaoler's fees which were necessary to obtain their release. Howard immediately proposed to the county justices that their gaolers should be paid a regular salary and should no longer have to rely on the charges they exacted from the unfortunate prisoners. He was told that his suggestion could not be adopted in Bedfordshire unless he could discover a precedent for it in some other county. In search of this, Howard journeyed all over England visiting prisons everywhere he went.

Howard's quest for a precedent proved to be unavailing, but what he saw of the general squalor and depravity in British gaols decided him to devote the remainder of his life to the cause of prison reform. In explanation of his motives he said: "To the pursuit of it, I was prompted by the sorrows of the sufferers and love to my country. The work grew on me insensibly : I could not enjoy my ease and leisure in the neglect of any opportunity, offered me by Providence, of attempting the relief of the miserable."

In his book *The State of the Prisons in England and Wales*, John Howard set out his views, not only on the manifold abuses of the existing system, but also on his own conception of the way in which the gaols should be organised. He believed that prisoners should be segregated during the night and should live in association with their fellows during the day. "I wish to have so many small rooms or cabins", he wrote, "that each criminal may sleep alone. If it be difficult to prevent their being together in the day-time, they should by all means be separated at night." Elsewhere he says : "Prisoners should not remain in the day-time in the rooms in which they sleep; they should have a common ward, day-room or kitchen."

Regarding the routine of prison life, Howard believed that the prisoners should be made to get up early in the morning. Idleness, he thought, was one of the besetting evils of prison existence, and he advocated sufficient labour for all in an organised work-room. Adequate food should be provided by the authorities. "I plead only for necessaries", he said, "in such moderate quantity as may support health and strength for labour." A devout Christian himself, he believed that every gaol should possess its own chapel. Further, he considered that the defects and abuses of the gaols would not be checked until a proper system of regular prison inspection had been instituted.

When Howard died in 1790 his fellow reformer, Jeremy Bentham, spoke his epitaph. "In the scale of moral desert the labours of the legislator and the writer are as far below his as earth is below heaven. His kingdom was of a better world; he died a martyr after living an apostle."

In spite of the movement for prison reform, and the labours and devotion of such men as Howard and Bentham, the conditions in the gaols of this country were still appalling in the first years of the nineteenth century.

Elizabeth Fry was only 10 when John Howard died, but in all probability when she was growing up in her respectable Quaker home in Norfolk she would have heard of his noble work from her father, John Gurney, who was himself something of a radical philanthropist.

The name of Elizabeth Fry is principally associated with Newgate, for it was amongst the women prisoners there that she performed the main part of her work. In 1813 a select committee had reported on the state of Newgate. The gaol could conveniently hold 427 prisoners, they reported, but there were, in fact, no fewer than 822 persons crammed within its walls. No bedding was provided, and those who could not afford to hire beds at 6*d*. a night had to sleep between two rags on the bare boards. Prisoners detained for debt were provided with no coal, no lighting, and no cleaning utensils, and the usual high fees were extorted by the gaolers both on admission and on discharge.

A visitor to the women's ward at Newgate around this time told of his experiences: "When I first entered the foulness of the air was almost insupportable; and everything that is base and depraved was so strongly depicted on the faces of the women that, for a while, my soul was greatly dismayed."

The section of Newgate in which the female prisoners were housed bore the nickname of "The Hell above Ground". It was filled with women who were, according to a contemporary report, "scarcely human, blaspheming, fighting, tearing each other's hair or gaming for the very clothes they wore, which often did not suffice even for decency".

Elizabeth Fry paid her first visit to Newgate in 1813 when she was 33 years of age and was the wife of a successful London merchant. Four years later she commenced the task to which she was going to dedicate the rest of her life. An entry in her personal journal a short while later was as simple as it was precise. "I have been lately much occupied", she wrote, "in forming a school in Newgate for the children of the poor prisoners, as well as the young criminals, which has brought much peace and satisfaction with it; but my mind has also been deeply affected in attending a poor woman who was executed this morning."

The Association for the Improvement of the Female Prisoners in Newgate was formed by Mrs. Fry early in 1817 with the purpose of ensuring that all the women should receive proper clothing, useful employment, and adequate religious instruction during their sentences. The Association also campaigned for the complete segregation of the sexes in every prison and for the stipulation that women prisoners would be wholly supervised by female janitors.

In a short while the Association succeeded in bringing about a considerable improvement in the conditions at Newgate. After they had been at work for about a year Mrs. Fry described the altered life of the women prisoners. "They knit about 60 to 100 pairs of stockings and socks every month", she said. "They spin a little. The earnings of their work, we think, average about eighteen pence per week for each person. Another very important point is the excellent effect we have found to result from religious education; our habit is constantly to read the Scriptures to them twice a day; it has had an astonishing effect."

An independent observer who re-visited the women's section of Newgate a few years after Mrs. Fry's Association had been formed confirmed that a complete transformation had taken place. He found, he said, that stillness and propriety now reigned. His account continues :

> I was conducted by a decently dressed person, the newly-appointed yard-woman, to the door of the ward where, at the head of a long table sat a lady belonging to the Society of Friends. She was reading aloud to about 16 women prisoners who were engaged in needlework around it. Each wore a clean-looking blue apron and bib. They all rose on my entrance, curtsied respectfully and then, at a signal given, resumed their seats and their employment.

Before her death in 1845 Mrs. Fry had visited prisons all over Europe and her suggestions and opinions exerted a powerful influence which extended far beyond the grim and massive walls of Newgate Gaol.

Although the conditions of a prisoner's existence have altered immeasurably since the days of Elizabeth Fry, we are, in fact, still using many of the prison buildings which were opened during or shortly after her lifetime. For instance : Dartmoor (1809), Pentonville (1843), Holloway (1851), and Parkhurst (1854). Newgate itself was not used as an ordinary prison after the end of 1881. The building was demolished in 1904 and the Central Criminal Court, better known as the Old Bailey, was built on the same site.

Lastly in this chapter I would like to mention Captain Alexander Maconochie, a Superintendent of Norfolk Island around the middle of the nineteenth century and a dedicated penal reformer. His close contact with the convicts under his charge made Captain Maconochie increasingly disturbed regarding the emotional and psychological stresses occasioned by a long prison sentence. "They go in weak", he wrote, "or they would not probably be prisoners, and they come out still more enfeebled." One of his most interesting theories was that the duration of a sentence should be measured in the context of labour performed rather than by a stated number of months or years. The convict would be released from prison when, and only when, he had performed the amount of work which had been allotted to him, irrespective of how quickly or how slowly he performed his task. Some such system was tried out for a time in the prisons of Ireland.

PART TWO

FACING THE PROBLEM

Chapter Twenty-one

The Sentencer

PERHAPS it is only natural that anyone sitting on the bench at a criminal court for the first time should try to formulate some rationalisation of his position and of his exact responsibility.

It is often supposed that to pass judgment on one's fellows must be an experience calculated to heighten one's self-esteem. On the contrary, there can be few activities which are more humbling or more likely to cause any normal person to have grave doubts about his own adequacy for his allotted role.

In the eyes of many the law is nearly always at fault and the judiciary are smug, pompous, and utterly removed from reality; the police force exercises an unheeding tyranny, and the rules and requirements of court procedure are tedious, restrictive, and completely alien to the cause of justice. Any association which criticises the established legal system and any reports which advocate the most sweeping changes in the law are usually received with a fairly general approbation.

It is frequently overlooked that the criminal law exists for the protection of the individual, for the safeguarding of personal and public property, and for the maintenance of orderliness and peace. Without an effective system of law enforcement a community would rapidly degenerate into a state of complete anarchy. The struggle between lawlessness, on the one side, and order, on the other, is both savage and unremitting, and it is in the criminal courts that the basic elements of communal existence are constantly being preserved.

In most countries the position has deteriorated alarmingly in recent years. The official criminal statistics for England and Wales speak for themselves. The total numbers of indictable offences known to the police during the last six years are given on p. 176.

In the face of this evidence nobody could possibly believe that we are now progressing into a stage of civilisation in which the trial and punishment of criminals will become increasingly unnecessary. In fact, throughout the foreseeable future we shall need more and more criminal courts and we shall have to have additional numbers

Indictable Offences during Last 6 Years

Year	Total
1961	806,900
1962	896,424
1963	978,076
1964	1,067,963
1965	1,133,882
1966	1,199,859

The figures for familiar types of crime during these years were:

Year	Larceny	Breaking and entering	Violence against the person
1961	531,430	164,986	17,601
1962	588,566	192,302	17,948
1963	635,627	219,138	20,083
1964	704,116	233,930	23,470
1965	744,155	252,733	25,549
1966	775,990	275,969	26,716

of judges and magistrates to pass sentence on the lawbreakers. The real problem concerns the nature of the penalties which ought to be imposed.

The totality of a penal system may be assessed by the most severe punishment it allows. One of the most mature and most civilised forms of extreme penalty is probably a sentence of banishment. In the majority of societies and clubs, if a member has been guilty of a grave breach of the rules, the management committee have the power to order his expulsion. The citizens in a democratic country must have their natural obligations as well as their natural rights, as was suggested by Rousseau, and any persons who refuse to conform to the prescribed code of behaviour might well be said to have made themselves liable to be expelled from the community.

Theoretically, an advanced penal system might have three different grades of punishment—admonition for minor offences, a fine or a period under supervision for the more serious, with banishment as the ultimate penalty.

It would, of course, be impossible to banish offenders unless there was some place to which they could be deported where they would be afforded adequate facilities for carrying on their daily lives. Otherwise the system would be both retrograde and cruel. But at the moment it would be totally unrealistic to imagine that any nation might be willing to receive an intake of the worst types of convicted criminal from other countries, and as there is little or no possibility of the re-establishment of overseas penal settlements in the few remaining British colonies, judicial penalties are likely to continue for a great many years to come to be based on conventional methods of punishment.

The day has passed when judges and magistrates regarded themselves as the mere instruments of social retribution. At the present time the ways in which a court can deal with an offender are more diverse than they have ever been before and, in consequence, the task of sentencing is becoming increasingly complex. There are different types of custodial institution, each with its own distinctive features and each catering for particular types of criminal. If a court does not wish to impose an immediate punishment there are various ways in which a penalty can be suspended. Further, there are methods whereby the defendant may be afforded moral guidance, medical attention, or psychiatric treatment. The object of a sentence today may be to punish an offender; on the other hand, it may be designed solely to bring about his social or emotional readjustment.

In this country we have no official training schools for the men and women who sit on our criminal benches. They learn the intricacies of sentencing from their personal experiences, supplemented by any researches they care to make of their own volition.

So far as the lay justices of the peace are concerned, they are nominated in the first place as suitable candidates, and later their credentials are carefully investigated before they receive their appointments. Until recently lay justices could take their places on the bench with no legal knowledge and no practical training whatsoever, although the Magistrates' Association and the chairmen of a great many benches took infinite care to organise comprehensive lectures and visits to penal institutions for them. It was true that a new justice was never plunged straight into the complications of sentencing, but always sat initially in the company of more experienced colleagues and under the ever-watchful eye of a legally qualified clerk. Nevertheless, for the most part, he used to learn as he went along. There is a new scheme now by which all lay justices have to undergo a course of study before they are permitted to exercise their judicial functions.

In England and Wales our High Court judges are drawn exclusively from the 2000 or so practising members of the Bar. For the most part, so are the other professional appointees to the criminal bench too, the chairmen and deputy chairmen of quarter sessions, the stipendiary magistrates, and the recorders.

It might well be imagined that a successful barrister, especially one who has practised in the criminal courts, would have little or nothing to learn on the subject of sentencing. He will know, of course, what are the maximum penalties prescribed by the law; he will know which defendants are eligible for certain forms of punishment; he will know the correct administrative procedure for passing sentence; and he will know the current penalty-tariff for the more common types of offence. If this sort of knowledge were all that is required of him, then he would, indeed, be fully prepared for his new and onerous responsibilities.

But as our penal system grows in complexity it is being suggested increasingly that those with the duty of passing sentence in the criminal courts should undergo a period of preliminary preparation for that task. The *Law Guardian* expressed this view very strongly in September 1967 when, in an editorial article, it was said :

> The criminal courts form an essential part of the English penal system, but are they properly trained and equipped to make the vital decisions required of them? . . . the fact is that in England the courts, that is the Judges, lawyers and laymen, are not trained in penology. First, the examinations for neither the Bar nor solicitors include criminology (the science concerned with the causes, treatment and prevention of crime), and thereafter there is no opportunity for the Judges to discuss with other professional lawyers, sociologists, psychiatrists, representatives of the prison, probation and police services and other skilled persons the admittedly difficult problems of penology, nor any opportunity to discover, in general or in particular, the consequences or efficacy of any sentence.

The article concluded: "The odd thing is that society allows, indeed obliges, its Judges (professional and lay) to do such important work without seeing they are qualified for the task. Our Judges are highly respected, are rightly so, but are we fair to them or to ourselves, let alone the offender, if we ask of them the impossible?"

Chapter Twenty-two

The Prospect of Conviction

THE majority of penologists from the time of Beccaria to the present day have agreed on the fact that one of the most effective deterrents to the potential criminal would be the certainty of capture. One might, indeed, go further and say that he should be aware not only of the certainty of capture but also of the likelihood of ultimate conviction.

In this country our cherished conception of liberty and our basic presumption of the innocence of the subject make it essential that the burden of proof which rests on the prosecution is a heavy one, but, all the same, if a criminal procedure is weighted too heavily in favour of the accused the lawbreaker will know that even if he should be caught he will stand a reasonable chance of acquittal at his subsequent trial.

Before considering the matter in greater detail it may be as well to mention another deterrent factor—the necessary moral stigma attaching to conviction. If this should be lacking, and if the common scale of punishment should become over-lenient, then the fear of capture will be almost completely nullified. The general attitude of the public is of paramount importance. Not only should they regard criminal behaviour with a universal opprobrium, but also they must be able to feel an undiminishing respect for the processes of law enforcement. The conduct of the police force must be above reproach, and the operation of the criminal courts must be approved for their dignity, their fairness, and their absolute integrity.

In the days of barbaric sentences the prisoner in the dock was apt to become the centre of a morbid curiosity. Charles Dickens, in *A Tale of Two Cities,* describes a treason trial at the Old Bailey. When Jerry Cruncher has squeezed his way into the crowded court-room he asks the man standing next to him about the prisoner. "Ah," returned the man with a relish, "he'll be drawn on a hurdle to be half hanged, and then he'll be taken down and sliced before his own face and then his inside will be taken out and burnt while he looks on, and then his head will be chopped off, and he'll be cut into quarters. That's the sentence."

Dickens comments: "The sort of interest with which this man was stared and breathed at was not a sort of elevated humanity. Had he stood in peril of a less horrible sentence—had there been a chance of any one of its savage details being spared—by just so much would he have lost his fascination."

Even in our own lifetime Charles Dickens's observation has been verified repeatedly. Prisoners who were destined to be tied up and flogged and those who were to suffer death by hanging were always the objects of an unhealthy, mesmeric interest. When a person was charged with a particularly revolting or a particularly sensational murder, a certain group of newspapers were accustomed to bid for his memoirs and for the opportunity of financing his defence, and vast numbers of the public used to pore avidly over the tawdry details of his life, little realising that his mystical attraction was due to the fact that at some preselected time and place he would be taken out to have his neck carefully and scientifically dislocated by the hangman. After the Homicide Act of 1957 it was remarkable what little interest was taken in the average non-capital murder.

The theory that the stigma of conviction can be regarded as a greater deterrent than the severity of punishment is naturally dependent on a highly developed public conscience. Such a conscience exists in some walks of life much more than in others. On a recent visit to an approved school, attended by boys between 13 and 15 years of age, the headmaster told me that there was an almost complete absence of penitence or shame on the part of either the inmates or their parents. Examples of our deteriorating moral standards are to be observed in the newspapers nearly every day, and the distinction between right and wrong, between honesty and dishonesty, is becoming more and more blurred. A recent occurrence* will illustrate this point. On 23 March 1965 a tally clerk at the London Docks was convicted of stealing twelve lamb carcasses and sentenced to six months' imprisonment. It was disclosed at the trial that vast quantities of goods were being stolen from the docks and that one of the habitual methods of theft, which was, in fact, used in this instance, was for a lorry driver with the complicity of a tally clerk to overload his lorry before driving away and later to sell his excess load for his and the clerk's private profit. This prosecution only succeeded because the lorry driver concerned

* Reported in the *Daily Telegraph*, 25 and 27 March 1965.

in the case had been an honest man and had reported what was taking place. The day after the trial more than 1300 dockers at the Royal Group of docks came out on unofficial strike in protest against the conviction of the tally clerk. A few days later 400 dockers, again acting against the advice of their union, refused to unload two lorries merely because they were owned by the firm which employed the honest lorry driver who had given evidence for the prosecution.

Nowadays all too many people seem to believe that the crime war is a private struggle waged between police and the criminals and that the rest of the community can stand on the side lines adopting a passively neutral attitude. In the summer of 1964 twelve men were convicted for their parts in what came to be known as the "Great Train Robbery" at Cheddington, Buckinghamshire, when a train was held up and over £2½ million in banknotes was stolen from it. Mr. Justice Edmund Davies, in passing sentence on the men, told them : "This conduct constitutes a menace to society. Let us clear any romantic notions of dare-devilry from our minds. It is nothing less than a sordid crime of violence inspired by vast greed." The judge went on to speak of the "nerve-shattered" condition of the engine driver who had been attacked and beaten up by the masked and armed robbers. During the months that followed the end of this trial it was quite customary to hear intelligent persons in England expressing admiration for the guilty men and regret that they had been captured at all. Again, when two of the robbers were rescued from prison many law-abiding citizens received the news with acclamations of joy and almost in a sense of personal triumph.

The position must surely be looked at realistically. The ceaseless and unremitting struggle between order and lawlessness is single and indivisible. Every citizen must stand on one side or on the other. The forces of the underworld are ranged, not only against the police, but against society in its entirety, and no person can declare himself to be uninvolved. Each one of us lives constantly under the shadow of criminality and violence; all of our homes are equally liable to ransack, and all of our property equally liable to plunder. This is the age of the thug and the hooligan.

A typical instance of the type of conduct which is prevalent throughout the country today was reported in *The Times* newspaper on 31 August 1965. A young man had fifteen stitches inserted in his head wounds and was detained in hospital suffering from severe concussion after being attacked by a gang on the previous evening. This victim, apparently, had been the witness of an accident in which a car had injured a small girl and then was driven away without stopping. The young man was about to fetch the police when the car had reappeared and the assault had taken place. This sort of behaviour will become more and more common if people continue to lose their respect for the law.

A factor which has undoubtedly had a considerable adverse effect on the relationship between the police and the public is the increasing use of private motor-cars. The majority of road traffic offences arise from negligence, forgetfulness, or momentary lack of attention, but they are dealt with in the ordinary criminal courts by the ordinary criminal process. Each time a motorist takes his car on to the roads he places himself in jeopardy of a summons and he feels, almost subconsciously, that every police officer has become his potential enemy. As well as that, many drivers will go on believing themselves to be in the right whatever happens. Indeed, it is surprising how many otherwise law-abiding men and women seem to be overcome by a partial megalomania, self-assertiveness, and entire lack of chivalry directly they sit down behind the steering wheels of their cars.

A committee of the Law Society recently suggested that this situation might be remedied if we were to have special traffic courts to deal with minor motoring offences. It has also been proposed that we should go a step further and have two completely separate bodies of police officers, one to enforce the ordinary criminal law and one to deal with minor road traffic offences. It may be argued that such a system would achieve nothing because a police officer is still a police officer whatever happens to be his immediate responsibility. It is true that in the U.S.A., which has virtually adopted this principle, the highway patrol are regarded simply as a branch of the ordinary police force. On the other hand, nobody looks upon the traffic wardens in our large cities as being police officers. Not only are their uniforms and their authority completely different, but it is well known that they belong to an entirely separate corps. At present traffic wardens only deal in the main with the irksome but essential task of supervising the correct parking of vehicles. If it was ever considered necessary it would be a comparatively simple matter to expand their numbers, their duties, and their powers so that they might take over the routine duties of patrolling the streets to keep observation of all minor derelictions by motorists. In this way the regular police force could be preserved solely for the struggle against the criminal. As well as the C.I.D., they would still require a uniformed branch, for the police officer in uniform will always provide the outward and visible symbol of the vigilance of the law.

It is essential that the general public of a nation should regard the police as being their allies and their guardians. The police officers themselves must also reflect this attitude. Many people believe that in the world today the role of the police is so important that every force should become a *corps d'élite* with stringent qualifications of entry, a respected status in the community, and a high scale of payment.

To revert to the question which was considered at the beginning of this chapter—Does our criminal procedure encourage crime by making it too simple for the guilty to evade conviction? It is abundantly clear from the statistics that only a small proportion, approximately one in four, of those who commit criminal offences are ever caught. This is partly due to the increased skill of the lawbreaker but mostly to the inadequate resources of the police. The report by Mr. Justice James in his inquiry into the case of Detective-Sergeant Challoner, published in September 1965, gave an example of the situation. Between 1959 and 1963 C Division of the Metropolitan Police, whose area included Soho and its environs, one of the principal criminal localities of London, had a C.I.D. strength comprising only forty-nine detectives. For three months in 1963 these officers were on duty for an average of over 60 hours a week. Indeed, one detective-sergeant had worked for an average of $12\frac{1}{2}$ hours on every working day throughout the year, and another had sometimes put in between 90 and 100 hours per week.

Further, in addition to their shortage in manpower, our police have not always been issued with the most modern technical and scientific appliances for crime detection and security which could have been made available to them. The principal reason is, undoubtedly, the comparatively high cost which would be involved in equipping them on a really up-to-date basis. One result of this has been that the police did not use scramblers on their wireless transmission sets and all their messages were habitually monitored by the better-organised gangs of criminals.

It is not altogether surprising that the proportion of undetected crimes is mounting steadily almost every year. The figures given in the official *The Criminal Statistics for England and Wales for the Year 1966* show that the percentages of indictable crimes which were known to the police but were never cleared up were :

Year	%
1962	56·1
1963	56·9
1964	60·4
1965	60·8
1966	59·8

The British people expect their police force to combat crime according to the strictest principles of fairness and propriety, considerations which in no way burden their adversaries.

In this country there are usually a number of highly successful practising criminals whose identities are well known to the police, but who remain immune from prosecution because they are too clever or too well protected to be caught by any of the permissible methods of detection. Probably the necessary evidence against them could be collected by means of telephone tapping, bugging, interception of mail, or in a number of other ways which would undoubtedly be regarded as an unwarrantable invasion of the privacy of the subject.

Our attitude towards extra-judicial admissions of guilt is, perhaps, symptomatic of the general policy of tolerance with which we treat our criminals. In a large proportion of cases the prosecution will rely, wholly or partially, on the confessions of the accused, or on patently false or contradictory statements he has made when questioned by the police. The admissibility of such evidence in court is governed by an unofficial, though strictly observed, code known as the Judges' Rules. In practice, the effect of these rules is to compel a police officer to discourage a suspect from making an incriminating statement. It is laid down that "As soon as a police officer has evidence which would afford reasonable grounds for suspecting that a person has committed an offence, he shall caution that person or cause him to be cautioned before putting to him any questions, or further questions, relating to that offence". The words of the caution are simple and categorical. "You are not obliged to say anything unless you wish to do so, but what you do say may be put down in writing and given in evidence." If a suspect offers to make a written statement, the caution appears at the head of the first page and must be signed by him before he goes on with what he wishes to say.

The procedure in British criminal courts is designed to tilt heavily in favour of the defence. Historically this might have arisen from the special emphasis we have always placed on the rights of the subject and the liberty of the individual. It may also have been influenced by a predominant sense of sportsmanship; a sympathy with the underdog, especially in the days when sentences were so harsh and barbaric.

The two principal advantages accruing to the accused at his trial are doctrine of the "burden of proof" and the right to trial by jury for all the more serious offences. The burden of proof and the presumption of innocence are analogous terms and are embedded in the principle that no defendant should be convicted unless he has been proved guilty beyond any reasonable doubt. Although this tenet implies a tacit acceptance of the fact that a not inconsiderable proportion of guilty persons will be acquitted, any alternative system by which the innocent were exposed to a greater risk of conviction would be completely unacceptable to the vast majority of people in this country today.

Trial by jury is regarded as one of the most cherished guarantees of civil liberties. The jury system has an old and venerated tradition, and in bygone generations a succession of anonymous jurors have withstood the truculence and the tyranny of some of the more ruthless of the judges in the causes of justice and humanity. Even today the jury acts as a safety-valve, preventing the law from becoming too much out-of-tune with the tendencies of current thought. Most juries prefer to reach their decisions according to the dictates of experience and common sense, and in doing so they will not hesitated to ignore any legal niceties or outworn doctrines which they believe to be in opposition to a rational point of view.

The aspect of the criminal jury system most criticised in the past was the requirement for unanimous verdicts, which applied equally to an acquittal or a conviction. Since October 1967 a jury has been permitted to bring in a majority verdict if the jurors have found it impossible to agree unanimously. This means that in certain instances when one or two individual jurors are either so stubborn or so illogical that they cannot follow the paths of reason acceptable to the rest, the trial will not be nullified as a result.

It is a basic principle of our criminal trials that the only evidence which can be adduced by the prosecution to establish the guilt of an offender must be of a purely objective nature. Although it is difficult to see how any variation of this rule could ensure absolute justice to the accused, it must also be recognised that almost inevitably such a doctrine must confer innumerable advantages on the guilty. For example, it is only in exceptional circumstances that it may be disclosed during the course of a trial that the defendant is a person of bad character. But in all probability a jury trying someone accused of, say, housebreaking, would think it of the greatest possible probative value if they could be told that the defendant had been convicted of several similar offences in the past. On the other hand, the presumption of innocence necessitates that the facts relating to a charge should be considered, whenever possible, in complete isolation. Naturally, after a conviction the defendant's full record is revealed before the passing of sentence.

Apart altogether from the strictly enforced rules, a convention exists in the legal profession for the prosecution, within reason, to offer every available assistance to the defence. It is contrary to the established etiquette for the defendant, or those acting for him, to be subjected to any premeditated surprises, or to be placed at any calculated disadvantage in the presentation of his case.

The advocate for the defence, on the other hand, owes his paramount duty to his client and is under no ethical obligation to make any advance disclosures which might assist those who are conducting the prosecution.

This system has been applied for a number of years and has given us a criminal procedure which is probably as fair to an accused person as any other in the world. In fact, it is remarkable how many guilty offenders are still convicted in spite of the manifold advantages which our present system lavishes on the defence.

If a situation should ever arise in Britain in which the criminal element of the community had gained a definite mastery over the forces of law and order, then we might be forced to consider whether we were justified in continuing a mode of trial quite so favourable to the wrongdoer. But this is a social speculation beyond the purview of a discussion on punishment.

For my present purpose it will be sufficient to reiterate that if it is true that one of the most effective deterrents to crime is the virtual certainty of capture and conviction, then it seems to follow that as few intending criminals as possible should be heartened by the belief that, even if they are caught, they would stand a good chance of an ultimate acquittal.

Chapter Twenty-three

The Treatment of Offenders

IN A modern civilised nation the criminal law exercises a dual function. On the one hand, it seeks to maintain a universal system of orderliness and honesty, and, on the other, to enforce a general conformity to an established pattern of behaviour. In the result the courts are dealing not only with the lawless element in the community, but also with the inadequates, the deviationists, and social misfits in general.

Even in a progressive welfare state like Britain today, there remains a not-inconsiderable section of the population who, although not criminals in the accepted sense of the term, either cannot or will not adapt themselves to a socially acceptable mode of living.

In a recent report entitled *Non-Citizens of 1964*, prepared by Christian Action and the Simon Community Trust, it was revealed that there had been at least 90,000 homeless men and women in Britain during the year 1964. These comprised the inhabitants of doss-houses and reception centres, and others who spent their nights sleeping rough. A survey conducted in London and several other large cities had indicated that the vagrant population was increasing from year to year.

The report provided some interesting, although alarming, statistical details. In London alone, between 1961 and 1962, about 12,000 men had been living in casual hostels and lodging houses. Worse still, approximately 1000 vagrants of both sexes had habitually slept out-of-doors, of whom an average of 87 men and 5 women spent each night on the benches at Waterloo Station. Out of the 2402 prisoners discharged from Wandsworth during the same period, no less than 1300 had had no homes. Indeed, it was estimated that about 40 per cent of the persistent criminals in Britain were always homeless on the completion of their sentences.

It was also disclosed in the report that every week around 200 homeless ex-patients from mental hospitals were drifting through London, and that each night schools of itinerant methylated spirits drinkers lit their bonfires on the derelict spaces in East London as they gathered for their nocturnal orgies.

This report was only concerned with the vagrant element of our new society. But there are many other categories of social outcast such as the alcoholics, the drug addicts, and the sexual deviationists, who move in a continual shadow-show before our criminal courts. With the inadequate facilities available to him, the task of the judge or the magistrate who has to pass sentence on these people is sometimes an invidious one. Occasionally he feels like the conductor of an orchestra from which the strings, the woodwind, or the brass are entirely missing.

The alcoholics present a constant problem, particularly in the magistrates' courts. The maximum penalty for the offence of being drunk in a public place is a fine of £5. When the defendant has been drunk and disorderly he is liable to a fine of £10 or a month's imprisonment. Such penalties are quite sufficient for the occasional inebriate or the casual reveller, but they leave unsolved the fundamental difficulties of dealing with the habitual drunkard.

A short while ago I spent an evening at a clinic for alcoholics in the West End of London. On the invitation of the doctor in charge I joined him in his surgery during the time when he was interviewing his patients privately. So that there would be no embarrassment or reservation he introduced me as a visiting doctor who was present for purposes of consultation.

Alcoholism is a condition which is virtually incurable, although it can be kept under control if the patient possesses both the desire and the will-power to bring this about. In its advanced stages it can undermine its victim in every way—physically, mentally, and morally. The ultimate end may be complete self-destruction.

I saw two patients at the clinic that night whose cases stand out particularly vividly in my memory. The first was a labourer, aged about 30. He told us he had been a secret whisky drinker since the age of 16. He had fallen in love a few years back with a very young girl and had married her without disclosing his condition—indeed, he had imagined at first that he might be strong enough to overcome it. But, unfortunately, this had not been so, and his experiences after his marriage had been typical. Out of his wages of £12 10s. 0d. a week, he had been spending over £5 on liquor. Consequently, there had been less and less money to spend on the necessities of life. Bills had mounted and the home had fallen into disrepair. Then his wife had discovered his drinking habits. There had been emotional scenes, tears, recriminations, lies, arguments, and unkept promises. Eventually the wife had walked out on him and he had not seen her since.

The second patient was a well-educated woman of about 40 whose husband, a civil servant, had accompanied her to the clinic. He knew all about her affliction and had been largely responsible in persuading her to seek medical advice. Obviously she had fought a bitter struggle against the condition which was slowly devouring her. She had lost her will to work, to form friendships, and even to go out-of-doors, but she had felt an infinite terror of the impulse which drove her towards her secret supply of whisky whenever she was left alone in her home. She kept repeating to the doctor, "This thing is stronger than I am. You must find some way of helping me."

In the courts one sees the wreckage of the men and the women who did not find the strength to overcome their weakness for drink. Some have been picked up drunk and incapable on the pavements and the roadways; others have caused distress and annoyance to passers-by by shouting and swearing in their presence, and even by molesting them. The lives of these people often consist of a regular cycle of drinking bouts, court appearances, paid and unpaid fines, and short spells of imprisonment. When they appear in the dock they are usually described as having no employment, no fixed abode, and little or no money in their possession. What sentence can be appropriate or beneficial to such people? If they are fined and allowed time to pay, the chances are that the fine will either be ignored or forgotten. If they are sent to prison, even for the maximum period, it will simply serve as a brief suspension of their customary way of life.

Because of their total degeneration, their inability to find a regular occupation, and their craving to obtain drink or money to purchase drink, alcoholics are frequently arrested for stealing or for committing other offences of dishonesty. Such behaviour is to a large extent a manifestation of their mental and moral disorder which can scarcely be remedied by the conventional methods of punishment.

The Royal London Prisoners' Aid Society has conducted a study amongst a thousand of the male alcoholics who habituate London prisons. It was discovered that out of these a third responded well to rehabilitative treatment, a third showed a measure of improvement, and a third had already deteriorated to an extent when they would require institutional care for the rest of their lives.

It has been estimated that there are at present over 400,000 alcoholics in the United Kingdom (in the United States of America the equivalent figure is said to be about a million).

The official statistics for England and Wales show that during the year 1966 a total of 66,599 men and women were convicted of offences relating to drunkenness. Of these, many served terms of imprisonment, either by way of initial sentences or on account of unpaid fines. It would be impossible to estimate how many others were imprisoned for offences which were directly or indirectly attributable to drinking.

Of late there has been a growing awareness here of the gravity of this situation. Branches of Alcoholics Anonymous have already been set up in a number of prisons, and in June 1965 Miss Alice Bacon, Minister of State at the Home Office, announced that the Government were considering the experimental transfer of some prisoners serving sentences for drunkenness to open prisons in the country where they could receive appropriate treatment for their condition. No doubt this progressive and enlightened step will be adopted in due course as a universal practice throughout the whole of our penal system.

Drug addiction presents the courts with a similar problem to alcoholism inasmuch as its victims suffer from the same sort of mental and moral degeneration. Although in this country there are considerably fewer drug addicts than there are alcoholics, the number is increasing by alarming proportions. It was recently estimated that there are now over four times as many cocaine and heroin addicts in the London area than there were two years ago and that the insidious growth is continuing unchecked.

In general, there are two methods of controlling drug addicts. Either they can be subjected to an immediate and absolute denial of their particular addiction drug, or else an attempt can be made to wean them away from their craving by allowing them to have a gradually decreasing dosage. It seems to be the opinion of the medical profession that the absolute denial method, even if imposed over a substantial period of time, will suspend rather than cure an addiction, and that as soon as the patient is free from restriction he will return once again to his old habit. On the other hand, the decreasing dosage form of control may sometimes effect a temporary, or even a permanent, cure.

At the moment there are no prisons in Britain which cater especially for drug addicts and these people normally serve their time under exactly the same conditions as any ordinary prisoners. Until very recently any prisoners who were seriously addicted to the more potent drugs such as heroin and cocaine had to manage without them completely for the duration of their sentences; this policy has now been slightly modified. In some cases, when drug-addiction had provided the motivation for a prisoner's criminal behaviour, it might have meant that he would leave prison with this tendency untreated and unchecked.

Apart from the alcoholics and the drug addicts, a not-inconsiderable proportion of the persons who commit criminal offences are suffering from mental illnesses and are in need of psychiatric treatment rather than punishment. It is obviously desirable that these defendants should be singled out as early as possible, but there can be no absolutely certain way of bringing this about. Sometimes the police officer concerned will suggest to a magistrate that he might be assisted by a mental and medical report; sometimes the magistrate himself will observe some peculiarity with regard to the defendant's appearance or behaviour which will put him on his guard. If there is any suspicion of mental instability a court will usually remand a person for the necessary examinations and tests. Generally speaking, the only satisfactory method by which these can be carried out will be by a prison medical staff, and so a remand for a mental and medical report will nearly always be in custody and not on bail. Unfortunately, this means that the defendant will have to be detained for two or three weeks in the prison hospital at a full security prison.

If anyone has been convicted of an offence which could be punished by imprisonment, and is found to be suffering from a mental disorder of sufficient gravity, the doctors can now make a recommendation for what is called a "hospital order". Although the imposition of sentence remains a matter for the court of trial, it is difficult to imagine that such a recommendation would ever be disregarded by a judge or a magistrate.

When courts make hospital orders they merely specify to which hospitals or clinics the defendants will be admitted without laying down the period for which the treatment will continue. It is then for the medical authorities concerned to decide at what stage a cure has been effected so that the order can be discharged. It is also open to the person who is the subject of an order, or to his relatives, to make periodical applications to the Medical Health Review Tribunal for the case to be reviewed. If the court which makes the hospital order considers that there is a risk of the defendant committing further offences if released too soon, it can impose a "restriction order", the practical result of which is to prevent the defendant from being discharged except with the consent of the Home Secretary.

Most psychiatric hospitals today have adopted the "open door" policy of treatment and retain only one closed ward in which patients subject to a restriction order may be confined. Dangerous and violent offenders are still sent to maximum security prison-hospitals like Broadmoor, Rampton, or Moss Side.

Many of the cases which come before the criminal courts are of a sexual nature. These may be crimes arising from brutality or lust, such as rape, incest, and serious indecent assaults, or they may be the more trivial offences committed by compulsive sexual deviants.

Every civilised society recognises a certain form of sexual behaviour and relationship as being "normal" and therefore socially acceptable. From the point of view of the psychiatrist the deviant is a person who, owing to an emotional or mental distortion, obtains sexual satisfaction in one of the "abnormal" ways. From the point of view of the criminal law, certain forms of sexual deviation are either socially abhorrent in themselves or constitute a possible source of corruption to others, especially to younger persons. At the present time, the causes of sexual deviation are not fully understood, and consequently no methods of treatment have so far proved to be particularly satisfactory.

The sex criminal, like the rapist or the paedophile, can obviously be dealt with by the conventional forms of punishment. But it is far more difficult to decide which penalties are appropriate for such offenders as the male homosexual who yields to an impulse to solicit other men in public lavatories, or the man who is afflicted by the compulsive urge to expose his genitals to females.

Experience has shown that very few of the deviant offenders are either violent or vicious types and, further, that only a comparatively small proportion of them are ever reconvicted on a subsequent occasion. Probably a moderate fine coupled with the shame and indignity of their court appearance will, in most cases, exercise a sufficient deterrent effect to keep them out of trouble in the future. It is the defendants who come back on a second and third occasion, perhaps even more often, who present the real difficulty. Heavier fines and sentences of imprisonment are probably of very little value with such people. One possible remedy for a deviant who cannot control his behaviour would be a course of treatment designed to neutralise his compulsive urges, for instance by induction of female hormones in order to reduce the activity of the testes. However, our courts have no power to compel a defendant to undergo such a process, and even if a man promised to submit himself to it on a voluntary basis there would be no way of forcing him to fulfil his undertaking.

In Scandinavian countries the courts can arrange in certain cases for a prisoner to be castrated with his prior consent. Naturally, this drastic step will only be taken with a dangerous or a persistent sexual offender when the alternative would be a prolonged period of imprisonment.

It is the duty of the bench in the criminal courts to give effect, as far as possible, to the attitude of the general public. In these days, when there is probably a greater enlightenment and far less humbug than ever before regarding matters of sex, very few people indeed would wish that the common prostitute, the male importuner, or the indecent exposer should be condemned to prison if there were adequate alternative methods of dealing with them. The imposition of increasingly severe fines may be an obvious solution, but it is one that can sometimes give rise to anomalous situations. For instance, the penalties for a prostitute who solicits or loiters in a public place for the purpose of prostitution are for the first offence a maximum fine of £10, for the second offence a maximum fine of £25, and for the third and subsequent offences a maximum fine of £25 or 3 months' imprisonment or both. Now a successful prostitute earns a very high income on which she pays little or nothing by way of taxation. In addition, she is accustomed to a very comfortable standard of living. If a prostitute is fined, the obvious way for her to raise the necessary money is by intensified soliciting. An experience which has, perhaps, befallen more than one inexperienced magistrate is that of fining a prostitute and giving her time to pay, and seeing the same woman appear before him a short time later giving the excuse that she was obliged to continue in her trade in order to be able to raise the amount of her fine.

The average prostitute has neither the temperament nor the ability to enable her to earn a high rate of remuneration in any other occupation. By the imposition of high fines the courts are merely driving them back to the streets. Prostitution *per se* is not unlawful in our criminal code and the sole purpose of the Street Offences Act of 1959 was to divert the harlot into alternative ways of practising her age-old trade or to induce her to abandon it completely. The threat of imprisonment on her third conviction is a prospect which fills the ordinary prostitute with dread and usually makes her particularly cautious as to the manner in which she carries out her calling. Once she has been imprisoned she will go to extreme lengths to avoid being convicted again. It is also the function of the criminal courts to interpret and to fulfil the intentions of Parliament, but for any bench which wished to pursue a sentencing policy which was both purposeful and con-structive, the prostitute undoubtedly presents a peculiarly difficult problem.

The male importuner can be punished on summary conviction by a maximum fine of £100 or by a sentence of up to six months' imprisonment. This particular offence is a manifestation of a form of homosexuality which the law can do little to curb or even to control. The defendant is punished, not because he suffers from a sexual aberration, but because he chooses to parade it publicly to the annoyance and disgust of the majority of his fellow men. A number of male importuners are people holding good positions and earning quite high salaries. On a first or a second conviction for this offence a fine, in most cases, is probably more desirable as a deterrent than a short term of imprisonment.

In the case of a man convicted of indecent exposure, the penalty on summary conviction is a fine of up to £25 or imprisonment for not more than three months. Here again the principal concern of the courts is to prevent the compulsive deviant from giving way to his impulses either by making him conscious of his social respon-sibility or by bringing it home to him that such behaviour will entail increasingly unpleasant consequences. If fines will prove sufficient penalties, they are naturally preferable to terms of imprisonment.

However, a large proportion of indecent exposers seem to be men of the vagrant class whose sole worldly wealth at the time of their arrest often comprises the loose change in their pockets. A defendant can only be allowed time to pay a fine provided there is a reasonable prospect of his being both willing and able to do so. Moreover, there must be some fairly certain method by which the police will be able to locate him if he should default in making payment. For these reasons punishment by way of fining is not always the easy and obvious solution that it might appear.

When a male sexual deviant is receiving a term of imprisonment he is frequently told that treatment will be available to him while he is serving his sentence. But prisons were devised for punishment, not for the administration of elaborate, long-term psychiatric attention, and with the best will in the world the average prison medical office is severely limited in regard to facilities and also in regard to time.

In 1954 Peter Wildeblood was sentenced to eighteen months' imprisonment for homosexual offences. In his book *Against the Law* he has described an interview which he had with the Principal Medical Officer at Wormwood Scrubs in order to discuss his abnormality. Wildeblood informed the doctor that he was willing to be cured, if possible, and suggested that he might receive glandular injections or hormone treatment, to which the doctor replied, "I most certainly wouldn't recommend it. We have tried courses of injections on a couple of sex cases here, but the results were far from satisfactory. One man came back quite shortly afterwards with a further conviction and the other has undergone physical changes of a somewhat alarming nature." The doctor went on to say, "The only thing that might answer, in your case, is a course of analysis and psychotherapy lasting perhaps years. Even if we had time, I rather doubt whether it could be carried out satisfactorily in prison. You might, perhaps, consult a psychiatrist about it when you are discharged."

Until we have special "hospital-prisons" at which alcoholics, drug addicts, and sexual deviants will receive adequate treatment, the powers of a court, at the highest, are to deter these people from committing similar offences, and, at the lowest, to postpone the day when they will offend again.

As regards the flotsam and jetsam of the streets—the tramps, the beggars, the mentally retarded, and all the other types of social inadequates whose way of life brings them into conflict with the law—it is said that some of them, even a very small proportion, would derive far more benefit from a special course at a rehabilitation centre than from a short sentence in an ordinary conventional prison.

Chapter Twenty-four

The Punishment of Criminals

IN THE earlier chapters of this book I have endeavoured to trace the gradual evolution of our penal system and to investigate the haphazard and often ill-conceived phases of its development. We are left today with a scheme of punishment which is essentially a legacy of the thinking and the practice of former centuries, and yet it would be difficult to suggest any rational alternatives which were not mere elaborations and refinements of our present forms of sentence. At the moment, in common with most other nations, we are losing the battle against the criminal—a situation which must emanate from a number of different factors besides the relative failure of our modern penal system. Nevertheless, one of the accepted purposes of punishment is to bring about the reformation of the wrongdoer, and it can be shown statistically that in this respect the majority of our methods are proving singularly unsuccessful.

In recent years the penal systems of the civilised world have aroused a great deal of public interest, and penologists in most countries have been studying the effectiveness and the consequences of various types of punishment. When all their data is assembled and analysed it may provide us with some valuable guidance for the future. But in the meantime the courts will have to carry on with the methods which are at present available.

It has been seriously suggested that the task of sentencing should be taken away from the bench and should be placed in the hands of a committee of so-called "experts". However, most experienced penologists contend that such a procedure would be likely to destroy the entire fabric of penal administration. Punishment must be flexible, but it must also be uniform inasmuch as it should be imposed according to a set of unvarying principles. It is a part of the duty of all judges and magistrates to study the dicta on sentencing which are being constantly formulated by the superior courts, and, indeed, to observe which sentences are upheld and which are varied on appeal. This is the only way in which a measure of uniformity can be achieved. Further, a just sentence must take into account both the gravity of an offence and the circumstances of the offender. In a criminal court room, where such matters are under continuous appraisal, the degree of culpability of the accused can be assessed with a fairly high degree of accuracy. It may be difficult to visualise how a specially convened committee, working in the detached seclusion of the conference room, could ever achieve the feel and the atmosphere of a case which is so essential in the measurement of punishment. Every court is aware of the social implications of the offences which come before it. The pattern and the significance of crime is ever changing, and varies from county to county and from district to district. A court, by its sentencing policy, has power to control the manifestations of crime within its particular jurisdiction. The extent to which this is necessary is gauged, not only by the number of persons who are actually convicted, but often by the evidence forthcoming in cases which terminate in an acquittal, perhaps because of some technical defence or of some flaw in the prosecution evidence.

Before a sentence is passed it is essential that as much information as possible about the defendant should be available to the court concerned. The views of such people as the probation officer, the doctor, the psychiatrist, or the welfare worker can be of immense value in appropriate cases, but only in an advisory capacity. The responsibility for evaluating their opinions and for making the final decision must, of necessity, be a matter entirely for the bench. In fact, the recommendations of these specialists, each approaching the problem from his own particular standpoint, are sometimes diametrically opposed to each other.

In 1957 the Advisory Council on the Treatment of Offenders published a report entitled *Alternatives to Short Terms of Imprisonment* in which they urged the courts to consider, in suitable cases, whether a heavy fine might not be the most effective form of penalty. It is generally accepted that the imposition of fines is one of the most convenient and humane ways of dealing with offenders, but, from the practical point of view, it may well suffer from three serious disadvantages. Firstly, the statutes under which many summary charges are laid frequently prescribe maximum pecuniary penalties which have remained unchanged for years and are altogether out of keeping with present-day money values. It follows that a court is often precluded from imposing a fine which is in any way commensurate with the gravity of an offence. Secondly, a defendant with dishonest inclinations might feel tempted to raise the amount of a large fine in an unlawful way. And thirdly, in the ordinary course of events there is no method by which a court can obtain any detailed and accurate information about the defendant's exact financial position before deciding the amount he should be made to pay. Fines will only be an equitable penalty if they are specifically related to the means of the offender.

It has been proposed that this last difficulty might be resolved if every criminal court had on its staff a professional financial assessment officer. Before the amount of a fine had been determined a defendant would be interviewed by this official to ascertain the true extent of his resources and his commitments. To deliberately mislead the financial assessment officer would naturally be considered a serious offence.

Sometimes it is quite impracticable for a court to deal with a guilty defendant by imposing a fine or by making use of any of the more lenient forms of sentence. In such a case a term of imprisonment might well be the only alternative. It is easy to criticise, even to deplore, a method of punishment which entails the physical incarceration of the offender. In *The Observer Weekend Review* on 10 October 1965, Sir Ian Horobin, who had himself just completed a four-year prison sentence, made an impassioned protest against the whole system. "Liberty is natural to man," he wrote. "Simply by being shut up anyone is as wretched as he is capable of being. Simply tie up a dog for a week and he'll bite. What do you imagine happens when you tie up a man for months or years?"

It is true, of course, that personal freedom is regarded today as one of the most priceless assets of the individual, but the salient fact remains that until an adequate alternative method of punishment has been devised, any civilised nation which decided to close down its prisons at the present time would drift rapidly into a state of general lawlessness bordering on complete anarchy. Moreover, the effects of imprisonment may not be wholly negative. Hugh Klare, the secretary of the Howard League for Penal Reform, in his book *The Anatomy of Prison*, said : "While I believe that some people are sent to prison who should never be sent there at all, I also think that treatment in a closed institution, given at the right moment and lasting for the right time, may be the only chance which many offenders may get of growing out of anti-social attitudes."

In Britain the judge or magistrate controls the length of a sentence of imprisonment, but he has no control whatsoever over the type of penal establishment to which a defendant will be sent. In practice all newly sentenced prisoners, ranging from first offenders to confirmed recidivists, are passed initially through the same procedure. They are sent straight from their courts of trial to closed, or maximum security, local prisons to be inducted into their life of captivity.

Whenever I visit a local prison I pause in the reception block and I try to visualise the reactions of a prisoner who is being admitted there for the very first time. It is impossible, of course; just as it is impossible to simulate any other deeply felt personal experience which one has never undergone. The worst part of it must be the sudden transition from being an individual to becoming a number; the complete divestment of personality and the merging into a uniformed mass. In most of the reception blocks at the old mid-Victorian prisons the prisoners first hand in their clothes and their private possessions. They are then medically examined and given a bath. Before being issued with prison uniform they go to a large room to be shut into detached cubicles, which resemble a cross between a sentry box and an upturned coffin. The delay at this stage may be considerable if there is a large intake from the courts on that particular day.

In his book *Against the Law* Peter Wildeblood said:

> Going to gaol is, in itself, a powerful shock. Suddenly, in the space of a few hours, a man's whole life is changed; he loses friends, possessions and free will and finds himself alone in a hostile place, wearing clothes designed to rob him of his last vestiges of self-respect and eating food which, for the first few days at least, makes him feel ill and depressed. Whatever values he may have are destroyed; whatever faith he may have is shaken.

After being sentenced Mr. Wildeblood was taken to Winchester Prison. He described his reactions on entering his cell.

> The first time that door clicked shut I sat down on the wooden chair, put my elbows on the table, and looked at my surroundings, making a mental inventory of them, examining their dingy colours and rough textures, and thinking, "I shall spend the next 365 days with these objects, or others like them, so I may as well get used to them."

His cell, he tells us, was 13 feet long by 9 feet wide with a small barred window opposite the door. "Previous occupants have defaced the whitewash", he says, "by scratching messages with a nail—'Elsie, Elsie, Elsie', or 'Trust in the Lord', or 'Roll on April 1949'." The floor at Winchester was of concrete stained black, which the prisoners were supposed to polish. There was a bed of wooden boards with a thin coir mattress and pillow, two sheets, three blankets, a small looking glass, a cake of soap, brushes for shaving, for hair, for teeth, a razor without a blade and a book of rules for the guidance of "Convicted Prisoners, Male".

Due to the shortage of prison staff and the absence of proper labour or recreational facilities, the prisoners in the majority of closed prisons spend a great deal of their time confined in their cells. At Pentonville, for instance, I was told in 1965 that prisoners were usually locked up at 5 o'clock in the afternoon, and, with the exception of those who were allowed to attend evening lectures, they stayed in their cells until 7 a.m. the next morning.

As is generally known, sanitation in the old-fashioned prisons is archaic. Normally, from the hour a prisoner is shut in his cell to the time of his morning release he has to rely on the use of a chamber-pot. Describing the scene at Winchester Prison every morning, Peter Wildeblood wrote :

> By 7 o'clock we were supposed to have our cells tidy and our beds made up in the approved manner, leaning against the wall with the bedding hanging over them. . . . Then our cells were unlocked, a razor blade was issued to each man, and after a quick shave in cold water we trooped out on to the landing for the ritual of Slopping Out.

There was, apparently, one flush-toilet for every twenty cells and the prisoners stood in a queue waiting to pour the contents of their chamber-pots down the drain.

In his autobiography *If Freedom Fail,* the late John Vidler, who was one of the most unorthodox of prison governors, gave a similar description of the conditions at Wandsworth : "The men worked for about sixteen hours a week", he says, "and spent most of the time in their cells. Early morning slopping out must have been a nightmare for the landing officers : the stench was terrible."

It might be said, with some truth, that the deterrent effect of imprisonment is heightened by the primitive discomfort and the nihilistic routine of ordinary prison existence. Indeed, it has been estimated that about 80 per cent of the men and women who go to prison for the first time never return to serve another sentence. In a forthright paper* which he read before the Third International Conference for Psychotherapy in London in August 1964, Dr. Melitta Schmidelberg described punishment as "the oldest aversion therapy known to man". He went on, "Swift, certain and brutal punishment is undoubtedly effective. The problem facing a civilised society is how humanely it can afford to treat its criminals and still protect the public." On the subject of imprisonment, Dr. Schmidelberg said :

> Anti-punishment enthusiasts dream of the day when prisons are replaced by hospitals, punishment by rehabilitation and an unspecified, glorified magical "psychiatry" will be the panacea. They are unaware that mental hospitals do not cater for offenders, that most psychiatrists do not wish to treat them, and those who do mostly demand such high standards of co-operation, character and intelligence as to rule out most offenders.

As the standards of living improve for all sections of the community, the greater will be the shock for most offenders of their early initiation into harsh realities of prison existence. Although this must be one of the dominant features of imprisonment, primitive discomforts are not a part of the official policy as laid down by prison rules, which state specifically that "the purpose of the training and treatment of convicted prisoners shall be to encourage and assist them to lead a good and useful life". A succession of Home Secretaries since the end of the 1939–45 war have sought to improve the general conditions by the reconstruction and replacement of the older prison buildings, but progress has been slow in the extreme as the expense involved in an immediate and total reorganisation of the whole of the prison system would be prodigious. It will probably be many years before Britain is equipped with an adequate number of modern prison buildings, and meanwhile the reformers will have to concentrate their attentions on alleviating any unnecessary hardship in the existing situation.

At the moment all prisoners go through the same initial procedure at the commencement of their sentences. Allocation takes place at a local prison and from there some are sent on to central prisons and others to open and regional training prisons. For certain

* Published in the *Magistrate*.

types of offender this preliminary period in a full-security prison can have a definite reformatory value. I have been told by a very experienced prison governor that the most effective first sentence of imprisonment is one of three months' duration, for although it will create a deep and lasting impression in the prisoner's mind, it will not be of sufficient length to accustom him to prison conditions.

Many people hold the view that for some offenders who are sent to prison this traumatic shock of initiation might be wholly unnecessary and even psychologically harmful. A term of imprisonment, like a fine, they say, ought to be adjusted to the individual circumstances of the offender, and the judge or magistrate who imposes the sentence might well be the best person to decide in what conditions it should be served.

In a model penal system no offenders would be sent to prison without the fullest inquiries first being made into their characters, backgrounds, and the circumstances of their offences. Information of this extent could not be collected at the court of trial and it would be necessary for every defendant who was being considered for a term of imprisonment to go to a special classification centre for detailed investigations to be carried out. Before making the ultimate decision on sentence the court would be shown all the available reports from the centre. If such a system ever came about there would be no reason why, in appropriate cases, a person should not be committed straight to an open or a regional training prison without serving any initial spell at a local prison.

Incidentally, this system is applied, to a certain extent, in the case of juveniles and young offenders who, after they have been sentenced to attend an approved school or to a term of Borstal training, are sent to a classification centre so that it may be decided for which particular institution they are most suited.

During recent years judges of the High Court wishing to impose maximum or near-maximum terms of imprisonment have sometimes avoided passing life sentences, and decided instead to specify a very long period of years. For instance, in 1961 George Blake received a sentence of 42 years for espionage, and two other spies were given terms of 25 and 20 years respectively. More recently, in 1964, seven of the men convicted of the Great Train Robbery were sent to prison for 30 years each, and several others for periods of over 20 years. As is generally known, the Home Secretary has power to review and to terminate a life sentence wherever he thinks fit. A judge is obliged to pass a sentence which is consistent with the circumstances of a particular crime, but he cannot be expected to foresee the possible changes which may take place over the years in an offender's character and outlook. For many years it had been suggested that if the prison authorities were of the opinion that a long-sentence prisoner may have qualified for his early release they should be able to submit his case for review to a superior judicial body consisting of a panel of judges of the Court of Appeal. The Criminal Justice Act, 1967 has introduced a new system by which the Home Secretary is empowered to appoint a parole board and local review committees whose function it will be to report to him on the suitability of prisoners for early release on licence.

Some penologists think that the courts should have a greater variety of penal establishments available to them. They point out that sending a defendant to prison involves far wider considerations than merely suspending his liberty. An absence from work for even a few months might well result in the loss of a good job, or even in completely wrecking a career. Further, when a married man is imprisoned, his wife and family very often go straight to the nearest office of the Ministry of Social Security and so, during the whole of his sentence, they are maintained by his law-abiding fellow citizens. Two forms of prison sentence have been proposed which could be used in special cases to overcome these difficulties. Firstly, the institution of weekend prisons, to which a person would be committed to work off a set number of Saturdays and Sundays. Secondly, the use of the short, deferred sentence. The defendant could elect to serve this at any time during the ensuing six months and it could, in practice, be arranged to coincide with a period which would otherwise have been his annual holiday.

Detainees who were undergoing either of these kinds of sentence would be expected not only to pay for their own keep but also to fulfil their financial obligations to their dependants. The establishments in which these sentences were served would be of the open or minimum security type. The régime would be hard, the discipline strict, and the amenities frugal. The punitive effect would derive both from the compulsory labour and the temporary deprivation of freedom. Only certain selected offenders would be suitable for these special sentences and the remainder would still have to go to the ordinary conventional prisons, which will inevitably be undergoing fairly sweeping changes and reforms during the years which lie ahead.

The proposal to introduce the suspended sentence into the British penal system was rejected by the Home Secretary's Advisory Council of the Treatment of Offenders in 1952 and again in 1957. "The task of sentencing an offender, already hard," they said, "would be made much harder by the knowledge that the sentence might never operate, or . . . would operate at an unknown future date and in circumstances which could not be foreseen."

However, in one country at least, the system has proved fairly successful, as was revealed by Mr. Nigel Walker, University Reader in Criminology at Oxford, in an article in *The Times* on 13 April 1965. Discussing the experiences of Israel, where suspended sentences have been employed for some years, Mr. Walker said that a large-scale investigation had revealed that "offenders dealt with in this way were if anything less likely to be convicted than offenders who received other sentences".

The suspended sentence was introduced in Britain by the Criminal Justice Act, 1967 in a series of provisions which came into effect on 1 January 1968. In general, any court which imposes a sentence of not more than two years' imprisonment can order that this will not be enforced unless the defendant commits another offence, punishable with imprisonment, during a specified period—which can be anything between one year and three years. The Act also lays down that sentences of six months or less, with certain exceptions, will automatically be suspended. This means that by far the majority of the sentences of imprisonment imposed by magistrates' courts will have to be suspended sentences whether the magistrates think it desirable or not.

One of the features of our present prison system which has been most criticised is the acute shortage of employment for the prisoners in local prisons. Open and regional prisons have fewer prisoners and have better facilities both for labour and for communal life.

The Home Office pamphlet, *The Sentence of the Court,* published in April 1964, said of work at local prisons: "The working week there is at present seldom more than 25 hours and sometimes falls as low as 16: and the trades and industries available are limited and of variable value, either for training or as preparation for good industrial habits outside."

It is intended that the working time in local prisons should be raised to a minimum of thirty hours a week, but this target depends on more prison officers and additional workshops becoming available. The situation at the closed central prisons appears to be more satisfactory. Sir Wilfred Anson, the Chairman of the Home Secretary's Advisory Council on the Employment of Prisoners, revealed in a letter to *The Times* on 18 November 1965 that most of the long-term prisoners at central prisons were working an average of forty hours a week.

Whether or not our penal establishments could ever be run on a completely self-supporting basis must be a matter of extreme doubt. The report on the work of the Prison Department for 1966 showed that the total expenditure on prisons, Borstals, detention centres, and remand centres for the year ending 31 March 1966, excluding capital expenditure, was £29,341,481. The income derived from prison industry and labour, including the sale of old stores during the same period, was £2,391,170.

It is sometimes thought that there might be trade union opposition to a fuller and more effective deployment of our prison labour force, especially because the rate of payment to prisoners is so low. (In 1966 it varied between 3s. 6d. and 11s. 3d. per week.) This supposition has been strenuously denied by the Chairman of the Advisory Council on the Employment of Prisoners, a body of which, in fact, a number of eminent trade unionists are members. In any event, our total prison labour force, if fully mobilised, would be only about 0·1 per cent of the entire British working population, so that the effective competition it could offer would be almost negligible. Those who are well acquainted with these matters contend that for the better economic management of our prisons as well as for the moral, mental, and physical well-being of the prisoners themselves, it is a matter of the utmost urgency that they should be given the opportunity of working ordinary hours at a productive trade for a normal rate of pay.

In 1964 the Advisory Council on the Employment of Prisoners published a report in which it was said:

> The Swedes have shown that, granted certain conditions, prison industries can successfully enter the open market. The first condition (apart from the all-pervading need for efficiency) is that there must be co-operation and understanding on the part of both sides of industry

outside prisons. This in turn involves a general acceptance that it is right and necessary that prisoners should be engaged on useful, productive work, and satisfactory assurances that prison industries will compete fairly and will make a helpful, not a disruptive, impact on the national economy.

Swedish experience, said the report, has confirmed the view that "for the majority of prisoners, the most suitable work is that which is generally known in industry as unskilled or semi-skilled repetitive work".

The Advisory Council went on to say that many prisoners in Sweden are paid amounts equivalent to £2 or £3 a week.

> In the new Swedish prisons trouble in the workshops is almost unknown. . . . While this is no doubt due in part to the exclusion from these workshops of prisoners who are constitutionally incapable of behaving themselves and working reasonably well, the Swedish authorities consider that the main factor is the higher pay which prisoners can earn there. It is a valued privilege to work in these workshops.

It may be said, indeed it is said very often, that there are many people in prisons who are simply incapable of doing a proper day's work. Dr. C. B. R. Pollock, a very experienced prison medical officer, writing in the *Magistrate* in April 1964, said :

> The type of psychopath most met in prison has been described as the ergophobic psychopath. Their distinguishing characteristic is a refusal to be employed or to engage in any steady work. They will not work for an employer nor keep regular hours. They will seldom keep a job for more than a week or two. They throw up employment with no prospect of finding another job. When unemployed, they turn to thieving and regard this as the natural thing to do. Not many bother to draw National Assistance as they regard it as too irksome to have to go round and fill up forms at the Labour Exchange. When they do work, it is at casual jobs to which they can go when they feel like it or stay away. They lie in bed until working members of the family have left the house and then loaf about till evening.

The sort of individuals whom Dr. Pollock describes would have to be strictly disciplined and constantly supervised in a prison where the majority of the inmates were doing a full and proper day's work. Perhaps if all prisoners had to purchase their own meals out of their earnings even the ergophobic psychopath would be stimulated to a newly discovered energy.

Should prisoners receive ordinary working wages, the immediate result would be that, not only would they be able to maintain their dependants while they were serving their sentences, but also they could make a substantial contribution towards the running costs of the prison. A compulsory deduction could be taken from their pay each week and placed in a savings account to be handed to them on discharge.

It has been suggested that the matter could be taken a step further and that every prisoner might be made to make the fullest possible financial retribution for his crime out of his prison wages. Dr. Julius Kay, in an article in the *Justice of the Peace and Local Government Review* in March, 1964, proposed that certain categories of criminal should be subjected to enforced bankruptcy as soon as they had been convicted. The court, said Dr. Kay, "would issue an order enabling the bailiffs to seize any and every property of the accused, including that in the possession of people with whom he habitually associates". Only the minimum, based on National Assistance Board standards, would be exempted from seizure. "The unmortgaged part of the house, the 'telly', the fitted carpets, even the wife's or girl-friend's fur coat would act as security against the coverage for caused loss or damage."

It should be added that the prison department of the Home Office has recently prepared a scheme for the consideration of the Home Secretary by which all prisoners would work between 37 and 42 hours a week and would receive wages between £10 and £12. They would have to pay £3 a week towards their own keep and also would have to support their families. No doubt, care would be taken to ensure that the prisoner, especially if he is only paying £3 a week for his keep, would not be financially better off in prison than he would have been in conditions of freedom.

The custodial treatment of young offenders is, perhaps, an even greater problem than the imprisonment of adults. On the face of it, it would be easy to say that the Borstal system has failed. A census was taken at the end of 1962 of the 13,560 youths who had been released from Borstal institutions in the period 1957–61. It was found that during the short intervening period no less than 53 per cent had already been re-convicted, and indeed it has now been estimated that the total success rate of Borstal training is as low as 35 per cent.

But statistics can be used far too readily for drawing false conclusions. No one can tell how much of the apparent failure of the

Borstal system is due to the training methods which are used, and how much to the basic qualities of the inmates themselves, and, indeed, to the deficiencies of their parents and the faultiness of their upbringing.

A sentence of Borstal training is indefinite in length but, in practice, can last for any period between six months and two years. Infinite care is taken to send the young person to an institution most suitable to his or her individual requirements. Some Borstals are open and some are closed; some are for the more intelligent and some for those needing medical or psychiatric assistance. It can truthfully be said that each institution caters for a different type of individual.

After receiving a sentence of Borstal training the young offender is sent to an allocation centre. For girls, this is at Bullwood and, for boys, at Wormwood Scrubs. They remain at the centre from two to three weeks and during this time they are interviewed by psychologists, medical officers, vocational guidance officers, and social workers. It is only after an exhaustive study that it is finally decided to which particular institution a boy or girl should be sent.

The Governor of the Boys' Prison at Wormwood Scrubs allowed me to attend an Allocation Board which was considering the future institutions of about thirty different boys, and I was impressed with the infinite care which was taken to choose a Borstal for which each one of them would be best suited. Afterwards, I asked the Governor if he could find any common characteristic among all the young offenders who were passing through his hands. He told me that the majority came from homes where the parents had either separated or were too preoccupied with their own lives to take a proper interest in their children. He also said that the amount of drug-taking amongst these adolescents was reaching alarming proportions.

It was difficult to form any estimate of the boys as each one appeared before the Allocation Board only for a matter of minutes, although their cases had been fully discussed before they were shown in. One 17-year-old apprentice, who had coshed an elderly woman in her sweet shop and had then robbed the till, told us he had done it because he wanted adventure. Another youth of about the same age, who had been employed at a wage far in excess of the national average, said he had gone out housebreaking, not because he needed the extra money but, as he put it, "for kicks".

Anyone who visits a boys' Borstal institution for the first time would be struck by the tidy and purposeful appearance of the inmates. Also by the complete absence of the customary atmosphere of a prison, a quality which is assisted, no doubt, by the fact that none of the staff is dressed in uniform.

Unfortunately "Borstal" has become an ugly word which conjures up a vision of a régime something similar to the old type of army "glasshouse". Nothing could be further from the truth. There has to be confinement and there have to be rules and a strict code of discipline, but apart from that the inmates of a Borstal receive a general academic education, indeed they can sit for their G.C.E. O and A levels at most institutions, and they are taught such trades as carpentry, plumbing, engineering, and bricklaying which will enable them to earn a living after they have completed their training.

I was told by the governor of a Borstal on the south coast that many of the boys suffer from a feeling of insecurity after they are released. One of his boys returned soon after his discharge and begged to be readmitted. He was told this was impossible, so he went away, deliberately committed another offence, and immediately gave himself up to the police.

I have been told repeatedly by the staffs of Borstal institutions and approved schools that effects of the training they administer and the standards they are able to implant are frequently dissipated as soon as the boy or girl is released and returns home. I have heard this confirmed by probation officers and social workers. Where parental example, or lack of example, or the general conditions of home life have contributed to a young person's original wrong-doing, it would surely be expecting too much from any system of corrective training to hope that it could provide a permanent shield against such dominant, adverse influences in the future.

A Borstal governor once told me that his inmates are profoundly affected by the behaviour of men and women in public life. A scandal involving a well-known person, he said, can cause a discernible psychological reaction throughout the institution. It is not merely that some of the boys tend to think, "See—in their own ways they are no better than we are", but also that they do quite genuinely expect a high standard to be set by the more eminent members of the community.

An alternative form of custodial treatment for young offenders is provided by the detention centres which are designed to administer what has been described as a "short, sharp shock". A sentence at a detention centre is specific in length and can be for any period from three months to six months. However, three months is recognised as the optimum duration, as the course is geared to a $2\frac{1}{2}$ months' training programme, allowing for two weeks remission on its conclusion.

The régime at a boys' detention centre is much more rigorous than that at a Borstal and is more reminiscent of the old-time recruits' course at an army barracks. For example, at Goudhurst in Kent the inmates rise at 6 a.m. and, apart from an hour's break for midday dinner and a further hour for tea, they are kept busy until 7.45 in the evening. A considerable period each day is spent in physical training, but there are also facilities for technical and general education. The routine is essentially military in pattern. The officers wear prison uniform and the programme is interspersed with parades and inspections. The squads of boys move from place to place, sometimes at a brisk march, sometimes at the double. The general living conditions compare very favourably with those encountered by many youths and men on first joining the colours during the 1939–45 war.

One of the prison officers at Goudhurst told me that the two features of the life at the institution which the boys found most difficult to endure were the total ban on smoking and the absence of any pop music.

Statistically, detention centres have proved no more successful than Borstals. It would be difficult to make any direct comparison between the two as so many of the inmates of Borstal institutes have previously passed through detention centres. Crime among the young can only be looked at in regard to the general pattern of behaviour. In this respect it is some indication of the seriousness of the progression into lawlessness that approximately half of the boys who receive their first conviction in the courts later develop into persistent criminals.

The total Borstal population on 31 December 1966 was:

Boys: 5624
Girls: 221

The figures for detention centres on the same date were:

Boys: 1537
Girls: 24

It is a social phenomenon, or perhaps a psychological one, that, in this country at any rate, there are far more male than female criminals. The distinction is equally marked with adults as it is with the young, for on 31 December 1966 the prison population of prisoners serving sentences was:

Men: 22,401
Women: 544

At the moment there is only one detention centre for girls with a régime which is based on a combination of firm discipline and hard work. From the point of view of a court sentencing a girl of under 21, it might be helpful if there were more places to which she could be sent for a short term as opposed to a comparatively long spell of Borstal training.

However much our penal institutions are improved and whatever new forms of custodial treatment are introduced, there can be no doubt that a great deal of the effectiveness of any detentive system will always depend on an adequate system of after-care. Writing with thirty years' experience in the Prison Service, John Vidler could say: "The most important end in view is to try to instil into the recidivist prisoner a feeling of hope. Institutional training has many defects, not least of them that a man having undergone this sort of training has ceased on discharge both to think for himself or to be in a state of mind to face up to the problems which he is bound to meet in the outside world."

When Mr. Vidler was Governor of Maidstone Prison one of his ex-prisoners wrote to him saying, "Most of the public first seem to think that when a man has been released his only need is money, until he gets a job to put him on his feet. What he really needs is the understanding, which very few seem to have or show."

The Council of the Central After-care Association drew attention in their annual report in 1963 to a further problem which frequently faces the discharged prisoner—homelessness. Not only the lack of somewhere to live, but also the absence of any person to share his life with him and to help him to pick up the threads of his existence.

It was a common experience during the six years of the last war that a great many marriages were unable to withstand a long, enforced separation. Moreover, it was often found that after an eventual reunion, the initial months or even years of living together as man and wife were beset with a host of difficulties. Any married prisoner serving a lengthy sentence must encounter the same sort of problems.

One must accept the need for long prison sentences in certain cases, but this does not mean that there would be no way of helping to preserve the marital relationship of the prisoners in question. One suggested method would be to establish separated houses within the confines of every long-term prison where husbands and wives could stay together for a set period every year. In certain prisons in Central and South American countries some such a scheme exists and male prisoners are allowed to receive what are termed "conjugal visits" from their wives. It is intended in the near future to introduce a similar arrangement in Britain.

The lot of the discharged prisoner has improved immeasurably in recent years. Before he leaves the prison he is given a free ticket to his home address and an introduction to the Ministry of Social Security. Until comparatively recently the homeless ex-prisoner might find himself in an immediate dilemma as he was unable to draw any National Assistance until he could show a fixed address, and in most cases he was unable to obtain a fixed address unless he could pay a week's rent in advance. However, special arrangements are now made to overcome this particular difficulty.

Another matter which still troubles the discharged prisoner is the fact that his insurance card is not stamped during his sentence, and an unstamped card is an almost certain give-away when he is looking for employment directly after his release.

A scheme for the fusion of the probation service and the after-care service has been accepted in principle by the Government. Under this plan every ex-prisoner would be entitled to receive the assistance of a probation officer in finding accommodation and work, as well as in solving his domestic and social problems. Unfortunately, the present size of our probation service is completely inadequate for this immense task and already many hard-pressed probation officers are finding it difficult to spare more than ten minutes a week in seeing each of the young people who are allocated to them for compulsory after-care following a detention centre or a Borstal sentence.

Conclusion

Thomas Hobbes, the seventeenth-century philosopher, in his book *Leviathan,* compared the natural state of man with an ordered society. He declared that in a state of nature there was no property, no justice, and no injustice : there was only war. And in war, force and fraud are the two cardinal virtues. Life without social order, he said, would be "nasty, brutish and short".

There can be few people today who would find much cause to differ from Hobbes's view. Indeed, the growth of civilisation has served to emphasise how completely society must depend on the maintenance of the rule of law, which is dependent, in its turn, on the effective administration of criminal justice, including the efficiency of the penal system.

On 20 January 1966 a leading article in *The Times* said :

> Britain is, in fact, being subjected to an increase in crimes of violence and offences against property of an unprecedented size. . . . What is to be done about it? Not even the most careful research has, so far, very much to offer by way of preventing crime. The causes of crime, when everything has been said about its being a function of environment, or of heredity, upbringing or educational deficiencies, remain entirely unclear.

How to reconcile the protection of the public, humanity to the individual, and the reformation of the wrongdoer—that is basically the problem of punishment.

Bibliography

Books
ARCHBOLD: *Criminal Pleading, Evidence and Practice.*
BECCARIA: *Treatise on Crimes and Punishments.*
BENTHAM: *The Panopticon or Inspection House.*
The Bible: Books of Deuteronomy, Exodus, and Leviticus.
BLACKSTONE: *Commentaries on the Laws of England.*
BURNS: *Justice of the Peace* (29th edition).
COKE: *Institutes.*
DEFOE: *Moll Flanders.*
DICKENS: *Sketches by Boz.*
DICKENS: *A Tale of Two Cities.*
EDDY: *Justice of the Peace.*
EDEN: *Principles of Penal Law.*
ELKIN: *The English Penal System.*
FITZGERALD: *Chronicles of Bow Street Police Office.*
FRY and CRESSWELL: *Memoirs of Elizabeth Fry.*
GORDON SMITH: *The Babington Plot.*
GRELLETT: *Memoirs of the Life and Gospel Labours of Stephen Grellett.*
HINDE: *The British Penal System (1773–1950).*
HOBBES: *Leviathan.*
HOWARD: *The State of the Prisons in England and Wales.*
HUTCHINSON: *Historical Essay concerning Witchcraft.*
JOHNSON: *The Idler.*
JONES: *Crime and the Penal System.*
KINGSMILL: *Prisons and Prisoners.*
KLARE: *The Anatomy of Prison.*
KNIGHT (Editor): *London.*
KOESTLER: *Reflections on Hanging.*
KOESTLER and ROLPH: *Hanged by the Neck.*
LAURENCE: *A History of Capital Punishment.*
LECKY: *History of Rationalism in Europe.*
MAINE: *Ancient Law.*
MERIVALE: *Lectures on Colonisation and Colonies.*
MOORE: *A Book of Australia.*
MUYDEN: *A Foreign View of England in the Reigns of George I and George II.*
NASH: *History of Worcestershire.*
NIELD: *The State of the Prisons in England, Scotland and Wales.*
PATERSON: *Principles of the Borstal System.*
RADZINOWICZ: *A History of English Criminal Law.*
ROUSSEAU: *The Social Contract.*
RUGGLES-BRISE: *The English Prison System.*
SAMUEL: *Memoirs.*

SHAKESPEARE: *Macbeth* and *Henry VI.*
SMITH: *The Common-Wealth of England.*
STAMPP: *The Peculiar Institution.*
State Trials: Vols. 7, 9, 18, 19, and 28; 2nd edition, Vol. 1.
STEPHEN: *A History of the Criminal Law of England, 1883.*
TREVELYAN: *English Social History.*
VIDLER: *If Freedom Fail.*
WILDE: *De Profundis.*
WILDEBLOOD: *Against the Law.*
WILKINSON: *The Newgate Calendar.*

Reports
Report of the Departmental Committee on Corporal Punishment, 1938.
Report of the Royal Commission on Capital Punishment, 1949.
Alternatives to Short Terms of Imprisonment, H.M.S.O., 1957.
Corporal Punishment, Report by the Advisory Council on the Treatment of
    Offenders, H.M.S.O., 1960.
Preventive Detention, Report by the Advisory Council on the Treatment of
    Offenders, H.M.S.O., 1963.
Annual Report of the Central Aftercare Association for 1963.
Non-Citizens of 1964, Report by Christian Action and the Simon Community
    Trust.
The Organisation of Work for Prisoners, Report by the Advisory Council on
    Employment of Prisoners, H.M.S.O., 1964.
Report of the Commissioner of Police of the Metropolis for the Year 1966,
    H.M.S.O.
The Sentence of the Court, H.M.S.O., 1964.
The Treatment of Offenders, Central Office of Information, Pamphlet 35.
Report on Alcoholics by the Royal London Prisoners' Aid Society.
The Criminal Statistics for England and Wales for the Year 1966, H.M.S.O.
Report on the Work of the Prison Department 1966, H.M.S.O.

Articles, etc., in Newspapers and Periodicals
    Daily Telegraph.
    The Observer.
    The Times.
    The Sunday Times.
    Magistrate.
    Justice of the Peace and Local Government Review.
    Law Guardian.

Index